The origins
of creativity

The origins of creativity

Edited by

KARL H. PFENNINGER

and

VALERIE R. SHUBIK

with contributions from

Bruce Adolphe	Françoise Gilot
Thomas R. Cech	Benoit B. Mandelbrot
Dale Chihuly	George E. Palade
Antonio R. Damasio	David E. Rogers
Janina Galler	Gunther S. Stent
Howard Gardner	Charles F. Stevens

OXFORD
UNIVERSITY PRESS

OXFORD

UNIVERSITY PRESS

Great Clarendon Street, Oxford OX2 6DP

Oxford University Press is a department of the University of Oxford.
It furthers the University's objective of excellence in research, scholarship,
and education by publishing worldwide in

Oxford New York

Athens Auckland Bangkok Bogotá Buenos Aires Calcutta
Cape Town Chennai Dar es Salaam Delhi Florence Hong Kong Istanbul
Karachi Kuala Lumpur Madrid Melbourne Mexico City Mumbai
Nairobi Paris São Paulo Singapore Taipei Tokyo Toronto Warsaw

with associated companies in Berlin Ibadan

Oxford is a registered trade mark of Oxford University Press
in the UK and in certain other countries

Published in the United States
by Oxford University Press Inc., New York

A catalogue record for this title is available from the British Library

Library of Congress Cataloging in Publication Data
The origins of creativity/edited by Karl H. Pfenninger and Valerie R. Shubik;
with contributions from Bruce Adolphe . . . [et al.].
Includes bibliographical references and index.
1. Creative thinking–Congresses. 2. Creative ability–Congresses.
I. Pfenninger, Karl H. II. Shubik, Valerie R. III. Adolphe, Bruce.
BF408.075 2001   153.3'5–dc21   00-045656
ISBN 0 19 850715 1

10 9 8 7 6 5 4 3 2 1

Typeset in Minion
by J&L Composition Ltd, Filey, North Yorkshire
Printed in Great Britain
on acid-free paper by
Biddles Ltd, Guildford & King's Lynn

Acknowledgements

This book benefited from the input, advice and efforts of many outstanding individuals.

Special thanks go to Oxford University Press. Without their efforts, there would not have been a book. We also want to express our gratitude to the anonymous reviewers whose important, constructive criticism helped us to sharpen the focus of the book.

This book evolved from a symposium entitled *Higher Brain Function, Art and Science: An Interdisciplinary Examination of the Creative Process* organized by Karl H. Pfenninger in honor of the 20th Anniversary of the Given Biomedical Institute in Aspen, Colorado.

The contributors listed on the cover of this book helped with the completion of the final manuscript and provided many of the illustrations. With sadness, we would like to note the death of one of our authors, Dr. David E. Rogers, a gifted physician and a dedicated artist. We want to thank his wife, Barbara L. Rogers, for her help with the photographs of his sculptures and for her permission to use his essay.

Many colleagues and friends on both sides of the Atlantic offered helpful advice and feedback: Prof. Henry H. Claman, Prof. Stephen I. Goodman, the late Prof. Fred Kern, and Brendan Essary at the University of Colorado's School of Medicine; and Dr. J.T. Hughes, Dr. Norman Heatley, Dr. Ken Fleming, Dr. David Millard and Prof. Geoffrey Lewis of Oxford University. Their invaluable contributions are gratefully acknowledged.

Particular thanks go to staff members at the University of Colorado who made the original conference possible and successful and devoted much effort to the preparation of the manuscript: Ms. Janet Ferrara, Given Biomedical Institute, and Mr. Mark Groth, Colorado Psychiatric Hospital; Ms. Gray Grether, Mr. David Oquist and Ms. Melissa Esquibel, Department of Cellular and Structural Biology; and especially Ms. Carmel McGuire.

We are also grateful to the librarians and staff of the following institutions for their help in making available to us information and illustrations: the Reader's Service Librarians at the Radcliffe Science Library; the Reference Librarians at The Library of Congress; Mary Walsh, MLS, Denison Memorial Library, University of Colorado Health Sciences Center; Ken Clark of the Chihuly Studio; Chrissy Illsey from the Whitney Museum in New York; Gloria Groom from The Art Institute of Chicago (David and Mary Winton Green Curator in the Department of European Painting); Lee Mooney from The Toledo Museum of Art; Barbara Plante at the Museum of Fine arts in Springfield, MA; Ellen Kutcher, the Collections Manager at Reynolda House, Museum of American Art in Winston-Salem, NC; Mariette Ineichen, Bündner Kunstmuseum, Chur; Ze've Rosenkranz, Curator at the Albert Einstein Archives of The Hebrew University of Jerusalem; Michael Molnar, Research Director at the Freud Museum in London; Stephanie Sloane, Pace Prints in New York; Jon Mason, Assistant Research & Archives, Pace Wildenstein Gallery in New York. Mr. Chuck Close kindly permitted reproduction of one of his paintings. Mr. Giacometti-Dolfi, Stampa, Switzerland generously gave permission to reproduce a painting by Augusto Giacometti.

On a personal note, Valerie Shubik would like to thank her husband, Dr. Philippe Shubik, for reading the manuscript and for offering suggestions. Karl Pfenninger would like to thank his wife, Dr. Marie-France Maylié-Pfenninger and his children, Jan Patrick and Alexandra, for their tolerance and support during the long hours spent over this book.

Denver, Colorado   Karl H. Pfenninger

Oxford, UK   Valerie R. Shubik

Editors' note

The chapters of this book are derived from talks given by the contributors at the symposium on *Higher Brain Function, Art and Science* mentioned above. They have been edited in the interests of clarity and enhanced with additional material, but the colloquial style of the talks has been maintained.

Contents

Colour plates

The colour plates are between pages 144 and 145.

Other illustrations

Part One
The DNA double helix.
Schematic structure of transfer RNA.
Pond organism, *Tetrahymena.*
Process of DNA transcription and RNA splicing.
Haystack in a Field, 1893, by Claude Monet.
Wheat Fields with Reaper, 1888, by Vincent van Gogh.
Team of glass blowers completing a *Venetian* in the Chihuly Studio.
Dale Chihuly's signature.
Pilchuck Glass Center in 1971.
Niijima Floats, with drawings, by Dale Chihuly.
The Chihuly Studio on Lake Union in Seattle.
Sketches and stage sets for *Pelléas and Mélisande*, 1993, by Dale Chihuly.

Part Two
Woman's Head by David Rogers.
Woman and Child by David Rogers.
Woman's Torso by David Rogers.
Togetherness by David Rogers.
Three-dimensional 'Brainvox' reconstruction of a brain.
Piano reduction of 'In Memories of . . .' by Bruce Adolphe.
Piano reduction of 'Bridgehampton Concerto' by Bruce Adolphe (two excerpts).
Improvised fragments by Bruce Adolphe.
Data integration in the nervous system.

Part Three
Rat learning to jump through unlocked window.
Barbados' National Nutrition Centre.
Typical Barbados home.
Children with protein-energy malnutrition and kwashiorkor.
Physical recovery after malnutrition.
Einstein: 1905 and early 1950s.
Picasso: 1904 and 1955.

Stravinsky: 1920 and 1958.
The young and older T.S. Eliot.
Two images of Gandhi: 1905 and the older Gandhi.
The young and older Martha Graham.
The young and older Sigmund Freud.
Illustrations from *De Humani Corporis Fabrica*, 1543, by Andrea Vesalius.
Two electron micrographs of a pancreatic exocrine cell.

Part Four
Rembrandt self-portrait (detail), 1669.
Line drawing of Rembrandt's self-portrait.
Large-pixel image of Abraham Lincoln by Leon Harmon.
No. 6 in *Keith Series*, 1979, by Chuck Close.
Schematic view of the visual system.
Self-similarity in the cauliflower.
The Sierpinski Gasket.
Artificial fractal coastline by R.F. Voss.
Fractal landscape by R.F. Voss.
A diffusion-limited fractal aggregate by C. Evertsz.
A fractal design by R.F. Voss.

Synthesis
African fractal and Cantor set.

The entangled bank:
an introduction

After Newton died in 1727, a monument was erected in what is now called the Scientist's Corner of Westminster Abbey. The sarcophagus was decorated with a pile of four books and two cherubs holding a prism, a telescope and newly minted coins. The implication is clear. Newton's towering intellect and god-given gift for creative thinking was the origin of his inspiration. Not far away, in front of the monument to Newton, is the tomb of Charles Darwin, whose *On the Origin of Species* first discussed the evolution of man. The proximity of the monuments is telling. If we are to define the single, most unique human attribute evolution has produced, it must be our ability to think creatively. Thinking is the ultimate human resource. Breaking through the barriers posed by dogma, and reaching beyond the limits of established patterns of thinking to discover what is new and useful is the engine that drives society.

What are the foundations of creativity? What is a plausible approach to this question in the twenty-first century, when the Faustian legend is a pre-Darwinian myth, and God is the Creator and infinitely unfathomable, but, as one wit said, religion is one of our best-kept secrets? How can we explain the genius of a Mozart or a Picasso? Throughout history, the analysis of human mental activity has been domineered by metaphysical discussions. This may be changing. Our understanding of creativity can no longer escape the influence of vastly improved knowledge in neuroscience. It is a major endeavor of this book to discuss creative activity in the light of this new science of the mind.

Is it reasonable for humans to try to comprehend creativity, the most advanced product of their minds? The molecular biologist and science philosopher Gunther Stent is not alone in arguing it might be beyond the capability of the brain to understand the full range of its own functions. This has been the starting point for unresolved metaphysical debates—two thousand years ago as well as today.

A landmark in the exploration of the mind was Descartes' theory of the 'res cogitans', a 'thinking substance' totally distinct from flesh and body and dissociated from the brain. The mind–body problem did not begin with Descartes, but his theory of the duality of mind and body has had profound and lasting impact. It took two hundred years of science and debate to move the thinking towards biology and away from Descartes' view. By this time, the end of the nineteenth century, an understanding of the biology of the brain had begun to emerge, neurologists had recognized that the cerebral cortex played a critical role in mental functions, and behavior had been linked to evolution (i.e. to biology and genetics). In the face of these advances, which heralded modern neuroscience, none other than Sigmund Freud argued that 'the relationship between the chain of physiological events in the nervous system and the mental processes is probably not one of cause and effect' (Freud, 1891). Perhaps not surprisingly, at that time, the explorers of the relationships between mental functions and the brain were preoccupied with the shape and size of the cerebral cortex rather than with its inner workings. So, even at the beginning of the twentieth century, Descartes' ideas permeated our thinking.

The mind–body problem continues to haunt scientists and philosophers. Bertrand Russell's grandmother teased the man who some regard as the most brilliant philosopher of the twentieth century with this mocking refrain: 'What is mind? Never matter! What is matter? Never mind!' Russell, after rejecting Descartes' fundamental Cartesian dualism, pointed out that those who reject Descartes' doctrine often retain a number of the underlying logical beliefs, which subsequently influence their thinking. He also noted that many philo-sophical debates center around scientific questions 'with which science is not yet ready to deal' (Russell, 1954). Is science ready today?

In 1859, Charles Darwin presented his theory of natural evolution. His pub-lication, *On the Origin of Species* (Darwin, 1859), in many ways marks the transition from the metaphysical to the biological. In the same book Darwin prophesied the emergence of a new natural science in which psychology would come to be based on a fresh, biological foundation. About one hundred years later, Paul Churchland, a philosopher of psychology, argues that our common-sense conception of psychological phenomena constitutes a fundamentally defective theory that is being displaced by modern neuroscience. Is this what Darwin foresaw in the final chapter of *On the Origin of Species*?

The cognitive psychologist, Howard Gardner, recognizes the importance of neuroscience. He cautions, however, that 'you could know every bit of neuro-circuitry in somebody's head, and you still would not know whether or not that person was creative' (Gardner, Part 3). Gardner is saying that the conscious mind will never be fully explained by the hard sciences, thus echoing Stent. We do not know the outcome of this debate, but for the time being the meta-physicians are members of the team.

The dawn of modern neuroscience came in the middle of the twentieth century, in the wake of a series of major technological advances: electrophysiology uncovered the nature of electrical currents in nerve cells, electron microscopy revealed the synapse (the strategic point where signals are transmitted chemically from one nerve cell to the next), and receptors for such chemical signals were identified because of advances in biochemistry and the availability of radioactive tracers. Soon, approaches of cell and molecular biology and genetics, as well as those of mathematical modeling using computers, were brought to bear on problems of neuroscience. More recently, non-invasive imaging techniques were developed that enable the neuroscientist to correlate particular mental functions in waking individuals with activity in specific brain regions. A whole new discipline has emerged, a science that encompasses the functions of the brain from the molecule to the mind.

As a result, many believe today that the schism between mind and body no longer exists. It is widely accepted that the physical entity that generates the mind and its creative output is the human brain. This underscores a critical point: regardless of one's position on the physical versus the metaphysical properties of the mind, whatever new theories on creativity emerge they must be compatible with our current knowledge of brain function. And if we are to reconcile the results from the many philosophical, historical, biographical and psychoanalytical studies of creativity and its origins, it is essential to combine this knowledge with biological evidence. The reason for this is simple: if the mind is indeed what the brain does, then our thinking about the mind must be consistent with the biology of the brain.

Framing definitions of creativity has been notoriously difficult; for example, psychologists look inward and theologians upward. The incorporation of neuroscience into the discourse on creativity changes the perspective and prompts the unexpected hypothesis that creativity embraces not only the whole range of higher mental functions, but body responses as well. This idea is most clearly articulated by neuroscientist Antonio Damasio. Scientific evidence supports his thesis that inherited mental images outside consciousness as well as physical body responses are involved in the selection of thoughts or images in one's mind. This selection process, and what is commonly called 'intuition' (the ability to arrive at a solution without reasoning), may well be based on mechanisms that emerged during evolution. Damasio's theory thus reconnects mind, brain and nature, as well as reason and emotion, on the basis of biological evidence. It begins to explain the '*Eureka!*' experience.

This book is organized around four central themes of creativity: the creative experience in art and science; the biological basis of imagination, emotion and reason; creative powers and the environment; and the mind's perception of patterns. These themes are addressed in a cross-disciplinary manner. The views of artists, who couch their ideas in more metaphorical language, mingle with the analytical thoughts of scientists, who strive to understand how the brain generates images and ideas. The voices of creators (artist, scientist, mathematician) and of those who study creative activity (neuroscientist, psychologist, philosopher) generate a broad spectrum of views on creativity whose integration offers new insights and becomes a creative act in itself.

A brief overview of the four main parts of the book follows.

Part 1

'Eureka! Discovery versus creation' compares the creative experiences of two individuals who have broken through traditional boundaries. One is an artist, and the other is a scientist. Their observations are followed by those of a philosopher who addresses the question of whether art and science are essentially similar or different. When Nobel Laureate, Thomas Cech, was a young molecular biologist, it was accepted universally that biological catalytic activity was confined to the realm of proteins. Cech's intuition, imaginative experimentation, sharp logic and radical thinking overturned that dogma and proved the existence of catalytic RNA, a discovery that impacts on many areas of biology and medicine.

Dale Chihuly, one of the world's great glass artists, created an art form out of a traditional craft. He broke with conventional wisdom and defied the limitations of this medium to create glass worlds that range from delicate vessels to huge installations, exhibited in major museums throughout the world.

'Is science discovery and art creation?' is the question addressed by Gunther Stent, a renowned molecular biologist. He makes the important distinction between creative works and their contents and explains that the natural scientist, like the artist, works in a world of abstractions. As he puts it, 'for the mind, reality is a set of structural transforms abstracted from the phenomenal world', a concept that is echoed later in Stevens' description of how visual perception works. Stent places creative works of art and science into a continuum that ranges from music and other arts (which draw on the inner human world) to science (which relates to our outer world)—all expressed in their distinct languages.

Part 2

'Body, brain and mind: Emotion and reason' addresses the roles of emotion and reason in creative activity. The traditional separation of these entities typically associates emotion with the arts and reason with science. The chapters in this section argue that emotion and reason are linked and essential for any form of creativity, across the continuum proposed by Gunther Stent.

David E. Rogers, a gifted physician–scientist who is an accomplished sculptor, balances creative expression in multiple, apparently unrelated domains. Rogers illustrates the power of emotion to fuel imagination, not only in the artistic realm, but also in scientific administration. Perhaps, he observes, working in both a rational and an emotional environment 'opens up more circuits in the brain'.

Antonio R. Damasio and his team of neuroscientists have discovered that emotional responses are inextricably linked to our 'rational' decision-making strategies. Modern scientific evidence thus challenges the foundation of Descartes' doctrine. In his essay, Damasio goes on to develop a scientific explanation for the laymen's phrase 'a good imagination,' which is based on a diversity-generating mechanism in our brains. Highly creative individuals can generate a rich array of images in this inner world, and they can modify these representations and discover novel configurations. Damasio links emotion and artistic expression to imagination, intuition and reason. His biological explanations are mirrored to a remarkable degree in the creative individual's personal experiences.

Bruce Adolphe is a prolific composer whose works range from solo pieces to opera and have been performed all over the world. Adolphe believes that music begins in the mind, and he speaks right from Damasio's inner, imaginary world. For Adolphe, the source of musical inspiration lies in memories that evoke feelings: the rasp of his 24-year-old parrot's voice, the rhythm of crowds crossing noisy New York streets or the sticky feel of eating thick chocolate icing are sublimated into new musical structures. He offers imagination exercises to stimulate the 'mind's ear' and argues that Damasio's working memory is 'really what composing is all about'.

The functions of specific brain regions (i.e. of large assemblies of nerve cells) form the basis for Damasio's explanations of the biology of imagination and emotion. The cell biologist and neuroscientist, Karl H. Pfenninger, uses a different but complementary strategy. He studies the elements or subunits such nerve cell assemblies are made of and analyzes how genes and the environment affect the construction of these assemblies during development and evolution. This raises the question of how imagination and creativity relate to the Darwinian concept of man's origins, specifically, the evolution of brain and mind.

Part 3

'The adaptive mind: deprivation versus rich stimulation' examines the influence of the environment on creative activity, from the individual's microenvironment to the societal macroenvironment. Janina Galler, a child psychiatrist and neurobiologist, describes studies that connect Pfenninger's cellular and molecular perspective to the developing human mind. Her results are based on work with children in Barbados and the Yucatan, as well as on experiments conducted with animals. Galler demonstrates that deprivation in early childhood (i.e. malnutrition and especially the lack of stimulus) interferes with the development of intelligence.

The cognitive psychologist, Howard Gardner, offers a different approach by analyzing the environments of acknowledged major creators of this century. Disregarding conventional IQ testing, he develops the concept of multiple intelligences. He finds that, regardless of the type of intelligence, creators typically grow up in nurturing environments that stimulate a rich imagination.

Nobel Laureate, George Palade, one of the creators of modern cell biology, takes a broad view of the history of creative achievement. Not unlike Gardner, he conjectures that there is a causal relationship between prosperity and creative output. He believes that people will look back on the twentieth century as a golden era of creativity, especially in the sciences, but wonders whether creative activity in the arts has suffered.

Part 4

This section is entitled 'Patterns of perception.' When Gardner discusses the interactions between creator and environment he points out that creative works must impact on society to reach their full significance. In other words, creative works must be recognized. The mechanism of how we recognize what is creative ultimately becomes a problem of perception of patterns—for example, patterns of shapes, sounds or logic. Pattern perception is examined in this section of the book from three different but complementary perspectives: from the point of view of the painter, the neuroscientist and the mathematician.

Françoise Gilot is an internationally recognized painter who wrote about her life with Picasso and her friendship with Matisse. Shape and color are the basic visual tools of the painter, but images and symbols, or what Gilot calls a 'language without a voice', affect our senses in many ways. She explains: 'Seeing is more than a visual experience; perception is more than a function of one sense . . . seeing is not a fixed perspective, but the synthesis of visual experiences that are not frozen, but constantly changing.'

Charles F. Stevens, a distinguished neuroscientist, explains that what we see is determined by how we see, or by the way our brain processes visual information. Two issues are central to this essay: the nervous system separates line and color information; and our response to specific patterns, shapes or color combinations depends on wiring of the visual system that is genetically predetermined. If you assume primordial symbols or archetypes are real, you need genetic underpinnings. Thus, Stevens offers insights into how Gilot thinks and explains the biological basis of the French Academy's 200-year debate on the superiority of line or color.

The mathematician, Benoit Mandelbrot, father of fractal geometry, broke with traditional Euclidean geometry and its symbols. Just like Gilot, he could have stepped right out of the pages of one of Gardner's books on creating minds, and he tells how he created a simple one-line mathematical formula that describes irregular shapes. This formula captures the essence or order of complex and apparently irregular forms in nature, all previously regarded as chaotic or without pattern. The laws governing fractal geometry were born out of visual thinking. We watch Gilot begin her painting by placing a circle in a context, while Mandelbrot shows us how a simple fractal formula can initiate a computer-generated image that appeals to one's artistic mind. Are fractal patterns a new form of art—one that is created without an artist—or does the human brain respond to fractal order inherent in works of art?

In Darwin's famous 'entangled bank' paragraph with which he concludes *On the Origin of Species*, the evolutionary biologist speaks of an environment in which a wide variety of plants and animals 'so different from each other, and dependent upon each other in so complex a manner', are all governed by the same laws. In some ways, this description applies to the contributors of the essays presented here. They are all very different. All search for the origins of creativity in their own way. But they are interdependent because not one of them alone can cover the whole problem. This is not a Gradgrindian world of facts out of Dickens, but an entangled bank in which biological mechanisms that evolved over millions of years provide the foundation for a new definition of creativity.

PART ONE

Eureka! Discovery versus creation

THOMAS R. CECH

Overturning the dogma: catalytic RNA

Most scientific hypotheses, including what seem the brightest and best, turn out to be wrong. I would guess that the luckiest and most productive of investigators is right in his original notion, the guess with which he starts his work, about once out of a hundred tries, at his peak. What counts is his instinct for spotting wrongness, his willingness to give up a favorite conviction, his readiness to quit and shift to a better project. Insoluble problems abound.

Lewis Thomas, 1980

I don't know nearly enough to tackle the general problem of creativity in the arts and sciences. Instead, I will tell you a personal story. I will then explain how I think this experience taps into many of the issues that are being discussed here. The basic story is the discovery that ribonucleic acid (RNA), a form of the genetic material, can act as a biocatalyst. What that means will be explained in detail in a moment. For a while, I tired of telling this story, and it seemed self-serving. But I found that after I had given a relatively dry scientific lecture, students would often ask for the story. They would say, 'How in the world did you come up with this idea in the first place?' Eventually, I realized that maybe it was important to tell the story to students since, if you read a textbook about some scientific discovery, it tends to give the impression that someone had an idea and did a linear series of experiments, marching from point A directly to point B. Maybe that happens when a theoretical physicist develops a hypothesis and tells an experimental physicist 'here is what you have to do to prove me correct'. Perhaps in some scientific areas such things do happen. But in those sciences I know, from chemistry through biology, few discoveries are made by such a straightforward path. My story involves a crooked path, which I believe is typical. I would certainly not be so bold as to call this a lesson in creativity, but you will notice here and there elements of creativity that have been discussed by others, in addition to some previously unemphasized elements. However, before I can tell you my story and make it understandable, I have to explain a little of molecular biology.

What is RNA and what is a biocatalyst?

Living cells need to know how to make particular proteins. For example, they need instructions to make pepsin, a stomach enzyme that helps you digest food, or myosin, the protein that helps you move your muscles. How do cells know how to make these particular proteins? The information is encoded in the chromosomes in a molecule called deoxyribonucleic acid (DNA)—the famous double helix. There are only four different building blocks in the strands of the helix. The order of those building blocks determines the sequence, eventually, of the amino acids in a protein.

How is this information transmitted? The cell copies the information stored in the DNA into a chemically related molecule, RNA. RNA differs from DNA only by one oxygen atom in each of the repeating units. Then, this RNA molecule is read out, three of its building blocks at a time, and each of these triplets specifies a particular amino acid. This process is called translation and results in protein synthesis. The order of the amino acids laid down into the protein determines how the protein folds, and how it folds ultimately determines what it does. These proteins can perform a large variety of functions: one may be an enzyme that digests food; another may be a building block of a cell— a structural component; yet another may participate in muscle contraction.

The process of encoding and synthesizing proteins can be likened to the following everyday example. The DNA can be thought of as a 'gold seal' master copy of your favorite movie, stored in a vault somewhere, and from which a limitless number of cheap copies can be made. These copies are the RNA equivalent; they hold the same information as the master copy. The protein synthetic process is akin to putting the videotape into a videocassette recorder. The equivalent of the tape machine in the cell is called a ribosome, which is responsible for translating the RNA information into the protein. What you finally get out is something useful—an image that you see on the television monitor. This is the equivalent of the cellular protein.

This role for RNA as a coding intermediary in the process of protein synthesis has been known for a long time. More recently, we found that RNA, in addition to being an information carrier, can also be a biocatalyst. That means it can speed up, by perhaps a billionfold or even many billionsfold, a chemical reaction that is necessary for life. Like other biocatalysts, it does this in a very specific way, speeding up one of the many reactions that a living cell needs to carry out, rather than all chemical reactions. Biocatalytic roles in the cell had previously been thought to be restricted to protein enzymes; now we know that in some cases RNA also can act as a biocatalyst.

It is useful to picture the players in this cellular chemistry game. Plate 2 shows the structure of a protein enzyme that binds a single sugar molecule (red) and

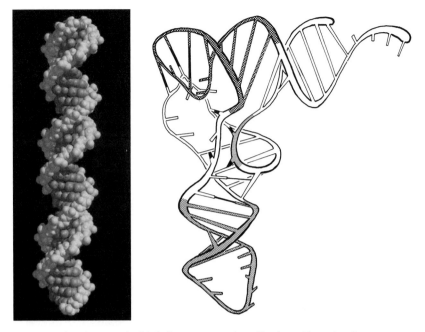

Fig. 1.1 *(Left)* The DNA double helix; reconstruction of its three-dimensional structure. (Image Library of Biological Macromolecules, Institute of Molecular Biotechnology, Jena).

Fig. 1.2 *(Right)* Schematic structure of transfer RNA. (Courtesy Professor Sung-Hou Kim, University of California, Berkeley).

catalyzes its chemical transformation. The protein has a complex, folded configuration. Why should it be a surprise that a nucleic acid can also catalyze a reaction? When people think of nucleic acid, they usually think of the double helix of DNA (Fig. 1.1)—a long, skinny molecule which seems to have neither the diversity of shape to fold around a variety of small molecules, nor the right sort of chemical active groups to enhance particular chemical transformations. On the other hand, if we go from DNA to its sister molecule, RNA, we see more conformational richness even in one of nature's smallest RNA molecules, the so-called transfer RNA (Fig. 1.2). This single chain folds back upon itself, forming local, double helical regions with the two strands connected by 'hairpin loops'. A variety of other features include a complex structural fold where the two rod-like regions come together, and several indentations or holes in the molecule. Thus, in terms of its structure, RNA has moved away from DNA towards the polymorphism characteristic of protein molecules.

Only very recently have we and others obtained similarly detailed pictures of catalytic RNA molecules or portions thereof (Plate 3). In the example shown in

Fig. 1.3 Drawing of the unicellular pond organism, *Tetrahymena.* (Actual size approximately 1/10 mm).

Plate 3, RNA achieves a degree of compactness reminiscent of proteins, with a distinct inner core and outer surface. For many other RNAs, we have only two-dimensional road maps, describing how these molecules are configured at a first level of folding. Even in these rather crude diagrams, however, one can see that catalytic RNAs have a complex folded shape, and it has been shown in a variety of ways that this folded shape is necessary for their activity.

RNA splices itself

> *Scientists try to make sense of the world by devising hypotheses, i.e., draft explanations of what the world is like; they examine these explanations as critically as they know how to, with the result that either they gain confidence in their beliefs or they modify or abandon them.*
>
> Peter Medawar, 1991

How was catalytic RNA first found? We were studying the organism shown in Fig. 1.3—a single-cell, microscopic pond animal called *Tetrahymena.* We were studying these organisms because, unlike bacteria, they have their genetic information in a cell nucleus and their protein synthesis takes place in the cytoplasm—which makes them, in a very fundamental way, similar to human cells. Yet, they are as easy to grow and to work with as bacteria, and their use does not antagonize animal rights' activists.

What we were trying to study in this organism was one of the steps in the expression of a gene—the step called transcription (the copying of a piece of information in the DNA into RNA). What we did not know when we started

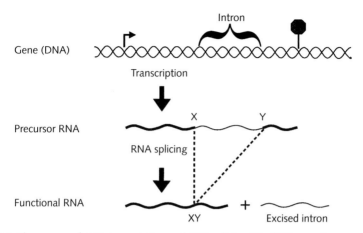

Fig. 1.4 The process of DNA transcription and RNA splicing. The DNA encoding a gene (between the arrow pointing to the right and the stop sign) may be interrupted by a so-called intron. The intron (between X and Y) is transcribed along with the gene and then excised from the precursor RNA.

these studies was that the coding region of the DNA was interrupted by a stretch of non-coding DNA called an intron, shown in Fig. 1.4 as a thin wavy line. I will not speculate here about why these introns occur in genes, but I will point out that, particularly as you go to higher and higher organisms and eventually to humans, you find that most genes are interrupted by quite a number of introns. When the cell copies the information in the DNA to form an RNA molecule, this interrupting portion of the DNA is not recognized as anything special. It is copied right along with the flanking, coding regions into a so-called precursor RNA.

We set up a simple test tube system with *Tetrahymena* extracts to try to follow the copying of the DNA into RNA. We saw that, yes, this reaction was working, but also that the intron was excised from the RNA and accumulated as a separate fragment. This result meant that, in addition to the copying, the next step of the expression of the gene, splicing, was going on in the test tube. The word 'splicing' comes from the nautical world: what does a sailor do with a rope that has a frayed portion in the middle? Nowadays, he buys a new rope. But in times past, he would cut the rope on either side of the frayed portion, throw out the bad part, and then splice the two flanking portions together. That is what 'splicing' is supposed to connote in molecular biology. So, in our test tube assays, the RNA was cut at points X and Y to remove the intron, and point X was joined to point Y to form the useful RNA (see Fig. 1.4). At this juncture we became more interested in this downstream step. There were a hundred laboratories in all parts of the world trying to study the copying of DNA into

RNA, but there was only one other laboratory, that of John Abelson in southern California, that had ever witnessed RNA splicing take place in a test tube. Abelson was looking at the splicing of a different kind of RNA in a different organism. We thought our information might well complement the data Abelson was collecting. So we decided to allow ourselves the luxury of a small diversion to examine the RNA splicing step.

What does a biochemist do to investigate such a process? One goal is to purify the enzyme that is responsible for recognizing two particular points along this long chain of RNA (containing in reality about 7000 individual units), for cutting at those two points, and for joining them together. Maybe there would be several enzymes involved, and we had no doubt these enzymes would be protein. After all, you could read in any biology or biochemistry textbook that any reaction that took place with such exquisite specificity would have to be catalyzed, and the catalyst, of course, would have to be a protein enzyme!

> *What is being tested in an experiment is the logical implication of the hypothesis, i.e. the logical consequences of accepting a hypothesis. A well-designed and technically successful experiment will yield results of two different kinds: the experimental results may square with the hypothesis, or they may be inconsistent with it.*
>
> Peter Medawar, 1991

Specifically, we were trying to find the proteins responsible for conversion of the precursor RNA into the RNA used for protein synthesis. How do you do that? Since we knew that the activity responsible for this conversion was present in our extracts from *Tetrahymena*, we isolated the precursor RNA—the RNA that had not yet undergone the transformation—and incubated it with a protein extract from *Tetrahymena* cells. The first time we did the experiment we saw splicing take place. It is quite unusual in science for an experiment to work the first time, so we were gratified. However, the result of a control experiment was another matter.

A control is a parallel assay consisting of a set of tubes identical to the experimental ones, except that various critical components have been left out—just to make sure that the reaction depends on the factors you presume are critical. One of the controls was to leave out the extract from the *Tetrahymena* cells, added as the source of the machinery that was supposed to be responsible for splicing. It turned out that that tube showed just as much RNA splicing as the one where we had added the extract! That was not one of the expected results of the experiment. It was incumbent upon me as the director of this young laboratory to come up with some explanations. As you will see, they turned out to be wrong. But it does not matter so much whether scientific hypotheses are correct or incorrect—as long as they flow logically from the information you have at the time, and as long as they are testable. Then, they either pass or fail the test, and along this type of branched pathway one can make progress in the understanding of a scientific problem.

At that time, the hypothesis was that what we were calling pure RNA must in fact not be pure. Some protein enzyme must be tightly associated with the RNA and responsible for catalyzing the splicing reaction. When we took the 'RNA' and incubated it with the small molecules present in all cells and necessary for this reaction, this RNA-protein complex would then go through all the splicing steps. How does one test such a hypothesis? Scientists know of many ways to destroy proteins, which, according to the hypothesis, should then block splicing. The methods are related to those you use when you wash your clothes. You add detergent, which is bad for proteins; detergents denature proteins and render them soluble in water so they float away. Thus, one test of our hypothesis was to add detergent to the test tube reaction and, of course, that was expected to stop the splicing activity. But it did not! The splicing activity did not care if there was detergent present. Another treatment that proteins hate is being boiled. Only a few proteins are able to refold properly after they have been boiled and unfolded. So we boiled the presumably protein-contaminated RNA, cooled it down, and then added the small molecules—and the splicing continued unabated. At that point the hypothesis was not looking so good, but we thought maybe this was an unusually stable protein enzyme. So we chose harsher treatments, like boiling in the presence of detergent or adding large amounts of non-specific proteases (enzymes that degrade protein)—but nothing seemed to prevent the splicing activity.

This brings us to our departmental Christmas party of 1981, when one of my graduate students, Paula Grabowski, gave me a picture of a daisy. Alternate petals were labeled 'it's a protein' and 'it's not'. Fortunately, we were able to think of something more scientific than picking the petals off the daisy to try to resolve the dilemma. We turned to genetic engineering, with which we had no prior experience at the time. We wished to synthesize this RNA in the test tube so that we would obtain RNA that had never seen the proteins of a *Tetrahymena* cell. Our thinking was as follows: if such RNA still underwent splicing we would be forced to conclude that there was no contaminating protein. In that case, the RNA itself might be the catalyst responsible for this very specific transformation, a phenomenon that had not been observed before.

We took part of the gene, the DNA that encodes this RNA, inserted it into a bacterial plasmid, amplified the artificial gene in bacteria, purified it, and added a purified RNA polymerase. This polymerase catalyzed the synthesis of multiple RNA copies that included the intron and the flanking regions of the DNA. Then we removed the one protein we had added, the well-characterized polymerase, and incubated the synthetic RNA with the small molecules, including magnesium ion. We made the astonishing discovery that the RNA underwent splicing. Importantly, the two sites along this long RNA chain at which the cutting and rejoining took place were exactly the same sites that were known to be spliced inside the living cell. This gave us some confidence that the observed so-called self-splicing reaction was relevant to the biological system.

Implications of catalytic RNA

What are the implications of this discovery? Two of the most fundamental functional complexes in the cell—machines that are necessary for the transfer and expression of genetic information—are the spliceosome, a large complex of RNA and protein that catalyzes splicing reactions in humans and other species, and the ribosome found in all cells, also a large complex of protein and nucleic acid (likened earlier to the videotape recorder), but responsible for synthesizing proteins. Our findings have given great encouragement to the current view that both of these complexes are essentially RNA-based machines whose activity is further enhanced by proteins. Thus, it is clear that RNA is involved in many very fundamental aspects of cell function.

The discovery of RNA catalysis has implications in another field—origin of life research. How did life on earth get started about four billion years ago? Over endless cocktail-hour discussions, scientists had argued that what you really need for even the most fundamental step of life, for any life form, is the reproduction of the genetic material—it may not be sufficient for life, but it is the most basic function. To achieve such reproduction, you need two things: the information molecule (which means nucleic acid in today's cells) and the catalytic machinery that copies the nucleic acid (which was thought to mean protein enzymes). So scientists were talking about rather complex scenarios in which there had to exist in some droplet of water somewhere on the earth, through random processes, just the right nucleic acid molecule and, simultaneously, just the right protein molecule that could copy that nucleic acid molecule. This seemed a little far-fetched! Now we know that one of these large molecules found in all cells, namely RNA, can play both games—that of an informational molecule and that of a biocatalyst. We also know that it can catalyze reactions of the very type required for copying the genetic information.

This opens the way for a much simplified hypothesis: namely, that at the beginning there was only RNA replicating itself and that the proteins were fitted into the scheme a little bit later. While such a scenario is exciting to think about, I am sure you can appreciate that it is very difficult to prove or disprove.

Serendipity, teamwork, and peer relations

All men occasionally stumble over the truth, but most hastily pick them-
selves up and hurry on as if nothing had happened.

Winston Churchill (attributed)

Let me look back on this story and analyze it with respect to the theme of creativity. Here are some ideas that have already been brought up and also some new ones. How about the role of luck in this research? No doubt you can see it in my story. We were looking for something very ordinary, with no hint or expectation that at the end of this trail would be a discovery that others would perceive as being of such special and fundamental importance. However, a better word than luck would be serendipity, best described by Louis Pasteur: '*chance favors only the prepared mind*'. Serendipity is a mixture of luck and the faculty of sensing it. That means both having your eyes open and having the necessary training so that when you stumble upon a bizarre result you recognize that it is worth pursuing and understanding rather than discarding.

A couple of years after our discovery, we realized that a number of laboratories throughout the world had had the appropriate cellular materials in their freezers to do the same experiments in 1982. French scientists in Gif-sur-Yvette were interested in the problem, but they were not investigating the process at the RNA level. They were trying to infer the answer from genetics and by looking at the DNA sequence, and thereby missed the fact that the RNA had catalytic activity. One Danish laboratory, in Aarhus, was neck and neck with us all the way, but they could not believe their results. They decided to quit working on the problem before the end—and felt bad about it later.

Another important aspect of the story is the team or group effort. Generally, we are discussing creativity as if it was exclusively, or almost by definition had to be, an individual effort. I am not so sure about this. Important to my story is the fact that several researchers in the laboratory, including Paula Grabowski, Art Zaug, and myself, were pursuing parallel yet distinct pathways. Had it just been me doing all of the experiments and getting strange results, I might have suspected my own technical abilities or my judgment. But I had great faith in my co-workers and knew they were good scientists. The fact that all of us were collecting some strange results validated the findings. Also, I was a step removed from the experiments of my collaborators, and I was not so enmeshed in the day-to-day problems of just getting the work done. Such distance often gives one a perspective of the whole landscape. Even so, it took me a long time to grasp the significance of what we were observing.

Howard Gardner discusses the issue of how one is perceived by one's peers as being important in any creative process. There has to be some support, and there also has to be some level of criticism. We certainly experienced both during this voyage of discovery. Acceptance by the *major domos* of the field was very encouraging. I remember a conference in about 1980 in Frederick, Maryland, involving most of the famous people in the RNA field—the people who had been the young 'turks' of the decade before and many of them already, or soon to be, elected to the National Academy of Sciences. They could have excluded me easily; instead, they embraced me and the work I presented. I do not know whether this acceptance was essential, but it certainly made things easy.

I also recall receiving some useful criticism and advice, often just the right word at the right time. For example, someone would take me aside at a conference in this field that I had just entered, and would point out how important it was to do experiments in a certain critical way, i.e. performing analyses that take into account every atom in the molecule and not just the gross chemistry. While I could appreciate the importance, when I returned to my laboratory the reality of the situation struck me: we would have to learn a whole new technology. Yet at the end of a long road, entirely new insights were gained.

This leads to another issue, again an example of serendipity: through this whole voyage I felt as if I had stumbled upon a particular field of science that I had not planned to enter—an area in the crack between biology and chemistry. It turned out to be a field for which my own way of thinking, my own mental processes, were particularly well suited. It is my belief that I was able to do much better work in this new field than I did previously. This makes me wonder how many people, who perform well or are perhaps even distinguished in their fields, might reach much greater achievements if they moved just a little bit from their specific area of interest into one where the powers of their own particular brain could be even better utilized. I imagine this holds true for all creative endeavors, in the arts as well as the sciences.

Science and art: similarities and differences

The last issue I would like to address is one of the similarities and differences between the creative processes in art and in science. Because I feel confident to discuss the creative process in science only, I will leave it to those who are artists to correct me if I misunderstand what it is to be an artist. I believe there are similarities. One feature that is shared by the creative processes in art and science is that the progress one makes is not linear with time. For any given amount of time spent, you often get nothing in return. And then, all of a sudden, the breakthrough comes, the flash of inspiration, and the problem is solved in a relatively short time. During those periods when you are laboring away and getting nowhere, the frustration can be very discouraging, but the rare periods of rapid insight are extremely exciting and uplifting, and for most of us they validate the whole endeavor. Another common feature is that we spend much time examining one particular property, for example, the fish in a well-known work by M.C. Escher. We try to understand why all the fish are swimming in one direction. Then, finally, we look at the scene from a new angle and realize there are birds flying in the opposite direction, and that is the key to the whole problem. So much for my attempt to bring some art into this discussion.

How about differences between art and science? I find Gunther Stent's discussion very provocative and I absolutely agree with most of it, but there is one point about which I have a different opinion. Stent compares a hundred scientists all using rather similar materials and trying to do the same thing as perceived by the artists, and one hundred artists, all using similar tools and trying to do the same thing. I think the scientists and the artists have rather different intentions. When different scientists are studying a particular problem— for example, how some signal is perceived by a cell and how that leads to a change in cellular metabolism, or how to identify the gene defects which are responsible for schizophrenia—their intent is to arrive at the same place, to achieve the same endpoint. After all, science is knowing nature. This implies that there exists a fixed set of facts that everyone wants to know. Some scientists might hope to solve a problem faster than their competitors, to do so more convincingly, more insightfully, or with more style, but they do not anticipate obtaining a different result. In fact, if two competing scientists generate different results and reach different conclusions, the field does not rest until this discrepancy has been resolved and it is understood why these different answers have been obtained. In contrast, I suspect that artists are not striving for commonality, but rather, that the content as well as the form of their work is unique.

Despite the different intent, it is still true that two exceedingly competent scientists who are investigating the same phenomenon will often come up with two related but distinct interpretations. Maybe that is not so different from art, after all. To illustrate this point, consider two paintings of similar subjects, chosen because they are both done in related palettes; Monet emphasizes pinks and van Gogh, yellows and blues. It is not the colors, however, but the way that they are used that is significant (Figs. 1.5 and 1.6; the two pictures are reproduced in black and white to emphasize the difference between the approaches). Even though one can imagine that Vincent van Gogh and Claude Jean Monet painted landscapes in the south of France with the same tubes of paint and the same brushes, their two paintings are unique. That is often the case in science as well.

Fig. 1.5 Claude Jean Monet, *Haystack in a Field*, 1893. (James Philip Gray Collection, Museum of Fine Arts, Springfield, Mass.) (Reproduced in black and white to emphasize stylistic differences from Fig. 1.6)

Fig. 1.6 Vincent van Gogh, *Wheat Fields with Reaper*, Auvers, 1888. (Toledo Museum of Art, Ohio.) (Reproduced in black and white to emphasize stylistic differences from Fig. 1.5)

What about creativity in science? . . . As a simple representative example of a creative process consider wit in its most popular form, a sudden juxtaposition of seemingly incongruous ideas that may be on the one hand laughter-provoking or on the other hand deeply illuminating or informative . . . The Reverend Sidney Smith was one day walking through the narrow streets of old Edinburgh when a furious altercation was heard between housewives addressing each other high up across the street where the buildings lean toward each other. Sidney Smith and his friend listened for a while and then Smith said 'They can never agree, sir, for they are arguing from different premises!'

Peter Medawar, 1991

DALE CHIHULY

Form from fire

Glass sculpture—a frozen fluid thought

*Who can still believe in the opacity of bodies, since our sharpened and
multiplied sensitiveness has already penetrated the obscure manifestations
of the medium? . . . Our bodies penetrate the sofas upon which we sit, and
the sofas penetrate our bodies.*

> Manifesto of Italian futurist sculptors issued in 1910;
> quoted by Herbert Read, 1964

*Glass is the most purely visual of all the art media, even more visual than
painting, because in it light, color, and material are one.*

> Art critic, J. Perreault, 1996

To me, glass is very different from any other material. Much of that has to
do with the transparency and translucency and the brilliant colors one
can get with glass—as anyone knows who walks into a Gothic cathedral
with stained glass windows. That is not to say that glass isn't also very interesting when it's opaque. Early on, as I got more interested in glass and gained
experience with it, I became aware of the concept of being able to blow the glass
with human breath. It is the one material that you can blow into a form. (The
only other material that comes close in its properties is plastic.) So, human
breath can shape this ancient material that is simply made from sand and fire.
All you have to do is melt sand, any sand, and you have glass. If you add soda,
it will melt at a lower temperature and you can sculpt it.

> *And glass itself, of course, is so much like water. If you let it go on its own,
> it almost ends up looking like something that came from the sea.*
>
> Dale Chihuly, 1993

*I had seen some beautiful Indian baskets at the Washington State
Historical Society and I was struck by the grace of their slumped, sagging
forms. I wanted to capture this grace in glass. The breakthrough for me*

was recognizing that heat was the tool to be used together with gravity to make these forms.

Dale Chihuly, 1993

*I've watched thousands of forms blown and I'm still amazed to see the first breath of air enter the hot gather of glass on the end of a blowpipe. The piece is always moving while it's in progress and one has to make decisions very quickly. I like the work to reflect these quick decisions, the end result being a **frozen fluid thought**—as direct as a drawing. Since the start of the Basket Series in 1977, my work has relied on spontaneous combinations of fire, molten glass, air, centrifugal force, and gravity.*

Dale Chihuly, 1986

Creative teamwork

I am a glass blower and a glass worker, a designer and an artist, and I work with dozens of people to create things. Figure 1.7 shows part of a team that might work on a project. In this case it's a series of glass objects called the *Venetians*. The team is headed by master glass blower, Lino Tagliapietra (he's working to my left), and he's assisted by a group of glass blowers, many of whom are artists in their own right, who have had exhibitions in the United States and around the world. Unlike film directors at the end of their movies, I don't have an easy way to credit what everybody does, which is what I would prefer to do. Because there is no alternative, the works go out with my signature on them only (see Fig. 1.8), but in many ways they are the result of a collaboration and the merger of several people's ideas and skills.

In the early days, however, I did not have the resources to build up a large team. I would often work with one or two people, usually students or other faculty members at the Rhode Island School of Design. So it's interesting to note that the idea of the artist working alone in the studio isn't always correct. It was very common for the masters of the Renaissance to have between ten and thirty people working with them on projects—unlike today's general concept.

In 1971, together with some friends, I founded the Pilchuck Glass Center, outside of Seattle, Washington, in the foothills of the Cascade Mountains over-looking Puget Sound (Fig. 1.9). We had a small grant of $2000 to start this little school and probably never thought it would last for a second summer. However, John and Anne Gould Hauberg of Seattle gave us the property, and John Hauberg single-handedly supported Pilchuck for about ten years as we constructed facilities and buildings. It has grown into an institution with a budget of over a million dollars. We run five, three-week programs in the summer, and we have 50 staff and 50 students. It was really this population of

Fig. 1.7 Team of glass blowers completing a *Venetian* in the Chihuly Studio. Dale Chihuly stands center back; on the right is the Murano artist, Lino Tagliapietra. (Photo: Russell Johnson)

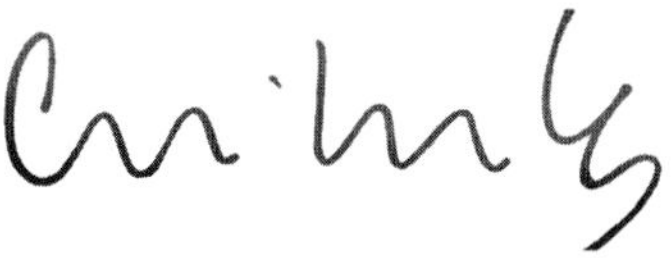

Fig. 1.8 Dale Chihuly's signature.

students and visiting artists that always provided a fresh source of people to work with. As Pilchuck became better known, people began to come from around the world—nowadays from about 25 different countries—to study glass and to work there. Many of them remain in Seattle. As a result, today Seattle has more glass shops than any place in the world outside of Murano.

Discovering installations

The show at the then brand new Seattle Art Museum, designed by the architect Robert Venturi, was the first time I had the opportunity and the resources to do

Fig. 1.9 The beginnings of the Pilchuck Glass Center in 1971. A young Chihuly is standing to the right.

whatever I wanted to with a large space. The exhibition was entitled 'Dale Chihuly Installations 1964–1992'. All the installations in this show were new, but the first part of the exhibition, in a darkened aisleway, consisted of large transparencies, six by nine feet, of about a dozen installations that had been done earlier in the 60s and the 70s. Beyond this, the first actual piece to be seen was installed in the only window in the Seattle Art Museum's gallery space; I called it *Venturi Window* (Plate 9). I extended the mullions of this window across the 45-foot wall and then placed on the window some large blown forms, which I call *Persian* wall pieces. Turning around from this *Venturi Window*, there was a series of 33 *Macchia* pieces. (Macchia is an Italian word for spot.) I combined these *Macchia* into a piece called *Macchia Forest* (Plate 11). (Many of the installations I developed in later years were really composed of what originally started as individual objects that were made to be seen on their own. However, glass blowing is limited somewhat by size. A glass blower is physically able to make a piece of glass no more than four or five feet in diameter. Thus, as opportunities to exhibit in museums increased, I used multiple pieces and worked them together.) The Seattle exhibit continued from

Macchia Forest, around a corner, to an installation called *Ikebana* (from Japanese flower arranging). This was another series I had developed a couple of years before; it started with large vases and the single flower stems that we would place in them. As a way to select from the stems, I had hung them on a wall in my studio. This flower stem array was transferred almost directly to the museum.

The next installation was a series called *Niijima Floats*. Niijima is a little island in Tokyo Bay that I had visited on the occasion of the opening of a new glass school. A Japanese student had come to Pilchuck a few years before. He went back to Japan and was able to raise the money to start a school patterned after Pilchuck, and I was invited to attend the celebration of this new school. Shortly thereafter, I started a new series of large spheres, each up to about 40 inches in diameter, which I chose to call the *Niijima Floats* after the Japanese floats. A view of the *Niijima Floats*, together with eight drawings or paintings on paper, is shown in Fig. 1.10. I will often draw and work with paint to show the glass blowers what I am trying to make.

Just before the opening of the exhibition at the Seattle Art Museum, there was a part of the show that I didn't like. I had mocked it up in a warehouse, but, as part of the exhibition, it wasn't working. So, I decided to make a large multi-tiered structure—a *Chandelier*. The first *Chandelier* I ever made was ten feet high.

In addition to these new installations for the Seattle exhibit, I recreated outside the actual museum building an earlier piece called *20 000 Pounds of Ice and Neon*. In 1971, in collaboration with Jamie Carpenter, who was a young student at the Rhode Island School of Design, we had created the original installation from neon frozen into ice at an old ice house at the back of the school. In any event, the ice piece that I did at the Seattle Art Museum show was the first of many accompanying the *Installations* exhibition. My favorite one, perhaps, was at the Honolulu Academy of Arts in Hawaii. When initially asked if I would do an exhibition there, I was simply going to have one installation. But they requested the ice and neon piece, outside, in a temperature of 80 °. I said, 'Well, it does not seem likely that you would have an ice house—an old ice house that makes the old-fashioned, 300-pound ice blocks.' But the director called me back and said, 'We do have an old ice house.' In fact, they had a 70-year-old ice house that made ice for fishing boats down on the waterfront of Honolulu. So, I ended up with a crew of ten, in Honolulu, working on a combination of different installations, and we increased the size of the exhibition.

The museum is housed in a beautiful building. In 1925, Mrs. Clark, who lived on this property, tore down her own house and built a 100 000-square foot museum for the city of Honolulu. It contains five interior courtyards, each one with a different name. When I went to visit the museum for the first time, I was

Fig. 1.10 *Niijima Floats*, on show with eight drawings at the Seattle Art Museum. (Photo: Eduardo Calderon)

only planning on an installation in the Central Court. But when I saw the rest of these courtyards, I extended the exhibition to include an installation for each. Plate 8 shows the first courtyard you see when you come into this beautiful museum; it is called the Central Court. We knew that there was no lighting in these courtyards and that the opening of the exhibit would be at night. So we searched for little lights for each piece of glass and for small batteries, calculated to last just the three hours of the opening and to be as small as possible. So, behind each of the *Niijima Floats* in the Central Court there was a little bulb lighting the piece, and this was done for all of the other installations as well. That night it rained. Actually, this worked out quite well, especially for the *Chandelier* in the Mediterranean Court, because the rain dripped off each of the little yellow 'hornet bellies' and filled up the *Macchia*. (The elements really don't hurt glass very much, unless the water freezes.) I chose to hang my second *Chandelier*, made about six months after the first one, over a little fountain, and the water splashed up against it (Plate 6).

In the Oriental Court, I installed two *Ikebanas*—large vases about three feet high, with one stem or leaf coming out of each piece. For another courtyard,

I simply took *Macchia* from *Macchia Forest* and placed them directly on the grass. The museum said that they would allow this only if I was sure that it wouldn't hurt the grass in any way. 'Of course it won't,' I said, 'How could it possibly hurt the grass?' This was one of the first installations my crew set up, and within about two hours the sun had completely burned the grass from the magnification through the glass pieces, and we had to spray the grass green.

Inside the building, one installation we did in the contemporary art area became a permanent part of the museum's collection. The museum requested that I also show some of the pieces that I am better known for, like *Seaforms* and *Baskets*. When people think of my work, they think of these organic forms, made primarily using the heat and the fire—hence the name, *Form from Fire*. The museum wanted me to put some glass pieces in one of the beautiful galleries, together with some working drawings. So, I thought about lining the walls with the drawings, and this was the first time I exhibited them in this way. I have done so in several other exhibitions since.

Many of the ideas for the installations come from my own studio, which is on a little lake in Seattle, Lake Union (Fig. 1.11). Lake Union is a freshwater lake almost in the center of Seattle, connected by canals and lochs to the ocean. I was very fortunate to get this beautiful building for my studio. I call it 'The Boathouse' because it was a factory for building 60-foot, 8-person boat shells, owned by a famous shell maker named Pocock. To give you examples of how some of the ideas for the installations emerge—if I make a series of drawings for a piece, the drawings are pinned to the wall. (It was seeing this display that made me want to exhibit the drawings in this way.) Going around the studio, you will find an *Ikebana* series. I would make a series of vases and then a series of stems and then lay them out and begin to work with the pieces. Continuing a tour of the studio, you would come to a long room overlooking the water, and you would see an example of the *Seaforms*. And, along the wall, there would be a series called the *Venetians*—lavishly decorated, colorful and exuberant pieces designed in the spirit of art deco Venetian glass. You would also find the second *Chandelier*, which uses several colors and gold and silver leaf, and, hanging down, two of the *Ikebana* stems. And, you would discover some framed drawings that I did for an opera some time ago. Then, on the coffee table in the front room, you would see a *Seaform* and, to the side, an *Ikebana* stem coming out of a *Venetian*.

Adding music: Pelléas and Mélisande

I had worked on the stage, but when Speight Jenkins, Director of the Seattle Opera, invited me to design the sets for Claude Debussy's opera, *Pelléas and*

Fig. 1.11 'The Boathouse' on Lake Union in Seattle. Location of the Chihuly Studio
(Photo: Russell Johnson)

Mélisande, I had never worked with opera before. I simply said I would, without thinking about it very much. But eventually, I had to transform this plan into reality, and the opera turned out to require a lot of sets. Fortunately, I had at my disposal a large budget and the great skills of the stage shop at the Seattle Opera.

> *I don't know why I said yes so quickly—I think I knew that I was being offered something that I might never be offered again. (Dale Chihuly in a television interview with KCTS 9, Seattle, 7 December 1993)*

> *Pelléas, the impressionist composer's first and only completed opera, consists of five acts and 12 tableaux connected by musical interludes, and it is based on an only slightly changed form of Maurice Maeterlinck's tragedy. Debussy's only significant alterations of the libretto involve the removal of servants and other minor characters, which is done in order to enhance the dramatic, symbolic core of the tragedy. The 'Drame lyrique' tells of the marriage of King Arkel's grandson, Golaud, to Mélisande, a mysterious girl he has found in the forest. King Arkel sends Golaud's half-brother, Pelléas, to carry the message that he consents to the marriage. During the first meeting between Pelléas and Mélisande her wedding ring falls*

*into a fountain or well. With time, Pelléas and Mélisande become increas-
ingly attracted to each other. A later encounter between them—lovers by
now—is interrupted by a jealous and furious Golaud, who then drags
Mélisande by her long golden hair across the stage. Eventually Golaud
kills Pelléas. But Golaud's insistence on knowing the full truth of
Mélisande's love for Pelléas remains unanswered; Mélisande dies in child-
birth. Debussy's music uses different motifs to evoke the spiritual climates,
the moods of the scenes (as opposed to the Wagnerian leitmotiv used
primarily for characters and their actions), and he overlays Maeterlinck's
symbolism with these motifs. The result is a highly abstract and poetic
work.*

I designed the opera set against an all-black background. The stage—floor,
back and sides—was all-black plexiglass; and the curtain was black too. For
the most part, each set consisted of just one single, usually very large element,
that would represent that scene (Fig. 1.12). The opening set, however, could
be more complicated because we had time to set it up beforehand; it was
composed of seven large trees. I made the drawings, and then we went into
the glass shop and made 2-inch high models of the sets out of glass. For the
stage, however, the sets had to be about 12 feet high. Seattle Opera first organized a conference of set designers and opera shops from around the country
to try to determine how to make these things. As a result, all of them were
made very cleverly out of plastic and then painted. Plastic has many qualities
similar to those of glass. You look at a piece of plastic—sometimes you do not
know whether it is glass or plastic. I didn't really have much to do with fabri-
cating the pieces; this was completely under the control of the very able
Robert Schaub, Technical Director of Seattle Opera, who directed the large
crew of people. Because some of the pieces were produced in different parts
of the country, I did not know how any of this would look and work in reality
until a few weeks before the opera was staged.

Thanks to technology, we were able to use new lighting fixtures run by
computers that can be pre-programmed. The light fixtures themselves can
move and change the beam and the color. So, the sets could be lit from the
front, from the back and in different colors. There were 28 of these programmed fixtures; it would have been very difficult to control the lighting by
hand, especially for all 12 sets. Also, it took 55 stage hands to move the sets in
the short periods of time, sometimes only 90 seconds, between scene changes.

During the 400 years of opera history, there were certainly transparent and
translucent materials available that people could have used on the stage, but, for
whatever reason, it seems they were seldom used. However, the transparency and

(a)

(b)

(c)

Fig. 1.12 *Pelléas and Mélisande*, from sketch to stage set: (a) Chihuly's sketch for the single structure in this scene (photo: Michael Seidl); (b) Seattle Opera's mock-up in glass and mixed media (photo: Claire Garoutte); (c) stage photo, Seattle Opera, 11 March 1993.

translucency of glass is what made our opera sets successful. It is that quality, of course, that we replicated with plastic. Having the option of beaming light from behind and, thus, having the sets glow, made *Pelléas* very unusual.

> *I find that this music is translucent, and I think you've got to see the light through it all the time in Debussy, you can't ever get murky. That's what glass does. (Speight Jenkins, Seattle Opera Director, commenting on* Pelléas and Mélisande *on KCTS 9, Seattle, 7 December 1993)*

A rather devastating scene from the opera takes place in a room in the castle. Mélisande is abused and dragged around the stage by her blond hair. To reflect my feelings about the scene, the set consisted of a single, very large, spiky structure, not unlike the bud of a thistle—an element often encountered in the *Venetians* (see Fig. 1.12). The first set in the castle was simply one large *Chandelier*, hanging in the middle of the stage. Again, that was the only element on stage. A lot of important action takes place near the well, and this is the only set that was used twice. My concept for this well was just the end of one of the *Ikebana* flowers, an *Anturium*. The set for the garden was simply one form, about 40 feet long.

The evolutionary process

Before concluding, I would like to trace my evolutionary process and briefly review some of my series that go back about 20 years. There are the *Soft Cylinders*, like the *Bright Yellow Soft Cylinder with Blue Lip Wrap*—the piece shown in Plate 7—which is based on a kind of Navajo Indian motif. Then, in a series called *Pilchuck Baskets*, I began to use gravity and centrifugal force and fire and heat to shape the forms. Another basket set that turned into a series called *Seaforms* is characterized by thin, ribbed structures. Next, I developed the spotted series I call *Macchia*. The *Persians* are a variation of the *Seaforms*. Then came *Venetians* and *Venetians with Putti*. *Mottled Red Venetian with Two Putti* is a piece from this series (see Plate 10).

Most artists—as is true for most architects as well—can be identified by one series of work that developed over a career. In the case of an architect, you may think of a style (e.g. Palladian style). An obvious exception is Frank Lloyd Wright, who made about five distinct style changes in his career. He had a long career, but still, such changes were uncommon at the time. They have, however, occurred more often in recent times, especially since expressionism. There are quite a few artists now who make distinct shifts in direction. Frank Stella would be a good example of a well-known contemporary artist who has made several style changes. However, an artist usually displays one type of identifiable style that evolves over time.

As far as I am concerned, I couldn't possibly have developed just one particular style or element—I would have become bored. I even get bored now with a concept once I have realized it. I am experimenting constantly and I am very lucky to have a crew of people who experiment for me, so that I can be developing ideas. When I first took on the young glass blower, Martin Blank, I had him work with two or three assistants on developing a new form that I wanted to realize. A year and a half passed before I decided to turn that work into a series—the series which finally became the *Persians*. Once I decide to create a series out of a particular work, then I feel obligated to develop it as far as I can, to take it to the extreme. When I reach that limit, then I either stop working on it for a while or, if there is something else that has emerged in the meantime and captured my interest, I develop that. However, because I have this team of people working with me, I can go back and recreate something that we already know how to do without a lot of effort. For example, when I decided on the *Macchia* installations, the individual pieces were fully developed, but we created something new by combining many of them. I could go back and say, 'Now let's do another 40 *Macchia* as big as we can, let's try to outdo ourselves.' But then, I may be repeating myself.

> *That winter Sylvia and I visited Venice and I had the opportunity to see a private collection of Venetian Art Deco vases unlike any I had ever seen in books or museums. They were very odd, with garish colors. Most were classical shapes with beautiful handles and other unusual additions . . . I began the blow with the idea of replicating the Italian Art Deco vases I had spotted that evening in Venice. I started with a simple drawing of a classical Etruscan form with several handles. After Lino (Tagliapietra) finished the first piece I quickly made another that was a little more complicated involving a bit more work . . . After a couple of days the pieces became much more involved. It wasn't long before something started to happen. It opened first in the drawings . . . The series started a drastic change from rather refined classical shapes to very bizarre pieces; handles changed to knots, points became claws, colors went from subtle to bright, big leaves and feathers appeared.*
>
> Dale Chihuly, 1989

GUNTHER S. STENT

Meaning in art and science

Ein echtes Kunstwerk bleibt, wie ein Naturwerk, fuer unseren Verstand immer unendlich: es wird angeschaut, empfunden, es wirkt; es kann aber nicht eigentlich erkannt, viel weniger sein Wesen, sein Verdienst mit Worten ausgesprochen werden.

[A true work of art, like a work of nature, remains always infinite for our understanding: it is perceived, felt, effective; but it cannot be really recognized, and even less can its essence, its merit be expressed in words.]

J.W. von Goethe (1749–1832), Ueber Laokoon

The relationship between art and science has been the subject of much confusing debate according to an essay that the musicologist, Leonard B. Meyer (1974), published 25 years ago. Meyer attributed much of the confusion in this debate to a viewpoint not infrequently espoused by scientists, and occasionally by artists and laymen as well, that in essential ways science and art are comparable. In his essay, Meyer expressed his sympathy for the attempts to bring together what C.P. Snow had called 'the two cultures' (1959). However, he warned that a wedding of art and science in which their important differences are ignored or glossed over is not a union made in heaven, but a shotgun marriage that is bound to fail.

To document his assertion that scientists tend to confuse the two-culture issue and are pushing towards such a shotgun marriage, Meyer referred to an article on art and science that I had published not long before in *Scientific American* (Stent, 1972). While I was proud that my paper had drawn the attention of a leading theorist of the arts, I was surprised by Meyer's holding me up as a terrible example, as an archetypal obscurant. All the while, I had been under the impression that I merely retailed what I thought were his own views, which he had set forth in his seminal book, *Music, the Arts and Ideas* (Meyer, 1967).

My article in *Scientific American* had been inspired by my preparing a review (Stent, 1968) of the many reviews of James Watson's memoir, *The Double Helix*, which describes Watson and Crick's discovery of the structure of DNA (Watson, 1968; 1980). Almost all of the reviewers were scientists, and they turned out to provide (mainly unwittingly) as much insight into the sociology and moral psychology of science as did Watson's memoir itself. One of these reviewers was the biochemist, Erwin Chargaff (1968), who played a major role in Watson's story (he had done important ground work on DNA composition). He found as little merit in Watson's literary attainments as he had in Watson and Crick's discovery of the DNA structure in the first place. Not only did Chargaff not care for Watson's book, he declared that scientific autobiography was a most awkward literary genre. Why? Because scientists lead monotonous and uneventful lives—that is, they are dull.

But why are the lives of scientists so monotonous and uneventful in contrast to the exciting lives of artists who make much less boring biographical subjects? Because, according to Chargaff, there is a profound difference in the uniqueness of the achievements of artists and of scientists. Chargaff wrote:

> Timon of Athens *could not have been written,* Les Demoiselles d'Avignon *could not have been painted, had Shakespeare and Picasso not existed. But of how many scientific achievements can this be claimed? One could almost say that, with very few exceptions, it is not the men that make science, it is science that makes the men. What A does today, B and C and D could surely do tomorrow.*

I was surprised that Chargaff regarded the development of art as wholly contingent upon the appearance of a particular succession of unique geniuses while, at the same time, regarding the development of science from the Hegelian or—God forbid!—Marxist perspective of historical determinism. In other words, he believed that progress in science was shaped by immutable forces rather than by contingent human agency. Since I found it hard to believe that Chargaff would really hold such incoherent ideas, I suspected at first that he had made his point only to put down Watson and Crick's discovery. But my unkind suspicion of Chargaff's motives was unjustified: most of my friends and colleagues, including Francis Crick himself (1974), turned out to agree with Chargaff that we would not have had *Timon of Athens* if Shakespeare had not existed; but if Watson and Crick had not existed we would have had the double helix structure of DNA anyhow. So, I wrote my *Scientific American* article to show them that the antinomy of contingent, unique achievements in art *versus* the inevitable and, therefore, banal achievements of science has little philosophical or historical merit.

The inner, emotional world and the outer, objective world

What do I mean by 'art' and 'science'? Both art and science, I asserted, are activities that endeavor to discover and communicate truth about the world: they share the central features of searching for, and encoding into a semantic medium, the meaning of novel truths. Where art and science differ fundamentally, however, is the domain of the world to which the semantic contents of their works mainly pertain. The domain addressed by the artist is the *inner, subjective world* of the emotions. Artistic communications, therefore, pertain mainly to the relations between private phenomena of affective significance. The domain addressed by the scientist is the *outer, objective world* of physical phenomena. Scientific communications, therefore, pertain mainly to relations between public events.

I had learned from Meyer's book that there is an important exception to this explication of the term 'art', which actually proves the rule. The feature of semantic communication between artists and audience pertains only to what Meyer called 'traditional' art (which is what most people think of as art), but not to what Meyer called 'transcendental' art (which includes aleatoric, or chance music, action painting, pop art and other manifestations that appeared after World War II). Because it had abandoned the semantic function, transcendental art represented the final phase in the millennia-long evolution of artistic styles. It was kind of a futuristic vision 25 years ago that the long road of artistic evolution had reached its end with transcendental art, and that novel successor styles were no longer possible. This prediction has been proven true meanwhile, by the rise of the eclectic and mannerist works of post-modernism which, rather than being innovative, 'cite' styles of the past.

Despite this fundamental difference in their principal foci of interest, traditional art and science form a thematic continuum, and there seems to be little point in trying to draw a sharp line of demarcation between them. After all, the transmission of information and the perception of its meaning constitute their very essence.

The uniqueness of great art versus the banality of great science: the great antinomy

I asked, in my article in the *Scientific American*, whether it's reasonable to assert that only Shakespeare could have formulated the semantic structure represented by *Timon*, whereas people other than Watson and Crick might have made the communication represented by their paper published in *Nature* in April 1953. It is immediately evident that the exact word sequence of Watson and Crick's paper would not have been written if the authors had not existed—no more than the exact word sequence of *Timon* would have been written without Shakespeare (at least not until the fabulous monkey typists complete their random work at the British Museum). Thus, Watson and Crick's paper and Shakespeare's play are both historically unique semantic structures. But in assessing the *creative* uniqueness of a linguistic structure, we are not concerned with its exact word sequence; we are concerned with the uniqueness of its semantic content. And so I readily admitted that meanwhile, even without Watson and Crick, other people were likely to have published a satisfactory molecular structure for DNA. Hence, the semantic content of the Watson–Crick paper would not be unique. As for the semantic content of Shakespeare's play, I pointed out that the story of the trials and tribulations of its main character, Timon, not only *might* have been written without Shakespeare but, in fact, *was* written without him. Shakespeare had merely reworked the story of Timon he had read in William Painter's collection of classic tales, *The Palace of Pleasure*, published 40 years earlier. Painter, in turn, had used as his sources the ancient, classical authors, Plutarch and Lucian.

But then the creative aspect of the play is not Timon's story; what counts is the novelty of the deep insights into the human emotions that Shakespeare communicates with his play. He shows us here how a man may make his response to the injuries of life, how he may turn from lighthearted benevolence to passionate hatred toward his fellow men. Can we be sure, however, that *Timon* is unique as regards the play's semantic essence? Negative, because who is to say that, had Shakespeare not existed, no other playwright would have communicated very similar insights? Another dramatist surely would have used an entirely different story to make his point, to treat the same theme—as Shakespeare himself did later in his much more successful *King Lear*.

So, we are finally reduced to asserting that *Timon* is uniquely Shakespeare's because no other dramatist, though he might have communicated to us more or less the same insights, would have done it in quite the same, exquisite way as the Great Bard. But then, what about Watson and Crick's double helix? Can we take it for granted that Drs B, C, and D, who eventually would have found the structure of DNA, would have found it in just the same elegant way and would have published a paper that produced the same revolutionary effect on contemporary biology? On the basis of my personal acquaintance with the people who were engaged in trying to uncover the structure of DNA in the early 1950s, I expressed my belief that if Watson and Crick had not existed, the insights they provided in a single package would have dribbled out much more gradually over a period of many months or years.

Why then is it that so many scientists seem to accept the antinomy of the uniqueness of great art versus the banality of great science? In my article, I put forward a variety of explanations, one of them being the scientist's lack of familiarity with the working methods of artists. Scientists tend to picture the artist's act of creation in terms of Hollywood movies: Cornel Wilde in the role of Frédéric Chopin is gazing fondly at Merle Oberon as his muse and mistress, George Sand, while he is sitting down at the Pleyel pianoforte and, one–two–three, he composes his 'Préludes'. As scientists know full well, science, of course, is done quite differently. Dozens of stereotyped and ambitious researchers are slaving away in as many identical laboratories, all trying to make similar discoveries, all using more or less the same knowledge and techniques, some of them succeeding and some not. Artists, we might note, tend to conceive of the scientific act of creation in equally unrealistic Hollywood terms: Paul Muni, in the role of Louis Pasteur, is burning the midnight oil in his laboratory at the Institut Pasteur; he has the inspiration to take some bottles from the shelf; he mixes the contents and, eureka, he has discovered the vaccine for rabies. Artists, in turn, know of course that art is done very differently. Dozens of stereotyped and ambitious writers, painters, and composers are slaving away in as many identical garrets, all trying to produce similar works, all using more or less the same knowledge and techniques, some succeeding and some not.

Works versus contents; discoveries versus creations

Another reason for the widespread acceptance of the antinomy between art and science is the confusion between *works* on the one hand and their *contents* on the other. A play or a painting is a work of art, whereas a scientific theory or discovery is not a work of science but the content of a work, such as a book, paper, letter, lecture, or conversation. Thus, as formulated, Chargaff's proposition of differential uniqueness is not even false. It is nonsensical because it compares *works* of art—that is Shakespeare's text of *Timon* or Picasso's painting of *Les Demoiselles d'Avignon*—not with a work of science (Watson and Crick's *Nature* paper) but with its *content* (the DNA double helix). The fundamental difference between work and its content is a tremendous source of confusion which even Meyer, I think, did not recognize. One must compare the Shakespeare text or the Picasso painting to the Watson–Crick paper; and as we have seen already, works of science are as unique as are works of art. What we have to address is the uniqueness of their contents.

It follows that the cause of confusion in the debate about the relationship between art and science can hardly be the one claimed by Meyer—namely that too many scientists espouse the viewpoint that in essential ways art and science are comparable. On the contrary, I have found that most scientists seem to believe, as does Meyer, that art and science are essentially *different*. While this belief is not wrong—in that the semantic contents of their works do address different domains of the world—art and science are, at the same time, also, essentially similar. Both seek to discover and communicate novel truths about the world (cf. Gilot's chapter 'A painter's perspective', Part 4).

But Meyer does not want to admit this similarity because he thinks that 'discovery' pertains only to works of science, whereas the works of art are not discoveries but 'creations.' He looks on the *outer world*, which science tries to fathom, from the standpoint of *naïve realism*, according to which phenomena and the relations between them have an objective existence independent of the human mind, and believes that this real world out there is as we see, hear, smell, and feel it. Hence, the outer world and its scientific laws are simply there, and it is the job of the scientist to discover them. According to Meyer, the DNA molecule was a double helix before Watson and Crick said that it was. This is a statement to which most scientists, agreeing with Meyer, would drink as well.

By contrast Meyer looks at the *inner* world, which art tries to fathom, from the standpoint of *idealism*, according to which phenomena and relations between them have no reality other than their invention by the human mind. Hence, there is nothing to be discovered in the inner world, and artists create their works *ex nihilo*. Shakespeare and Picasso simply cut *Timon* and *Les Demoiselles* from whole cloth. Meyer's insistence on the antinomy of 'discovery' versus 'creation' suggests that he had not fully appreciated Immanuel Kant's (1724–1804) definitive resolution of the epistemological conflict between naïve realism and idealism. Kant's theory of knowledge made its impact on the human sciences under the general banner of structuralism in the 1960s and 1970s. Structuralism emerged simultaneously, independently, and in different guises in several diverse fields of study—psychology, linguistics, anthropology, and biology.

Reality as a set of structural transforms abstracted by the mind from the phenomenal world

Naïve realism and idealism both take it for granted that all the information gathered by our senses actually reaches our mind. Naïve realism envisions that thanks to this sensory information, reality is *mirrored* in the mind, while idealism envisions that thanks to this sensory information reality is *invented* by the mind. Structuralism provided the insight, however, that knowledge about the world of phenomena enters the mind not as raw data but in an already highly abstract form, namely as 'structures' (cf. chapters in this book by Stevens and Damasio). In the preconscious process of converting the primary sensory data, step by step, into structures, information is necessarily lost because the creation of structures, or the recognition of patterns, is nothing other than the selective destruction of information. The mind creates a pattern from the mass of sensory data by throwing away this, throwing away that. Finally, what's left of the data is a structure in which the mind perceives something meaningful. (This eliminative view of cognition has been substantiated by recent advances in neurobiology—I think this is one of the few philosophical implications neurobiology has so far produced; cf. Stevens' chapter 'Line versus color', Part 4.)

Thus, since the mind does not gain access to the full set of data about the world, it cannot mirror reality. But neither does the mind freely invent reality. Instead, according to structuralist realism, the mind interprets reality as a set of structural transforms abstracted from the phenomenal world.

Thus, the structure of the DNA molecule was not what it was before Watson and Crick defined it, because there was and there still is no such thing as the DNA molecule in the natural world. The DNA molecule is an abstraction created by century-long efforts of a succession of biochemists, all of whom selected for their attention certain ensembles of natural phenomena. The DNA double helix is as much a creation as it is a discovery; the realm of existence of the double-helical DNA molecule is the mind of scientists and the literature of science, but not the natural world (except insofar as that world also includes minds and books). Hence, as applied to art and science, the antinomy of discovery versus creation has little philosophical merit.

Structuralist realism tells us that every creative act in art and science is both banal and unique. Banal in the sense that there is an innate correspondence in the transformational operations that different persons perform on the same primary data, from inner and outer worlds—that is, simply, we are all human beings. Unique in the sense that no two persons are quite the same, and hence never perform exactly the same transformational operations on a given set of raw data. As developmental neurobiologists have shown, there are no two individuals—not even identical twins—with identical nervous systems (cf. Pfenninger's chapter 'The evolving brain', Part 2). So, all human minds are different, and yet they are similar. That is the reason why there is something unique and something banal in every discovery.

Truth in art and science

According to Meyer there is another profound and basic difference between art and science that is related to the discovery–versus–creation antinomy. Scientific theories, he says, are *propositional*, whereas works of art are *presentational*. Meyer's second antinomy adds further confusion to the debate because *all* works, of science as well as of art—indeed all semantic structures—are presentational. They are presentational in the sense of being concrete patterns that can occasion enjoyable, intriguing, and moving human experiences. By contrast, the quality of being propositional pertains not to works but to their contents. The contents are propositional in the sense of being statements that affirm or deny something, so that they can be characterized as either true or false. So, when we talk about presentational nature, we refer to the work; and when we talk about its propositional nature, we refer to its content.

Not every presentational structure necessarily has a propositional content of course. Meyer rightly points out that a natural phenomenon, such as a sunset or Mount Everest, is a presentational structure without propositional content. There is nothing true or false about it; it's just there. But by denying propositional content to works of art, Meyer implies that there can be nothing true or false about them either. Yet, as a theorist of the arts, Meyer can hardly maintain that it is characteristic of most works of art that their contents cannot be judged as true or false. He would drive himself out of business. So he concedes that, unlike sunsets or Everest, great works of traditional art command our assent. That is what makes them great, in fact. Like validated theories, they seem self-evident and incontrovertible, meaningful and necessary, infallible and illuminating. There is, without doubt, an aura of 'truth' about them. But then Meyer insists that 'truth' pertains to art only in a metaphorical sense. Why? Because according to the naïve realist standpoint from which Meyer approaches this deep problem, a literally true proposition states what is objectively the case (i.e. is directly or indirectly observable in the real world). And since there are no imaginable observations that could test the validity of the *content* of the work of art, it could be said to be 'true' only in a metaphorical but not in a *literal* sense. How is one going to test if *Les Demoiselles d'Avignon* is true? So Meyer, guided by naïve realism, concludes that works of science are propositions in that they can be literally true, but in works of art the contents are true only metaphorically.

Structuralist realism, however, leads to a different literal concept of truth inasmuch as reality, to which truth relates, is something that each person abstracts from the world of things. A proposition is true (for me) insofar as it is in harmony with my internalized picture of the world (i.e. my reality) and commands *my* assent. This literal meaning of truth is obviously not an objective one, but a subjective one. It leads to the concept of objective truth only as long as I am convinced that a proposition that is true for me would command also the assent of every other person qualified to make this judgment. Here, the ideal of an absolutely objective truth is reached only if God also assents to the proposition. So, from the structuralist–realist point of view, the use of the term 'truth' in connection with the content of a work of art is not metaphorical at all: it is the very same literal usage as that applied to the content of a work of science. It is exactly by their command of assent that we come to believe also in the truth of scientific propositions. In the 50 years that I have spent as a working scientist, I have personally validated (if indeed validation is at all possible) or examined the published records of the validation by others, of only a tiny fraction of all the scientific propositions that I believe to be true. The remainder simply command my assent, for the same reasons that Meyer cites as the basis of the aura of truth of great works of art.

A thematic continuum between art and science

Let us now reconsider the thematic continuum presented by art and science with regard to their principal foci of interest in inner and outer worlds (Table 1.1). Music, which appears to be the purest art form and has the least to say about the outer world, lies at one end of this continuum. Accordingly, music shows the least thematic overlap with science, which lies at the other end. The content of works of music is more purely emotional than that of any other art form because musical symbolism very rarely refers to any models of the outer world—to which it could never do justice anyway. The meaning of musical structures thus relates almost exclusively to inner models. That is the reason why 'program music,' such as Respighi's *The Pines of Rome*, is not very highly thought of among musicologists: it tries to do something for which music is not appropriate. Musical symbolism is able to dispense with outer models because according to Susanne Langer (1948), the great twentieth-century philosopher of art, 'the forms of human feelings are much more congruent with musical forms than are the forms of spoken language; music can *reveal* the nature of feelings with a detail and truth that language cannot approach' (see also Adolphe's chapter 'with music in mind', Part 2). Hence, music conveys the unspeakable; it is incommensurable with language, and even with the representational symbols, such as the images of painting and the gestures of dance.

The position of an art form on this continuum—that is, how close it is to science and the extent to which it addresses the outer world—seems closely related to the degree to which its symbolism is embedded in language. The visual arts, painting, and sculpture, are still relatively 'pure' art forms, as is Poetry. Poetry—although it does resort to language as its medium—uses words in a quasi-musical form. Literature and drama, however, with their mainly linguistic symbolism and their close thematic ties to the outer world—but still

Domain	Modality
Inner world Music Poetry Dance Painting Sculpture Drama Literature Science Outer world	Non-linguistic Linguistic

Table 1.1 The continuum of art and science.

addressing the inner world of emotions—seem to lie halfway between music and science. Science is, of course, wholly dependent on language as its exclusive semantic modality.

All the same, the semantic transactions of art still pose a most difficult problem. What is the meaning of the propositions implicitly formulated in works of art? What do the relationships exemplified by works of art actually refer to? What are they about? Evidently the difficulty of answering these questions increases as we progress from science towards music in the thematic continuum. At the musical end of the continuum, where symbolism is incommensurable with language, these questions cannot be answered (verbally) at all. Meyer quotes the following incident concerning Beethoven: when asked what the *Moonlight Sonata* meant, what it was *about*, Beethoven returned to the piano and played it for a second time. Meyer finds Beethoven's answer not only appropriate but compelling. But Meyer thinks that, if a physicist was asked what the law of gravity is all about, and he answered by letting some object fall to the ground, our inference would be that he was trying to be funny. I agree that Beethoven's response seems more reasonable than that of the uncooperative physicist, but not for the reason given by Meyer, namely that the *Moonlight Sonata* is not about the world and does not refer to anything, whereas the law of gravity is about the world and does refer to something. Rather, Beethoven's response was reasonable because he was asked a question for which there is no adequate *verbal* reply. In contrast, the physicist's response was unreasonable because he *could* explain gravity.

This then is the paradox: since the *Moonlight Sonata*, exemplifying a relationship, has some meaningful content—as opposed to a sunset or Mount Everest, which do not—logic demands that it must refer to something, must be about something, yet we cannot say what that something is. In thus being generally speechless regarding the meaning of music, we resemble the split-brain patients studied by Roger Sperry: the patients can recognize familiar objects seen in the left half of their visual field but are unable to identify them verbally. They know what they are seeing but can't say what it is.

As we move away from music towards science in the thematic continuum, through the visual arts to literature and drama, verbal explanations of the meaning of artworks and their contents, though still formidably difficult, become at least possible. Indeed, this is the very task of hermeneutics, the discipline dedicated to the explicit interpretation of meanings that are hidden implicitly in a broad range of semantic structures, especially artistic structures (Gadamer, 1976). There would be massive unemployment among hermeneuticians if Meyer's assertion were actually true and if the contents of works of art did not refer to anything and were not about the world.

Suppose we stay with our original example. Having just seen a performance of *Timon*, we ask a Shakespearian scholar, 'What does the play mean, what is it all about?' and he simply takes us back to the theater to see *Timon* for a second time. Would we not consider his response as disingenuously witty and nearly as improper as that of the physicist? That is not to say that if the scholar did give us his verbal interpretation of *Timon*, it would fully capture the semantic essence of the play. Depending on his hermeneutic skills, he could go some considerable distance towards giving us an idea of what the play's deep meaning, and not just its plot, is all about. But what would be most likely missing from the scholar's verbal interpretation of *Timon* is precisely that part of the play's meaningful content which is not embedded denotatively in the text and which arises from it connotatively, thanks to the contextual situation created by Shakespeare.

The union of the two cultures as an ordinary marriage

So, we have traveled a long way from Chargaff's reflections on the banality of scientific autobiography to the bottomless depths of epistemology and cognitive philosophy. We saw en route that 'art' and 'science' are semantic activities that seek to discover and communicate truths about the world in which we live our lives, with art addressing mainly the inner world of emotions and science mainly the outer world of objects. That explication allowed us to identify one common source of confusion in discussions about the relationship between the arts and sciences, namely the false antinomy of the uniqueness of *works* of art versus the banality of the semantic *contents* of works of science. Once that confusion had been cleared up, it became plain that works are unique in both art and science.

We then noted one deep source of confusion in the discussion of the relationship between art and science, namely that the outer world, which science tries to fathom, is often viewed from the standpoint of *naïve realism*, whereas the inner world, which art tries to fathom, is often viewed from the standpoint of *idealism*. This incoherent epistemological attitude leads to the false distinction that scientists merely discover what is already there—they don't create anything, whereas artists create something that had no prior existence—they don't discover anything, However, as soon as our relation to the world is viewed from the standpoint of *structuralist realism*, it becomes evident that in both art and science, discovery and creation actually refer to the same process.

The most difficult aspect of this discussion turned out to be the nature of the *semantic contents* of works of art. Does the concept of 'truth', which clearly applies to the contents of works of science, apply also to the content of works of art? Here we saw that when viewed from the standpoint of structuralism, the concept of truth, as applied to scientific propositions, amounts to harmony with my internalized picture of the world, that is, *my* reality, and hence commands *my* assent. Since great works of art similarly harmonize with reality and command assent, this concept of truth would apply to their contents as well. Nevertheless, concerning the communication of truth, there is an important difference between art and science: works of science communicate their truths explicitly in spoken language, whereas the truths of works of art are communicated implicitly in linguistic, tonal, and visual structures.

What *is* the meaning of the truths implicit in works of art? What is the *Moonlight Sonata* actually about? Here we finally encounter a deep semantic paradox: although we can capture the meaning of the content of a work of art, we may not be able to say what that meaning is. So even if the union of the two cultures, art and science, *were* made in heaven, theirs would merely be one of those ordinary marriages in which the spouses have some difficulties talking to each other.

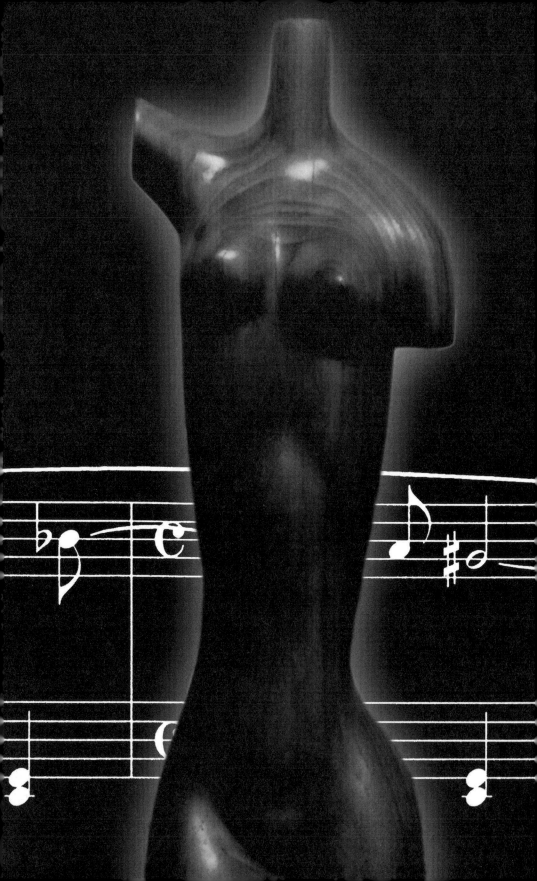

PART TWO

Body, brain, and mind: emotion and reason

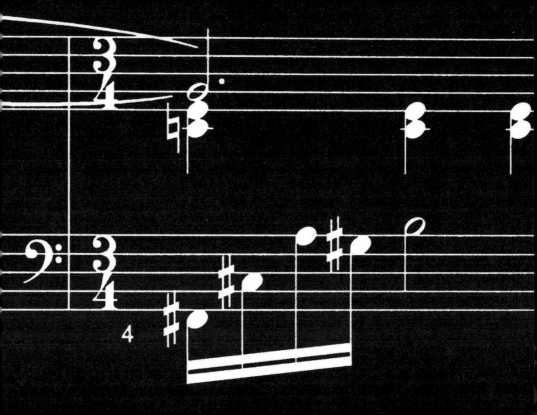

Embracing the range

Creative adventures: of balance and leadership

It is fairly unusual for somebody who is in scientific or medical research to have a secondary career in the visual arts or music, but it is not that uncommon. What I found interesting in reading your biography is that you work in another area which—I think at least—involves a lot of creativity, though it is not often recognized as such: that is running big organizations, whether it is foundations or being in a high administrative position in a medical setting. What I would like to ask you is, do you think that that involves creativity, or do you think it is just part of a job that you are able to do? And if you do think it involves creativity as I do, do you see relationships between that and what you do as a researcher and a sculptor or do you think, so to speak, it uses very different kinds of skills and capacities?

Howard Gardner addressing David Rogers, July 1993

I do regard leading a large organization as a creative process. I think it is an activity that really requires a lot of attention and talent. It is not trivial to lead well, to see to it that groups feel good about themselves and reach consensus, and to proceed in constructive ways. It takes a lot of creativity to accomplish that, and I am pleased with that facet of myself; I find that I do it well. To feel comfortable in letting others be themselves, I think, helps. I do not put down those who are feeling angry or dissident; I try to encourage them. My artwork gives me some personal security. In giant organizations, there are many ways in which one can fail, and not to be destroyed by that and to go back the next day and give it another crack is a great asset.

Perhaps some of my confidence comes from the security I feel in expressing myself in some different, very isolated, self-centered activity. I regard my artwork as very, very selfish. I used to trivialize that. I remember one time a rather gushy woman said to me, 'Oh, I don't see how you can do this sort of thing.' I was feeling a little irritated; I looked at her and said, 'Because I'm God-damned serious about it.' I think that this was the first time I recognized that I really am serious about my artwork, and when I do it I need big periods of time by myself. I am quite moved by Françoise Gilot's response to young painters who asked her how they could know if they would ever be any good as painters. She asked them in return, 'How many hours can you remain alone?' I thought this implied a rather profound statement. To do sculpture takes uninterrupted blocks of time; it takes a considerable period of immersion before I can really get into sculpting; short shots at it do not achieve anything. I would guess that is probably characteristic of most creative efforts of value.

Let me place another thought tentatively on the table: I am putting enormous creative effort into something that is not my primary professional life. I have not invested all of my security eggs, if you will, in one basket. My satisfactions in life, my security, my feelings of self-worth, are not totally tied to my professional success. If I am absolutely honest, they are not tied to my professional success plus my sculptural work. Relationships with my wife and with my family and my friends are an equally important source of considerable security and satisfaction to me. So, to overwork a tired analogy, my satisfactions in life rest on a three-legged stool.

My point is the following: divesting of my own feelings of pleasure or self-worth in more than one arena has, I think, allowed me to be a more consistent risk taker. I think my science was perhaps braver because of that. I know I am a more adventurous teacher. I am less afraid of expressing my views no matter how outrageous and, in turn, am quite comfortable in allowing others to do the same. I can live for long and rather intense periods within my own intellect without panicking. And that, I think, is what Françoise Gilot is saying to us. Perhaps that is what good scientific or creative activity is all about. New leaps of the mind, the recognition of new relationships, new adventurous inquiries into the nature of things requires that one live for significant periods within one's own head to permit that wonderful structure we call the brain to do its thing. And maybe that is where a chance to be creative with hands or heart in satisfying ways can contribute. Maybe it opens up more circuits in the brain; maybe it allows more alternative neuronal pathways to fire; maybe it mobilizes more neurons.

> Hat man mit dem Schuhwerk nicht seine Not!
> Waer ich nicht noch Poet dazu,
> ich machte laenger keine Schuh'!
>
> [Doesn't one have one's trials with those shoes!
> If I wasn't a poet, too
> I wouldn't make any shoes any more!]
>
> The cobbler–poet, Hans Sachs, in Richard Wagner's
> Die Meistersinger

Searching for the source of ideas

I have the feeling—it is no longer an uncomfortable one—that, while our knowledge base about creativity will be significantly extended, it is my bet that the precise ways in which the right half of the brain influences the left half of our brain, or what music or painting or other artistic adventures do to influence some of our more pedestrian activities, will remain, rather tantalizingly, just outside of our understanding.

Let me tell you a story. Some years ago, Carl Rogers, a psychologist who happens to be my father, and a man whom I still regard as one of our most adventurous and creative minds of this century, recounted an experience to me that I have always remembered. It happened apparently at a conference, at which the organizers had assembled a small group of people—all men incidentally—who were thought at that time to have the most creative minds. The purpose was to find out how these creative contributors to science actually functioned—how they got their ideas: in essence, how their brains worked. And they were to tell it all to one another.

My father told me that the first day of that conference was surprisingly painful, awkward and unrevealing. No one seemed willing to say very much. Then something interesting happened on the second day. One of the participants, actually the man who was regarded by his peers as the most creative of the group, said he had a confession to make. He indicated that he was scared to death to be there because he knew deep in his own heart he had absolutely no concept of how he got his ideas, or what drove him, or what made him more creative than his fellow man, but that he had come to the conference because of his admiration for the other nine conferees. He was convinced that, if he could simply hide his own uncertainties for a day or so, these other nine people, who clearly knew what they were doing, would cue him in on how the creative process actually worked. Apparently, his revelation was greeted with a sense of profound relief by all who were there, and then, one by one, they all told very similar stories. It is my understanding they did not go off a great deal more knowledgeable about creativity, but they did all develop considerable affection and admiration one for another.

Medicine and a passion for sculpting

Conceive form in depth.
Clearly indicate the dominant planes.
Imagine forms as directed towards you;
all life surges from a centre,
expands from within outwards.

In drawing, observe relief, not outline.
The relief determines the contour.
The main thing is to be moved, to love,
to hope, to tremble, to live.
Be a man before being an artist.

A. Rodin (quoted in H. Read, 1964)

I would like to advance some personal speculation about certain necessary, but not determinative, ingredients that encourage creativity, using sculpture as a backdrop for those views.

For more than half my life, I was a closet sculptor. I was considerably embarrassed by the fact that I did this rather odd creative thing: I made wood sculptures. Although I couldn't seem to stop doing it, I kept my obsession a secret from my friends. I felt like the compulsive gambler or drinker who keeps his problem bottled up inside. However, about thirty years ago—quite reluctantly —I was talked into a one-man show of my work. This experience changed my attitudes: I found that others actually enjoyed my work, and that I enjoyed their interaction with my work. A new dialogue had begun. Now I am quite comfortable about admitting that I work with wood, and I feel that being a sculptor is an important, integral part of my being. I have absolutely no idea why I felt as I did then or now, but it is true.

When do I sculpt? I have thought a lot about this. I sculpt when I am worried or when I am stressed; I sculpt when I am feeling professionally unproductive; I sculpt when I am happy and feeling fulfilled; I sculpt when I have free, contemplative time that I could use to think about how to improve the world of medicine; I sculpt when I am enormously overcommitted. And I feel vaguely uncomfortable if I do not have a sculpture in progress. In other words, I sculpt all the bloody time. And I will lie, cheat or steal to have weekends free to do my thing. Obviously, I have asked myself whether this obsession with wood, this creative adventure with forms and carving, improves my creativity in other areas of my life. I do not know. But I can offer some observations, and perhaps you can relate them to some of the other discussions in this book.

Apprenticeship

It takes about 10 years to get to a point where you really can do something in your area, which both Howard Gardner and Antonio Damasio confirm (see their chapters in this book). And some period of apprenticeship is probably required. I carved a lady—I think it was the second thing I tried—some 54 years ago. I was 13 then. I do not recall having had any formal training in art at that time. Three years later, when I was 16, I carved a woman and child. Since that time I have improved, but my work has always had a life of its own, even then. Perhaps my lack of conventional training was to my advantage.

My mother was a very good painter; my sister was a good painter; my father got to be quite a good painter. We would have these damned artistic weekends, and everyone in my family would paint. But I could not paint at all. Nor could I draw. So, out of self-defense, I took up whittling. I began to carve sculptures. Everybody was reasonably pleased. My father was very permissive about what I was doing, but I do not think that my sculpting was treated as a great gift. Indeed, this reminds me of a story. At one time, when I began to get somewhat better—I think I was in medical school—I was visiting my parents in Chicago. I was looking for a sculpture I had given my parents with considerable pride. It was a big piece. When I asked my mother where it was, she said, 'Oh, when we moved we put it in the fireplace.' They had burned it up. So I don't think my artwork was admired with great reverence.

Because I never have had any formal training in art, I just get on with my sculpting. Today, I am more intellectually involved, but I vividly remember a one-man show that the Art Department of Vanderbilt University invited me to put on. At that time, they had a rather distinguished sculptor-in-residence who asked me to talk to his sculpture class. The students were looking at my work, and they would ask, 'Oh, were you thinking about Brancusi? Were you thinking about so and so?' I did not know one of the names, and afterwards the professor was so disgusted that he said, 'You set sculpture back about three hundred years.' So I had to go and read a little bit.

I did not know then that artists like Brancusi and Rodin, both great modern sculptors, were rooted in practicality and concreteness. That is also true for me. But art is not an intellectual exercise for me—it is an emotional outlet. Actually, I use the *process* as an outlet for torment; I can bang the hell out of a piece of wood with a mallet and a chisel. I realize that, paradoxically, my sculptures are basically happy forms. Which modern artist said that sculpture is affirmative?

The process: you will never have more to work with than when you started

> When I carve, I look for the Buddha in the wood. And, when I am carv-
> ing, I need to bring the Buddha out of the wood. I have to be very careful
> not to cut the Buddha.
>
> Carver of Buddha figures in Kyoto (quoted in
> Goleman, Kaufman and Ray, 1992)

As you probably know, a wood sculptor uses a mallet, a few chisels, some wood files. I just thought I would explain the process to you. The piece of wood suggests the shapes: I had a big cedar stump, and that was the start of a polar bear. It is important to me to keep the geometry of the forms within the shape of the piece of wood. One thing about this kind of sculpture, in contrast to painting or perhaps blowing glass, is that I know that I am never, never going to have any more material to work with than when I started. If I make a mistake, there's no going back. The trick is to do better the next time, and to remember to take care not to cut off a piece of wood that you subsequently wish was there. I am interested to know that Dale Chihuly creates beautiful paintings in preparation for his glass sculptures; but I don't do that. I get so discouraged when I take pen to paper. You'd be appalled at how little I can sketch. Instead, I just start with a piece of wood. I will put some lines on it sometimes to tell myself not to cut off a particular piece—yet. As I look at that piece of wood, a new relationship between it and my mind develops: the new form emerges. So I carved away on that big cedar stump, and the polar bear began to take shape.

I do not articulate all the forms; so I stopped when the piece of wood looked like a bear. I did not try to carry it very far, but I wanted to give it that wonderful sway that bears have in their hindquarters. It took me some time to learn to stop when something looked like the idea I had in my mind. I used to try and get cute and go beyond my own talent; now, when I can see the form come to life, I stop carving.

Sometimes, just a very small change will make all the difference. I was working on one of my favorite forms—the head of a woman. I believed I had finished, and then looked at the carving with my physician's eye. 'She looks like she's got a big goiter,' I thought. Just changing the line of her throat changed her expression slightly, and that change was enough to balance the sculpture (Fig. 2.1).

A kaleidoscope

> In addition to the sensations one derives from a drawing, a sculpture must invite us to handle it as an object, just so the sculptor must feel, in making it, the particular demands for volume and mass. The smaller the bit of sculpture, the more the essentials of form must exist.
>
> Henri Matisse (quoted in H. Read, 1964)

Françoise Gilot says painting is a language without words; well, sculpture also is a language without words. But, unlike a painted canvas, a sculpture has a tactile side to it. Sculpture appeals as much to the hand as it does to the eye. You can walk through a sculpture or stroke it.

My carvings are independent objects that reach out to the viewers and interact with them. Some time ago, I carved a figure of a woman that some of my

Fig. 2.1 David Rogers, *Woman's Head*, driftwood.

female activist friends did not like very much. One angry woman said. 'This is your view of womanhood—fat thighs and a very small brain'. I had not thought about it that way!

Women have preoccupied me in one form or another since I first began to carve. The female figure is one of my most cherished themes. Figure 2.2 shows *Woman and Child* carved from cedar. Cedar, with its subtle curves, enhances the rhythms of the joyous female form. I use quite a bit of cedar. The big roots fall over the cliff at our summer place, and the contrasts in the wood add to the sculptural illusion. I also have carved a number of female torsos. The one shown in Fig. 2.3 started as a piece of rotting teak that I picked up on the shores of Tortola in the British Virgin Islands.

I am influenced by what I see, either directly or indirectly. I have sculpted many birds; the forms are simple and fun to do. However, I do not work in series, and I do not think that I have ever done a particular piece twice. After a trip to Peru, where they make those ordinary little bulls you see in every shop, I felt challenged to do something better. On another occasion, I was delayed in Anchorage Airport because my flight was grounded. While waiting, I had to look at a big, miserable, stuffed musk ox for about four hours. When I came home, I carved a musk ox. Sometimes I begin to carve and the wood itself dictates the form I carve; other times I start with a more independent idea. One piece started out as a flower—but I was not satisfied; something was wrong. I

Fig. 2.2 David Rogers, *Woman and Child*, cedar.

took a chain-saw and cut off one piece of the flower and the wood took on the shape of an animal.

My objects are not as stylized and simplified as those of Brancusi; I usually try to express some literal meaning in my carvings. When the sculpture is non-objective, I often give it an emotive title. For example, I call the piece shown in Fig. 2.4 *Togetherness*. It is made from an unidentifiable piece of driftwood. Sometimes I finish a piece in finer detail; and sometimes, as in Fig. 2.4, I leave large portions uncarved. Very often I try to leave some of the natural shapes of the wood itself in place. Not every part of every figure is articulated.

I have carved a great many dancers. Although I am not a student of the ballet, I am a student of the female form. I carved a piece of driftwood; I do not know what kind of wood. It evolved into the carving of a dancer. I will end with the thought that a female form in space can transcend pure anatomy. So, this is what I do when I am not being medical.

Fig. 2.3 David Rogers,
Woman's Torso, teak.

Art and science

*You are physician–scientist and, at the same time, a sculptor. Do you
think that these activities are carried out by you in parallel, completely
independent from one another, or do you think that your art affects your
science and vice versa?*

George Palade addressing David Rogers, July 1993

Art is a form of communication, and I have realized that a great deal of success
in science depends on the communicative process as well. I mean by this that
successful science is not pushing the frontiers of knowledge forward just in
your own mind; you need to advance them in that of others as well. Sculpture
or painting, it seems to me, makes a statement that others can take or leave—
or interpret as they see fit. Sometimes I have heard people interpreting my work

Fig. 2.4 David Rogers, *Togetherness*, driftwood.

or discussing what I must have been thinking about when I was doing a sculpture, and my reaction is, 'Hell, I wasn't thinking about that at all.' However, I do not think that any message that I am communicating with my science is ambiguous. Thus, I believe the nature of the message in art and science is different.

I have been inclined to think of my activities as a physician–scientist and as a sculptor as parallel, quite separate tracks, except as they relate to my own feelings about what I am doing. If I am having difficulties in the laboratory or organizationally, but I have had a very satisfying weekend of carving a piece, it certainly changes my outlook. I feel reinvigorated, creatively recharged in going back to the first set of problems. It is difficult to remain angry if you are doing something creative—though Françoise Gilot says she is often annoyed at her canvas. Well, I am annoyed when I mess up my sculpture, and that happens fairly frequently. But if the carving is going well I relax, and my mind can wander off to other things, and can sometimes work on fairly complicated scientific problems.

> *[Regarding] the topic of the relation between an activity such as your sculpture and science. It looks like in your case there's a superb, invigorating and calming and inspiring effect from the sculpture, but it does seem to be relatively independent of your activity as a scientist and of your activity as a creator in another realm, that of administration. However, there are other examples. Since Hanna [Damasio] is too modest or perhaps too shy to tell it, and Howard [Gardner] was suggesting it, [I would like to mention that] Hanna is a very accomplished sculptor and also a neurologist and neuroanatomist. I think the fact that she has become a very good neuroanatomist and a wizard with neuroimaging is clearly related to her talent as a sculptor. There's one case in which the [connection] is very visible to all of us who know her.*
>
> Antonio Damasio commenting to David Rogers, July 1993

ANTONIO R. DAMASIO

Some notes on brain, imagination and creativity

From an evolutionary perspective, the oldest decision-making device per-
tains to basic biological regulation; the next, to the personal and social
realm; and the most recent, to a collection of abstract–symbolic operations
under which we can find artistic and scientific reasoning,
utilitarian–engineering reasoning, and the development of language and
mathematics. But although ages of evolution and dedicated neural sys-
tems may confer some independence to each of these reasoning/decision-
making 'modules,' I suspect they are all interdependent. When we witness
signs of creativity in contemporary humans, we are probably witnessing
the integrated operation of sundry combinations of these devices.

Antonio Damasio, 1994

It is not possible to discuss the neuroscience of creativity without considering
information from a variety of disciplines outside neuroscience. The reason
is simple. We come into this world with a brain equipped with a variety of
preset circuits. Most of these have to do with life regulation; they are located in
the diencephalon and brain stem and they regulate basic biological functions
which ensure our survival. After birth, most of the non-preset brain circuitry
begins to be shaped by our own activities and experiences. The term 'plasticity'
refers to that reshaping (cf. the chapters by Pfenninger and Stevens in this
book). Because our encounters with the environment are unique, the brain
circuitries are shaped somewhat differently in each of us. In other words, interactions between the organism and the environment give a certain shape and
function to the plastic circuits, notwithstanding the fact that the innate bioregulatory circuitry affects how those plastic circuits develop under the
influence of physical and social environmental interactions.

From the interactions between individuals and environment emerge the social
and cultural artifacts that we talk about when we discuss creativity. These artifacts cannot be reduced simply to the neural circuitry of an adult brain and even
less to the genes behind our brains. It follows that the sort of brain activity that
leads to creative behavior involves three functional levels: a genome-specified
level of brain circuitry, an activity-specified level of brain circuitry, and then

something that results from the interactions of the brain with physical, social and cultural environments. That is why extremely reductionist views cannot capture all the issues we wish to understand when we discuss creativity.

Modern approaches to the study of higher brain function

> *There is a sense of excitement and optimism in the brain sciences today, a sense that we may soon have some new insights into several previously intractable problems—into the development of the brain and the mechanisms of perception, motor coordination, and learning. This optimism is not completely new to neural science, but it is probably fair to say that it is more realistic now than ever before.*
>
> Eric R. Kandel and James H. Schwartz, 1981

Before I say a word about the structures and functions of the brain that I believe have something to do with creativity, I would like to introduce the type of research we practice. In general terms, our work is described under the banner of cognitive neuroscience: it relates to the understanding of how the so-called higher functions—perception, emotion, memory, language, decision making and planning—relate to the large-scale systems of the primate brain (that is, to those regions in the cerebral cortex and subcortical areas whose circuits support these important mental processes). This work depends largely on the study of both healthy humans and those affected by neurological disease (usually by stroke, but also by other disorders that cause damage to specific parts of the brain). In these latter patients, we can correlate specific functional deficits with the presence of lesions in certain brain regions. Moreover, we can also study the microscopic detail of the regions we investigate in humans by analyzing the brains of non-human primates, such as monkeys. Another important approach in our studies involves function imaging—techniques such as positron emission tomography (PET) and functional magnetic resonance (fMR)—which allow us to investigate how a mental task activates or deactivates a brain region in a normal individual.

Table 2.1 shows the different constituents of a nervous system in terms of the levels of complexity and of the relative sizes of those regions. Although these regions are obviously composed of the functional elements—the individual neurons, synapses and molecules (see Pfenninger's chapter 'The evolving brain')—the present discussion is aimed at the higher organizational levels of the brain: the large-scale systems which are made up of several macroscopic regions. At these levels, we have a better chance of making a transparent connection with the sort of mental processes studied in the cognitive sciences, and with complex phenomena, such as creativity.

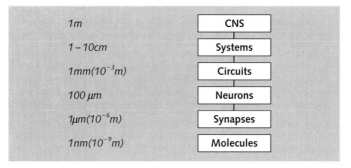

1m	**CNS**
1 – 10cm	**Systems**
1mm(10^{-3}m)	**Circuits**
100 μm	**Neurons**
1μm(10^{-6}m)	**Synapses**
1nm(10^{-9}m)	**Molecules**

Table 2.1 Scales and levels of complexity of the human central nervous system.

A critical ingredient for our research is the ability to relate human behavior to brain structure and to brain function in a meaningful way. To establish such a meaningful relationship, it is necessary to have theories and hypotheses. Then, armed with a variety of cognitive experiments in which a normal individual or a patient is asked to perform a particular task, we can test a hypothesis and decide whether the results conform to the anatomical, behavioral, or cognitive predictions.

How can this be achieved? A brain lesion (an area of brain damage) can be used as a probe to test the hypothesis; or differences in brain activity in a PET scan can be used to support a given prediction. All of this depends, of course, on the remarkable development of new brain imaging technologies. Take, for instance, the image shown in Fig. 2.5. You might think this is the picture of a post-mortem brain with a lesion in the cerebral cortex—the brain of someone who died and is being studied at autopsy. Well, that is not so. You are looking at a three-dimensional reconstruction of the brain of a *living* person and a subject in one of our behavioral experiments. This brain image has been generated from the raw data of a magnetic resonance scan. The technique used here, called 'Brainvox,' was developed in Hanna Damasio's laboratory and can be used to reconstruct a three-dimensional image of the brain at the computer screen. Unlike an autopsy, this technique allows you to cut the brain, on the computer screen, from every angle, and to analyze it at the microscopic level. Also, and most important, you can relate the site of damage *now* to the *current* behavioral or cognitive performance of the patient.

Another advance in neuroimaging makes it possible to map nerve cell activity in the living brain, as it occurs during a behavioral or cognitive task. The colored slices you are looking at in Plate 5 were generated by PET scan analysis. PET enables us to map the amount of radio signal emitted from regions of the living brain. For these studies, one first injects a radio tracer into the bloodstream. The

(a)

(b)

(c)

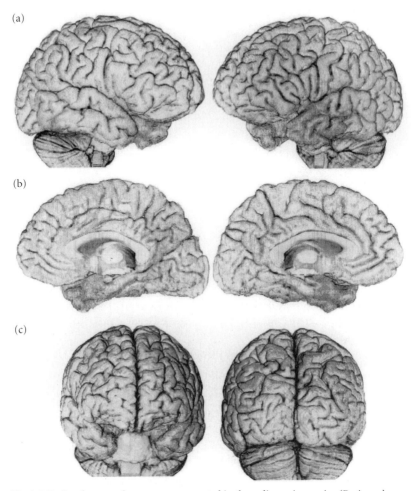

Fig. 2.5 Brain of a normal person reconstructed in three dimensions using 'Brainvox':
(a) Brain seen from its lateral views, right and left. (b) Internal views of the right and left
hemispheres, separated by splitting the corpus callosum and the midline deep structures.
The cerebellum was also removed. (c) Both hemispheres from the front and from the back.

scanner then locates increases or decreases of the radio signal which are related
to the amount of activity in a particular brain area. Such localized changes in
activity are, in turn, associated with the particular task being carried out by the
subject at that moment. In other words, this allows a direct correlation between
mental activity and the dynamic change in the activity of a specific anatomical
structure of a unique brain.

To illustrate the power of the functional neuroimaging approach, consider the result of a recent experiment. We knew that the human brain uses distinct systems to handle concepts of *entities* as opposed to concepts of *actions*. But we also wanted to know whether or not the word forms that describe concrete entities and actions are handled separately by different brain systems. Is the system used to retrieve the common nouns that designate the concepts screen, chair, person and so on, independent from the one that handles the verbs that denote actions such as jumping or swimming or talking? To see if our hypothesis might be supported, we compared the performance of normal individuals with that of patients with differently localized brain lesions. Each group was asked to perform two contrasting tasks: in the first, they had to come up with a word corresponding to an object, such as a chair or table; in the second task, they had to retrieve a word corresponding to an action performed by a person or by an object. We found a complete double dissociation.

One group of patients was not able to name concrete entities normally, but when it came to producing names of actions, they performed in a manner comparable to the controls. The patients that had this particular defect shared a lesion in the *left temporal cortex*, as our hypothesis had predicted. In another group of patients, we found that the production of words for concrete entities was perfectly normal, comparable to controls, and yet, when it came to naming actions, we noted a significant drop in performance. These patients had lesions that clustered in the *left frontal cortex*—and there was no overlap with the previous group. We were able to conclude that there are structures in the left *frontal* cortex of humans that are related to the process of retrieving words that denote activity, whereas there are structures in the left *temporal* cortex that are related to the retrieval of words that denote entities. We can assume that closely related functions, such as the handling of the words for actions and entities, depend on partially segregated systems in the human brain.

This segregation is a functional principle you can find in other domains of brain function. The separation of different types of learning or the separation of color and shape information in the visual system are good examples (see Stevens' chapter 'Line versus color', Part 4). Functions may appear seamlessly integrated but their neural basis is often distributed in several cooperating regions.

Requirements for creativity

> *Donald Campbell reasoned that in human creativity, a cognate process must be at work: human creativity must be a rapid combination and recombination and reassortment of ideas, the memory retaining the more plausible juxtapositions rather as if the computer were programmed to*

produce jokes of the random kind while a selective process would have sorted out those that were genuinely funny from others that were merely silly or meaningless. I suppose it is possible that such a process does go on below the surface of the mind and that it is an element in the sub-conscious processes which must be presumed to precede the irruption of a hypothesis or explanation into the mind.

Peter Medawar, 1991

The physicist Leo Szilard believed that scientists had much in common with artists and the poets. He did note, however, that 'logical thinking and an analytical ability are necessary attributes to a scientist, but they are far from sufficient for creative work.'

Antonio Damasio, 1994

My list of requirements for creativity begins with *motivation* and *courage.* I think courage is important for an artist and equally important if you want to be a scientist. You must be ambitious enough to want to do the work, and you must have the courage to face the criticism and rejection that inevitably will come at some point or another. My second requirement is *extensive experience* and *apprenticeship.* I borrow the word 'apprenticeship' from Howard Gardner's writings on creativity because it describes particularly well a whole collection of critical attributes that include expertise, connoisseurship, technical proficiency and scholarship. If you think about those who have produced important works of art or of science and try to identify characteristics they all shared, extensive apprenticeship is certainly one of them. Great creators are highly expert, have extensive knowledge of their fields and know what works and what doesn't. They know what is original and what is not; they know what people like and dislike, what people admire and do not; they know how a final result can be achieved. However, if you do not know a lot about how to manipulate the creative components—that is, the technique needed for a scientific or artistic endeavor—you have little chance of becoming a successful artist or scientist. Although it is possible that someone without extensive aesthetic experience might produce one interesting piece of art, it is unlikely that such a person could continue to create significant works.

The picture gets even more complicated with the next requirement: *insight into the workings of the self and into the workings of other minds.* This applies mostly to the arts. Being able to know how your own mind works and how other minds work is an underlying prerequisite for creating great art. Great art is unthinkable without this knowledge. But some of my favorite scientists—the ones I have known personally—have this attribute as well. Conversely, I can think of some scientists who do not and who, I believe, have not done so well.

Next, I would like to focus on some of the neural systems and functions relevant for creativity. The first requirement here is the *strong generation of representational diversity*. What I mean by this is the ability to generate—to bring to your conscious mind—a variety of novel combinations of entities and parts of entities as images. These 'images' are prompted by a stimulus that comes either from the world outside or from the inside world (one that you generate and recall). For example, it would be hard to imagine that someone creative enough to design an interesting experiment or to produce the *Demoiselles d'Avignon* would not have a strong generator of diversity, continuously bringing images or representations 'on line'. Many of these representations have to be discarded because they are not relevant; but the images are there to choose from. This process is not unlike the generation of diversity that has permitted the process of natural selection in evolution. If this amazing natural diversity had not been available, humans would not exist as they are today. I believe that this strong generator of representational diversity is linked to the pre-frontal cortices. The images are not realized as such in the pre-frontal cortices—but rather in the early sensory cortices—but they are conducted or ordered *from* there. The lay term 'a very good imagination' really is an effective description of this diversity generating mechanism.

Another requirement is for *working memory* with a large capacity. Because working memory tends to be a misunderstood concept, let me explain what it stands for. Working memory is what permits us not only to retrieve and generate representations internally, but also to hold such representations actively 'on line' and to operate on them—that is, rearrange them in space, recombine them and so on. If I ask you to repeat a phone number, you can do that with plain short-term memory; that task does not require working memory. But if I ask you to retain a phone number and then give it back to me backwards, or backwards and skipping all the odd digits, *that* requires a working memory. You need to hold the set of digits 'on line' and perform a manipulation on them. It is hard to imagine how someone could be creative without having this sort of capacity in abundance. Creativity probably requires the capacity to hold many different data sets 'on line' and the ability to manipulate items and parts of items in those representations such that novel combinations can be formed. Artistic editing can only work, in short, if a great diversity of items is generated, and if the different items are co-displayed for approximate manipulations.

Let me mention two other requirements for creativity. One is the *ability to recognize novel representations*—that is, to judge the aesthetic or scientific value of certain items or item combinations and decide that they are indeed novel and deserve to be saved. I suspect that a marvelous pre-frontal cortex generating many new items and holding them 'on line' would be of little use if we did not have the ability to execute good selections based on an aesthetic or scientific goal. As far as aesthetic selections are concerned, one key aspect of their fine-tuning is the ability to recognize when a particular configuration that is being held in working memory is likely to produce an emotion in others as well as in yourself. The other requirement is for a sharply tuned *decision-making apparatus*. If one is not capable of effective decision making—even if one generates representations abundantly and has a good working memory—the gradual process of choosing what to keep and what to discard will block the possibility of reaching the best results.

The neural basis of decision making and emotional responses

> *This perspective on emotion, feeling, and knowing is unorthodox. First, I am suggesting that there is no central feeling state before the respective emotion occurs, that expression (emotion) precedes feeling. Second, I am suggesting that 'having a feeling' is not the same as 'knowing and feeling', that reflection on feeling is yet another step up. Overall, this curious situation reminds me of E.M. Forster's words: 'How can I know what I think before I say it!'*
>
> Antonio Damasio, 1999

Plate 4 is a rather extreme simplification of a working model of these complex brain functions, and it is meant as a framework for understanding higher brain functions. The visual and auditory cortices generate 'on line' neural patterns corresponding to particular items (shapes of objects, sounds of objects and so on). If we penetrate one of these cortices with many electrodes simultaneously, we find a pattern of neuronal activity—a map—that holds some relationship to the configuration of the signals present in the retina or cochlea and also some relationship to the object being looked at or that is producing a sound. It is important to note, however, that the memory of such a representation is not stored as facsimile image but, rather, as an extensive modification of the firing properties of numerous circuits in 'association cortices' (the properties that allow each nerve cell in a circuit to be on or off). If you penetrated these circuits with many electrodes simultaneously, you would never have a chance of finding a pattern that looks like an object you know. I call these records 'dispositional representations.'

  These neuronal systems are all wired with both forward and backward connections, so that a mapped representation, for instance, that of a face, can become a dispositional representation without the iconic features of the face but with the potential to replicate it or nearly so. The most important feature of this model is that the dispositional representation contains non-explicit records for an entire mapped representation, and that, through backward projections from the dispositional record into the mapping area, the brain attempts to reconstitute the original image. When you see my face now, you represent it in the mapping visual cortex. But if you learn my face, you build a dispositional representation of it, and you could bring back some version later when I am not here. Humans have this ability in abundance—the ability to represent, learn in dispositional mode, and bring back images in recall. When you hold an image in working memory, you hold it in explicit form.

There is another group of cortical areas known as pre-frontal, and they also hold acquired dispositional representations. Interestingly, however, many of them are not so much concerned with the features of a representation (e.g. the structure of a face) as with the relevance of that representation for the entire system or organism. This relevance is established by connecting the dispositional representations of a given item with the innate dispositions contained in the circuitries that regulate the fundamental life processes. The regulatory levels of the brain (the diencephalon and brain stem) are neuroanatomically interwoven with the cortical levels so that when we acquire the representation of a given item, we do so under the influence of circuitries in the lower brain levels. In other words, just as there is no such thing as Kantian pure reason, there is nothing like a pure intellectual representation of a face or of an object.

How does the brain know how to treat a particular object specially? In essence, the brain responds to an object not just intellectually, with facts evoked from memory, but also emotionally. Because of the bioregulatory dispositional knowledge available in the diencephalon and brain stem, the brain responds to a particularly relevant object in a special way while disregarding the others. Suppose that one of those objects is the face of a friend you love, or that of someone you detest. Whether you want it or not, there will be a number of responses that will affect the muscles of your own face and musculo-skeletal frame, the viscera and the internal milieu (e.g. the secretion of chemical substances). Moreover, there will also be neurochemical responses within the brain itself which alter the functioning of other brain circuits. The dopamine system is an example of the kind of brain device that is activated by stimuli whose nature or learning history makes them relevant for the organism. Other comparable brain devices are those that use neurotransmitters such as norepinephrine, serotonin and acetylcholine.

In the context of art and creativity, the arrangement just described is especially relevant. The brain is probably designed to respond with an emotional signal when it encounters certain stimuli—for instance, certain colors and combinations of colors, certain tones and their combinations, certain shapes or their combinations. The emotional responses, which are an ingredient of the aesthetic experience, are first triggered by those stimuli which lend themselves naturally to an emotional response. Later however, by means of an associative process, individuals learn to extend such emotional responses to many other stimuli.

As explained, the autonomic and musculoskeletal responses that are part of the emotions modify the state of the body. When a picture or a musical piece generates a state of pleasure, a great part of that state of pleasure is based on the somatic responses. Somatic responses can happen in two ways. When you are thrilled at hearing a musical piece or looking at an especially beautiful painting, the response is truly somatic—there are changes in skin conductivity, heart rate, breathing rhythm and so on which are easily detectable. This is what I call the 'body loop'. But sometimes you do not actually need to go through the body loop. Little by little, especially with aesthetic objects to which you become habituated over time or with emotional situations to which you become adapted, you actually bypass the body and use what we call the '*as-if body loop*'.

This bypass is possible because the pre-frontal cortex has an important two-way connection to the brain structures that map the body state, namely those known as the somatic cortices. Initially, when an emotion changes the body, the body signals back to the somatic cortices, and those cortices map out the changed state of the body. At the same time, there is two-way signalling between the pre-frontal cortex and those somatic maps so that, after some time, the pre-frontal cortex can lead the somatic cortices to assume the mapping state that they usually assume when the body is engaged by an emotion. In short, we can generate an 'as-if' body state without using the body.

> *Creativity itself—the ability to generate new ideas and artifacts—requires more than consciousness can ever provide. It requires abundant fact and skill memory, abundant working memory, fine reasoning ability, language. But consciousness is ever present in the process of creativity; not only because its light is indispensable, but because the nature of its revelations guide the process of creation, in one way or another, more or less intensely. In a curious way, whatever we do invent, from norms of ethics and law to music and literature to science and technology, is either directly mandated or inspired by the revelations of existence that consciousness offers us. Moreover, in one way or another, more so or less, the inventions have an effect on existence as revealed, they alter it for better or for worse. There is a circle of influence—existence, consciousness, creativity—and the circle closes.*
>
> Antonio Damasio, 1999

BRUCE ADOLPHE

With music in mind

Where does inspiration reside?

A composer may be inspired by mathematical equations,
moonlight, a stranger's glances, money, traffic patterns,
birdsong, a death, an historical fact, sex, a formula for
gambling, chaos, chocolate cake,
an ancient song, a river, a garden, a story,
a piece of music, a card trick, a joke, or the wind.

The quality of inspiration resides in the composer.

Bruce Adolphe, 1996

I was at a music festival a number of years ago. Because I was there as a composer, I was not directly involved in rehearsals and would sit outside on the porch and listen to the music. This particular day, I happened to be sitting next to someone who turned to me and asked, 'Aren't you a composer with the festival?' 'Yes,' I answered. 'Well,' he remarked, 'we both do the same thing, we project abstract thought into a logical format, making it available.' 'Oh,' I said, 'what kind of music do you write?' And he answered, 'I design weapons systems.'

That conversation has bothered me ever since. I have been trying to think what the difference is between his abstract thought and the projection of it, and what I do. Perhaps it is that I look forward to performances.

I would like to discuss a few things, such as imagination generally and, especially, what I call musical imagination. Part of that will be a discussion about teaching and developing a musical imagination, or creativity. I specialize in training young composers and I've spent a lot of time over many years with students. I was only partially joking when I acknowledged thanks in my second book to 'my many students over many years at Juilliard, New York University and Yale who taught me how to teach'. I try to teach imaginative thinking, or I should say I try to encourage my students' imaginative thinking through exercises.

This is the theme of my first book. *The Mind's Ear (Exercises for Improving the Musical Imagination)* (1991) is about creative spontaneity—freeing up the mind to think in ways that academic theory might miss. My second book, *What to Listen for in the World* (1996) probes the nature of music and explores its meaning in our lives.

> *Music can slip by all words,*
> *dissolve past and future into the moment,*
> *release illusions,*
> *and reach the reality of the heart.*
>
> *A good composer*
> *enjoys tradition and is happy to ignore it.*
>
> *Bruce Adolphe, 1996*

I also want to talk about the process of composing a little bit and, if I can get up the nerve, try to compose a piece at the end as a kind of parlor trick. It might not really be composing, but perhaps it will be memorable.

Also, I want to talk about musical performers, who have not been discussed very much because they are not thought to be 'creative' in the initial sense. Perhaps they are re-creators—but they're a very important part of the life of a composer. You can't think as a composer without them, or without having heard the composition played; so, I'm going to mention the performers.

The mind–body continuum

In fact, I'm going to begin with a story about a famous performer. We were both the same age, both at Juilliard in New York City at the same time as students. The Juilliard School has a Pre-College Division where I have been teaching for many years. The Pre-College is for students prior to college age, who seem to be very talented, and who want to be musicians. Those who don't, by the way, often go to medical school (and that's a real statistic!). Anyway, back to this experience. It was 1970, Yo-Yo Ma and I were both fifteen years old. I had written my first cello piece, and I wasn't quite sure whether it would all work because I was a real novice. Yo-Yo said that he would read through the piece with me at the piano and play it at sight. However, before Yo-Yo could do this, I had shown the piece to a cello teacher who pointed out one chord which could not be played on that instrument. He looked at my piece and said, 'Well, this is all fine, but there's a chord right here which can't be played on the cello across four strings. It's just not going to work. There is no way a cello player can get the fingers of the left hand in that position on the fingerboard.' So, I said: 'Well, what should I do about it?' The teacher suggested rolling the chord a little bit so that it didn't happen all at once. Too excited about the music to bother rewriting the passage, I simply placed a squiggly line in front of the impossible chord—a line which indicates that the notes should be 'broken' in an arpeggio rather than played 'flat' together.

Going back to Yo-Yo, he played through my composition, and when that impossible chord came, he played it—straight across all four strings with his bow! Afterwards, I asked him how he did it, because I had been told that it couldn't be done. He said, 'What?' I said, 'this chord here.' So he looked at it again—he had been sight reading—and said, 'I'm not sure that it can be done.' 'Well,' I said, 'you did do it'.

We started over again, and when the moment came, I said 'stop!'; we both looked at his left hand in amazement. It was completely contorted on the fingerboard. The hand position he had somehow magically found was uncomfortable for him to hold; his fingers were twisted in a most unnatural way. 'Oh,' Yo-Yo said, 'you're right, you really can't play that'. This is an absolutely true story, and it points out the difference between my friend and a great many other cellists.

Yo-Yo Ma has another neurological phenomenon attached to his playing that I witnessed many times. When you play the cello, if you have to play very high notes (which in fact look very 'low' because you have to reach way down), you have somehow to place the note just before it's going to happen, playing it very quietly with the fingers. My friend never needs to do that. I remember one recital, where he was listening to the introduction and the piano, with his bow ready, his hands relaxed, and his eyes closed. At the moment that this note came, he went straight in and hit the note right on. And that's the kind of thing that can't be explained, can't be taught, and is bizarre.

> *Musicians have a special biology . . . I have often found that musicians the world over are more like each other than they are like other people in their own countries . . . Music integrates the mind and body in a unique manner which often surprises non-musicians. Sometimes musicians astound other musicians with the level of mind–body coordination.*
>
> *Musicians are formed as human beings, to some extraordinary degree, by music itself.*
>
> Bruce Adolphe, 1996

The neuroscientists are in agreement (see the chapters in this book by Galler, Pfenninger, Stevens): the practice of skillful tasks helps shape the brain's circuitry, especially in our childhood. All of this has something to do with the mind controlling the physical movement. And with a musician—a great musician—the music is so completely in the mind, so fully takes over, that technique is simply the realization of your thoughts. That is true for a composer, too.

> Look out the window of a train as you ride,
> and pretend you are someone else:
> a poet, a novelist, a painter, a politician,
> a composer . . .
> The composer sees the houses,
> streets and clouds rush by
> and feels the stillness inside
> the train, aware of time's
> conflicting rhythms,
> its persistent ironies and
> flowing architecture.
>
> Bruce Adolphe, 1996

A real composer is someone with the ability to do what they want, without impediments. And, as Françoise Gilot says, what is frustrating, what might be a failure, is not something that others can say is obviously wrong (like in science). You feel that it's not what you wanted; it's not what you set out to say. After a little while, you don't even recognize it as yours; you don't like it anymore. In fact, it may be very good, but you no longer find it personal and an expression of what you had in mind. In that sense . . . it's a failure.

> The silent screams of Picasso's Guernica,
> the tears which never fall from Michelangelo's Madonna
> are true music–
>
> As we look we wait
> for the impossible moment
> when the screams will be heard
> and the tears will fall
>
> and we understand eternity.
>
> Bruce Adolphe, 1996

Mind and body loops

> We all have something to say if only we
> will learn to really use our imaginations
> and explore our inner lives.
>
> Bruce Adolphe, 1991

The 'as-if loop' and the 'body loop' concepts discussed by Damasio in the previous chapter, have given me a lot of thoughts about what I usually say. I didn't teach music at New York University; I was involved in the drama department, and the Stanislavsky method was popular then. I won't go into it too much now, but his drama exercises had to do with speech and accent and body language, and also hearing things. What an actor's training is all about is getting into the 'body loop' instead of the 'as-if loop'. In other words, the question is whether your memory is physical—in which case you would have the actual reactions that you had at the time—or intellectual. Great actors who can really laugh when it's necessary, at the same joke after hundreds of performances, have found a way through exercises—the Stanislavsky method is part of it— and they are stimulating that other part of the brain that really makes you fully react. How does an actor cry on cue? By using the right loop, I would imagine.

Aural memory—or how to listen to your inner voice

Before I go on to some other points, I'd like to talk about imagination exercises. Let's actually do some of the ones I've done before with my students. Close your eyes and try; there's no way that anyone can know if you're doing the exercise. Now, one of the things that I tell my students is that visual memory seems to be very good for most people—at least better than aural memory. I have no idea whether that's built in or taught or encouraged. It may be genetic; it may be environmental (or encouraged). I don't really know. But musicians often find that they have a much greater aural imagination/memory than other people.

One way a musician can improve is to work on the aural memory. By that, I don't just mean perfect pitch, which is trivial. Perfect pitch is helpful, but not essential. A lot of great musicians don't have it; others who have perfect pitch don't use it. Now, for example, if I were to ask you to recall—it does help to close your eyes—the face of someone you know well, it would probably be not too difficult for most of you to see that face. But if I were to ask you to take a sentence like, 'Hello, how are you?' and then to hear that same sentence said in the voice of someone you know well, can you do that? Can you hear it? Loudly? Some people tell me that exercise is extremely difficult; some people can't do it at all.

Sometimes I suggest substituting the voice of a celebrity; a lot of people find that easier. Trying to hear your own voice is more difficult. Now, here's a little exercise in timbre (the distinctive quality of an individual sound produced by the voice or an instrument). That is what we were just working on. I'm sure that most of you are familiar with the sounds of orchestral instruments. If I were to ask you to imagine for a moment the sound of one note (it isn't important which one) you might or might not have difficulty. See if you can hear one note being played on a violin as clearly as you can picture a violin. I would bet that by saying the word 'violin' the image of a violin comes immediately to your mind. However, it is not as easy to hear the sound of one note. For some people it is. For some musicians, of course, it's extremely easy.

This is only the beginning of a whole set of exercises that become increasingly complex and difficult. I guarantee—well, of course I can't guarantee this, but I am convinced—that you can improve your mind's ear and your aural memory if you work on it. However, the exercises can become very intricate and can involve far more than just hearing sound.

> *In order to compare the visual and aural imagination/memory, I have frequently asked people in workshops and seminars to imagine first visual then aural situations as I describe them. I might say: 'Imagine a street . . . in the street is a chair . . . on the chair is a car . . . on the car is a person standing . . . on the person's head is a violin . . . on the violin is a piece of fruit.'*
>
> Bruce Adolphe, 1996

No one has trouble seeing this scenario in far greater detail than the actual description. People have suddenly remembered a street from childhood or imagined a street unlike any they can remember. People have imagined plush thrones for chairs or remembered the kitchen chair from when they were four years old or imagined a strangely designed steel chair which they had never seen in real life. People see exact cars, with clear shapes and colors, whether or not they know one car from another; sometimes they imagine toy cars so as not the break the chair. People see their relatives, friends, movie stars or faceless people with familiar bodies standing on the car—they see their clothes down to the last detail. The violins may be realistic or like an abstract drawing. Everyone picks a specific fruit, and many are quite sure that I told them which fruit to see.

> *Then comes the aural suggestion. I ask the same group to hear the voice of someone you know well saying, 'Hi, how are you? Would you like to come over for dinner?'*
>
> Bruce Adolphe, 1996

Many people struggle with this. They can see the person's face but cannot hear the voice. Often, they see the face floating, detached from the body, in a dark background. Or they hear the voice, but keep 'losing it' to silence. Sometimes it is easier when they pretend to hear the voice on a telephone. It is important to realize that even though the visual suggestion was a completely unrealistic fantasy, most people found it easier to imagine than the mundane aural suggestion. Practicing hearing memories and imagining sounds in silence can improve one's musical imagination and heighten the ability to listen to music in a meaningful way.

Here is an exercise that has to do with composing. I sometimes do this to get going on a composition. Try to remember an incident in your life that was very dramatic in some way—it doesn't matter whether it was very happy or sad or awful. Now, try to remove whatever visual images you have associated with this event, and substitute just energy—a feeling, in other words. Maybe I can say, from what Damasio explained in the previous chapter, enter the 'body loop' and see what feelings actually do get into your body by remembering only the energy or feeling of some event after the visual images have receded. Next, depending on your familiarity with instruments in an orchestra, choose one instrument and see if there is some gesture on the instrument, some sound, that in any way captures that remembered feeling.

This exercise is not in my book *The Mind's Ear*, but it certainly is an integral part of my second book, the first chapter of which, 'Chocolate legato,' revolves around an experience in which Itzhak Perlman associates sound with ideas and images. I had written a solo violin piece for Itzhak based on Louise Gikow's poems about food. One piece reminded her of brandy, but when Itzhak was sight reading the piece, he stopped in the middle of playing.

> *His face suddenly lit up, 'It's chocolate cake! Let's call it chocolate cake!'*
> *Before I could react to the suggestion, he began to play it with a deliciously*
> *gooey, chocolate legato. The notes sounded like pieces of cake strung*
> *together by sticky strands of chocolate icing. 'Chocolate it is.' I agreed*
> *completely. And it was.*
>
> Bruce Adolphe, 1996

Itzhak Perlman's playing, informed by sensual memory, captured forgotten things which helped us all to remember not merely things, but feelings and ourselves.

Working memory; the virtual orchestra

Damasio's 'working memory' is really what composing is all about. The great performers in music must feel things deeply, rather than just intellectualizing them or doing them with great technical skill. Perhaps all other creativity at some level has to do with what you remember and how it affects what you want to make.

Your working memory must include some knowledge of the history of music. For example, you need to know at least a body of information in order to think in a medium. If you don't know anything about music, you can't do it. So, the more you know about what other people have written and the more pieces you are familiar with, the more sources you have to draw on. You can even be inspired by mistakes. But ultimately, you have to let your memory for the actual events in your life inspire you. For example, two people could be standing at the same train station. One person will see a little clump of flowers and think that they're beautiful. Someone else will see them and have some kind of memory jolt. This person will see the flowers in his childhood backyard and have a strange Proustian revelation. Then when the train actually comes, that person will have to come back to reality as if from a dream. That feeling is very stimulating. As a composer, you're not going to draw the flowers, but you may feel inspired to work because of the rhythm of that memory jolt.

The idea of inspiration

Someone mentioned that the mind prepared for inspiration; it happens continually. I have an exercise that I can do by myself on a train. This exercise involves looking out of the window in various disciplines. For example, try looking out of the window as a dog. Now that's not exactly a discipline, but the exercise has to start somewhere. Now who knows what a dog sees? His mind might be a blank. But if you look out of the window as a dog, you observe everything differently. Actors do this exercise all the time.

What you do see is all of the shapes and all of the forms, even though you don't know what they mean or what they are called. You just see them very clearly, as if for the first time. It's a kind of a pre-language feeling—if you can make it happen.

The next step in the exercise is to look at the same scene using the eyes and ears of a composer. In other words, if you're sitting in a train and you're speeding through a landscape you don't just see the shapes and forms, you also see rhythm and line. I've written some pieces where I really do capture this—for me anyway. I've always found it fascinating how things move by out there. Sometimes I can't look at it anymore, and I look inside the train to calm my eyes. That difference between the two speeds is very stimulating rhythmically. The difference between the calm inside and the lights flashing by at night, or of trees or leaves going by is also very stimulating. And let's face it, if you're going to blot out the outer world then it's going to be harder to be inspired.

I've written pieces that have been inspired by the rhythm of trains specifically. I've also found inspiration from walking along the streets of New York City, which is in itself an athletic feat. In other words, trying to get across the street in a crowd, the feeling of moving around—that spatial feeling, like a dancer's, of trying to get from one place to another—has its own rhythm. You can become incredibly frustrated and/or you can add to it a sense of exploring the rhythm of that experience. The experience can become a source of inspiration. I did find rather an amusing rhythm from it once that overlaid my feelings of frustration. I used this in a little dance piece of mine, over and over, until the rhythm became quite obsessive; it's a short piece, thank God. It's only three minutes long, and it's one part of a much larger work, but the basic rhythm came from this business of avoiding people on the street. Ironically, I must add that I didn't ever compose that way until I started to try to help my students by suggesting these exercises to develop their musical imagination. After making the suggestion I thought I had better try it too. And it works!

Let me add an amusing story about this idea of getting inspiration. At the Chamber Music Society, one part of my job involves looking at all the scores and ideas that are presented to see if anybody has a good one. The funniest letter came from some guy who wrote, 'I have a great piece for your organization. It's a piece for two violins, a viola and a cello. If this interests you, please call immediately.'

Theories, rationalization, and intuition

Experiencing music requires a suspension of judgment while the music unfolds. In Mandelbrot's discussion (in Part 4), we see a complete blur between science and art. The truth is, I couldn't tell the difference between the thinking and work of a mathematician and those of an artist. In fact, I noticed a real similarity between Mandelbrot's projections of fractal images and the multi-colored images of Dale Chihuly's glass. To me, both are art. One man is an artist, the other a scientist. I need to think about the implications.

I think that inspiration in science has to do with understanding. In my experience, inspiration in music may or may not have to do with understanding, because what inspires musical thought is often mysterious. It may have more to do with confusion; it may come as a result of being confused and challenged. That may be true in science too, but I will not expand on inspiration in science because I don't know much about it. But I will say that I did study with Milton Babbitt, who was a mathematician before he was a composer. Although my music is nothing like his, I learned a lot about thinking about music from him.

> *Hear the world around you*
> *without identifying the sources.*
>
> *Free from names, sounds reveal mystery.*
>
> *Not only birdsong and rhythms of the rain,*
> *but the hum of human actions*

> *and the din of our inventions*
> *heard without names*
> *in a grand mosaic*
> *reveals the spinning mystery of all*
> *music.*
>
> Bruce Adolphe, 1996

The best lesson that I ever had from Milton Babbitt—which he forgets ever happened—was about twenty years ago at Juilliard. At the Juilliard Composer's Forum, in the early 1970s, a seminar was taught by a well-known musician who also claimed to be, and was, fascinated by science. Anyway, the famous composer, Xenakis, had come to lecture and present his music to the Forum, which was made up of young composers and the faculty. Xenakis put a whole series of equations and calculations on the chalkboard, and when he had filled the whole board with these complex mathematical equations, he stopped. 'These mathematical symbols will explain the music you are about to hear. I have been inspired by these equations representing gasses in the air, and by my childhood experiences in Greece,' Xenakis announced.

I listened to the music and happened to like the piece a lot. I could understand this composer's childhood in Greece, I could recognize various highly abstract and distilled elements of Greek rhythm all coming together in a collage. But I had no idea what the numbers on the board meant. None of them made any sense to me. However, I knew that I was going to have a lesson immediately afterward with Milton Babbitt.

> *After the Forum, I asked my teacher, Milton Babbitt, about the equations.*
> *Babbitt had been a mathematician and is well known to be a fan of*
> *numerical complexity. He smiled his embarrassed smile, turned the usual*
> *red he turns when asked such a question, and said, 'The numbers were all*
> *wrong, Bruce.'*
>
> Bruce Adolphe, 1996

So I asked, 'What do you mean it was all wrong?' 'The arithmetic was wrong, it was just completely wrong,' he said. I was stunned, and really upset. 'Does that mean that this famous composer is a phony?' 'Oh no,' Milton explained, 'Xenakis didn't say that he understood the mathematics, he said that he was inspired by it!'

I have been inspired by many things I don't understand. This feeling helps you to write music. One of the things that is most inspiring for a musician is when you can capture that feeling that you had when you were a child and you couldn't completely understand things.

It's quite true, of course, that understanding a mountain and being inspired by it are entirely different things. I have been inspired by rivers, skies, traffic and various people, none of which has anything to do with understanding. And yet, studying a piece of music can lead to a kind of understanding which can in turn lead to inspiration. Discovering subtle musical details that relate to larger formal structures in a work of Bach or Beethoven can bring a rush of energy and a desire to compose. Understanding how a formal tradition was broken or given new meaning by Mozart is a remarkable feeling.

Understanding is often a matter of noticing and naming. Inspiration is often a matter of seeing without naming. This is a mysteriously simple idea.

Bruce Adolphe, 1996

Music becomes boring for a composer when you're working in a technical area of music and you become obsessed with how it's done and forget what the mystery is all about. As Oscar Wilde wrote in *The Importance of Being Earnest*: 'I don't play accurately—anyone can play accurately—but I play with a wonderful expression. As far as the piano is concerned, sentiment is my forte. I keep science for life.' I ask you, 'Have you ever heard a pianist who was "all fingers and no soul"?'

Let me remind you that by technique, good technique, I mean that you can do what you want and think in sound as a composer. Or for that matter, good technique allows you to think in visual images as an artist. But if you allow technique to overwhelm you as an artist, it is absolutely useless. When technique becomes important enough to an artist, then it is actually destructive.

I can think of composers who have been overcome by technique; it is a while before they can create a really good piece. They are pressured by peers or conferences to convince people that their music is completely mathematically worked out. There is always some truth in that approach. Françoise Gilot puts it well when she says that she can explain her paintings after the fact. For me, after the fact is much easier. And I know lots of composers who can chart fantastic mathematical equations out of their pieces after the fact. Some do pre-compositional work that is like that—but I'm not one of them. I am very different. But Milton Babbitt, whose own pieces are completely worked out in advance, has convinced me, on and off, that my way is not so different. It's just a different mind set.

The important thing is to liberate the imagination. Teachers must teach more than procedures, methods, and techniques. They must challenge musicians to free their imagination.

How composers think

Composers do think in sound. It's an extremely verbal world in which most composers have to teach or occasionally write articles about music to make a living. So they end up being very good at explaining things to other people. But those words almost never interfere with the process of actually composing music. When they do, it's frustrating.

There is a difference between what I call 'doing a job' and making an individual and highly personal statement when composing music. For example, writing for a film is not very personal for me; I put something together like a machine and attach it to something. I've stopped doing that kind of work. But when I needed money more, I did plenty of it, mostly for the theatre, where I'd just slap things together as little designs. I don't regret it because along the way I learned a lot about the process of composing music. But the difference is that I didn't put myself totally into that kind of work. Musicians call that 'doing a job' because there is nothing at risk as an identity statement. A piece of music that comes directly from me is in no way a 'job'. Although it's hard work, I would never call it an occupation in that sense.

> I have urged you to listen
> to the music of the world around you,
> and to the world revealed by music.
> Music is not merely feelings:
> it is the form and pattern of experience
> the space before words and after
> the echo of dreams
> the axis of energy
> the resonance of action;
> Music is the sum of all of our memories,
> even those we have forgotten,
> reborn as gesture and inflection,
> the shape of memory itself.

Bruce Adolphe, 1996

There are many different kinds of composers. Some, such as Janàcek or Bartòk, speak directly in the medium of music, very subconsciously. You may be shocked to find that Arnold Schoenberg only discovered 12-tone music after he had written a lot of it. This is a well-documented fact; he says it himself. Only after Schoenberg had composed his work did he make up a theory to describe in words the sound world he had stumbled on. People still have to ask whether a particular composition of Schoenberg's is 12-tone or not. Some famous early pieces sound like they are rooted in his 12-tone theory, but they were written before he developed it. Subconsciously, he understood his achievement, but he needed to devise a conscious theory, in words, that could explain what he already knew and had developed.

> *Debussy listened to shadows,*
> *he heard the sound of light*
> *playing clear and bright on glass, on water—*
> *on things unknown and unnamed.*
>
> *Hinting at secret pleasures,*
> *precise yet elusive,*
> *he revealed his private harmony.*
>
> Bruce Adolphe, 1996

Stravinsky is in many ways a much less fundamentally creative revolutionary in his domain than we often think. I won't go on about Stravinsky, but I will say he was very self-conscious, and that he designed and drew upon other people's work. Rimsky–Korsakov and Debussy were more intuitive, like Schoenberg. That doesn't take away in any sense from Stravinsky, whose genius was just a different and more accessible kind. This underlines the thought that composers work in many different ways, but the common thread is that *they all think in sound.*

Exploring the message encoded in music

> *Music is never mere information*
>
> Bruce Adolphe, 1996

Let me explain a student exercise that had a very interesting result. I had started a series of seminars at Juilliard which were a kind of master class. Actually, it wasn't clear what they were. For example, I would try to help students be better at playing their instruments—when I didn't play that instrument. It was pretty scary at first, but some interesting things came out of this experiment.

A student got up and played a solo Bach movement on the violin. I'm not a violinist, and I had no technical suggestions to offer, especially to someone who played the violin as well as this person. I didn't want to discuss Bach's style either, because that wasn't what this class was supposed to be about, and the student did have a private teacher. I said, 'Let's play a little imagination game with this. When you play the music again in a few minutes, pretend you are a spy, that your cover is that you are a violinist, and that you are on stage playing this piece. You know that encoded in this piece is a secret message which will save the lives of the people when someone in the audience understands the message, but you don't know what the message is because you're just the messenger, the spy. If you got captured, it wouldn't be very nice if you knew what that message was. So that is the reason you don't know.' The young man stood there a long time, getting quite serious. Luckily, he was very talented, otherwise this whole thing could have been terrible. He thought, and then he played the music again. It was absolutely impossible to tell what he did differently, but it was much better. Everyone knew it, and there was tremendous applause. 'How did it feel?' I asked him. 'Well, it felt incredibly important this time,' he answered, 'because it had a kind of life and death quality.' 'So,' I responded, 'let me ask you something. Is there a message encoded in the music?' 'Yes.'

One of the great musicians that I had the honor to study with at Juilliard said to me—it sounds corny now, but he said it to me at a good time in my life—'I just heard Beethoven's "Fifth" for the first time *again*.' I warned you that it was corny, and that you probably have said something like that yourself. But it's an important thought! What he meant was that you can hear a great piece of music forever and thrill to it each time as if you were hearing it for the first time. If you get bored, maybe you should leave it alone because in that way you can discover it all over again. In other words, you can play games with your memory.

You can memorize Beethoven's 'Fifth' and learn a lot about it; you can also forget the music, hear it again some time later and be very inspired. It might be a performance, a live performance perhaps, in which there is a subtle alteration, which makes it not the same piece exactly; it's pretty close, but something will be different. And that small difference that results from the interpretation of the musicians and the acoustics of the room might reveal a whole new world— a whole new message.

Not every piece is capable of that. Unfortunately, some of the most famous and popular works, by composers such as Mozart, will not go through such dramatic transformations. But many of Mozart's much less familiar works, such as the G minor String Quintet, can be endlessly revealing.

Projecting abstract thought into a logical format

Now, I'm going to say one or two words about how I was inspired to write a particular piece called 'Turning, Returning' (for two violins, viola, and cello). Like all of my pieces, the title came quite a bit afterwards. I didn't want to call it 'String Quartet No. 2' because people don't like those titles anymore; they think you're not interesting, and that your music won't be interesting. This is a good title for me because it does express something about the piece. And more than that, it says something about all pieces of music.

Some thoughts are like a gift. Usually this kind of inspiration comes unsolicited. I could also make it happen, but it doesn't feel the same. And it usually isn't as good if it's forced. Leonard Bernstein used to say all the time, if you lie down on the couch and think about inspiration maybe, it will come. I have spent many, many hours lying on the couch and telling people, 'Quiet, I'm working!'

You try to work with a thought, like a painter or like a sculptor. You play with it, you fuss with it, you turn it around, and look at it from different angles. And the more technique you have in the traditional sense, the better you can express your thoughts through sound and give them form. Do you know what a fugue is? What a sonata is? Do you know how to write counterpoint?

Actually, these are fairly trivial things because, in a few minutes, you can teach sonata form to almost anyone who is willing to listen. You can teach fugue, which is not as complex as a thought or an idea. People, especially musicians, like to make of it a complex thing in order to teach courses that seem almost incomprehensible. Actually, it's very simple; its structure is almost fractal-like (see Mandelbrot's chapter 'The fractal universe, Part 4). Only when Bach writes a fugue is it complicated, but the idea itself is not. And it's the idea that is important—not technique.

Melody, context, and modulations

The difference between a pop song and what I like to call art music is context. For example, create a wonderful melody and it will be a song; you can have no melody or a wonderful melody (it doesn't matter), but when you create a context, or structure, then you have an art form. And of course when you combine the two, it's even better. Schubert was able to combine a wonderful tune with a structure that seems to have a life of its own as an organism.

From the beginning, 'Turning, Returning' had a very simple idea. All I tried to do was pull threads out of the idea; the music spins around the central idea constantly, turning and returning. I pulled out threads and then pieces shot off it. And then I did it again, only this time a little longer and a little slower. Everything in this particular work stemmed from the initial idea, even if it isn't always obvious at first hearing. That's why Mandelbrot's fractal concept actually has me deeply worried—maybe everything is like that, even this simple little piece of music.

The piece is in four movements; it's full of memory things. An unresolved movement flows right into a movement that's all about childhood. As you might expect, this movement is very simple. Then things get recycled, and they come together in a kind of nightmare movement; at this point the piece ends.

Recently—and this is not a normal way for writing music, even for me—I've acquired this idea that, instead of developing the motif or the germ or the idea, I just go on trying to find a new context.

So, here's a very simple idea, which first of all has book ends: there is the same passage at the beginning and at the end of the music (Fig. 2.6; see bars 1 and 11) to signal that within, there is one idea. That's why I call them book ends. And then the idea is basically contained within that supporting framework.

You hear a little gesture (Fig. 2.6; see bar 2); a note is added at the beginning (see bar 4); two notes are added at the beginning (see bar 5). And after that happens, I take this chord which is the basis of the whole piece and I repeat it, transposed to two other levels (Fig. 2.6; see bars 6, 7, 8). And I add rhythm, too. So it begins to sound different.

One more quick example is from a piece that isn't as sophisticated as most of my work; I call it my summer festival piece. I mean by that title that I still put a lot of creative effort into the music and enjoyed the experience. But at the same time I felt that people were passing through, deciding what to do, so they really couldn't be hit over the head too hard. I tried to make these pieces of music a little more enjoyable, and they became challenging for me as well.

The particular piece from which Fig. 2.7 is taken has a melody that is very brief (see bars 1–3), and an answer to it (see bars 4–6), and the point of this piece is that those two elements keep happening within a continually changing harmonic context. So, the feeling of the melodies changes because the context changes.

Also, sometimes I transpose a part of the piece. In traditional music, and especially tonal music, when you transpose a melody you transpose the whole thing to another key. So here, I might transpose the excerpt in Fig. 2.7 into the key of Fig. 2.8.

So the music is the same, and yet it is different. Parts of the music change, while parts of it remain the same. It isn't really new, but it's endlessly interesting!

A question of style

I once asked a famous composer if he was stuck in a rut. I was only 16, and it was a very rude question. 'Are you stuck in a rut?' I asked. 'No,' he answered. 'But these pieces all sound the same,' I persisted. 'That's called style,' he answered. And he was right.

There are a lot of ways to listen to music. If you heard a piece of music and, by the time it was over, you realized that you were sort of daydreaming, or you were just taking in a total effect, that would not be at all unusual. It is also not unusual to take in a total effect without listening carefully—and then to have a

Fig. 2.6 Piano reduction of 'In memories of . . .' by Bruce Adolphe. Copyright MMB Music Inc., 1993.

very strong opinion about what you have just heard. In fact, it can be a career. That's just a joke!

Improvisation

I don't improvise very much; some people do. But when I am composing, I do improvise in my head a lot—I will think about ideas, but I won't write them

Fig. 2.7 Piano reduction of 'Bridgehampton Concerto' by Bruce Adolphe. Copyright MMB Music Inc., 1993.

Fig. 2.8 Piano reduction of 'Bridgehampton Concerto' by Bruce Adolphe. Copyright MMB Music Inc., 1993.

down until I have thought them through and the ideas are clear in my head. My relationship to the keyboard and improvisation has practically nothing to do with my composing. I do love to improvise jazz, but I don't compose jazz. I improvise jazz because it's a nice release for me, but it is not interesting for me personally to compose in that style.

Some composers have worked on the keyboard and insist on it, others never go near the keyboard. The reason that I don't work at the keyboard is that when I sit down at the piano my hands go through all of those pre-learned gestures and formulas and trivial things that I'm not interested in. My fingers do them right away. So, I don't work at the piano very much.

Fig. 2.9 Fragments by Bruce Adolphe, improvised to demonstrate varied implications of random notes.

Figure 2.9 is the interesting result of some random note suggestions from an audience—B, E flat (which is also D sharp), C and F sharp. I took the notes as they were suggested and moved them around a little bit from a compositional point of view. In bars 1 and 2, there is a major chord and a diminished chord. You could be Cole Porter with the music in bars 3–6. I could also take the suggested notes and use them as a bass configuration, low enough that you would not even recognize them (see bars 7 and 8). Then I use those same notes, transposed, to do something linear (see bars 9 and 10). An harmonic context from that might be to take the major chord that was suggested accidentally, and the one note that was dissonant to it, and make that the whole point of the piece. I just stopped myself, however, because some of my thinking was directly related to those notes and some wasn't. I pull out the same dissonances in relationship to all the notes. Hack composers of various periods would immediately have found a traditional accompaniment for the notes, and then gone directly to the dissonant note. In other words, this composing thing is endless on one level, and very provocative and fascinating; but it can also be very trivial and dull, with the creative process existing at a very, very low level.

Improvisation can run from incredibly low levels of creativity, where hack composers 'burp out' melodies, to the other extreme, where it discloses extremely complex and brilliant revelations, by making known a truth that was previously secret. If I was going to improvise in some brilliant or revealing way, I would try to get into a mood and then just do something. I can't get into a mood before an audience; at least, not a good one from the standpoint of creating music. One way of improvising successfully is to start off by doing things that you know; hopefully, that will lead to things that you don't know.

Often I sit down at the piano and do that very thing. Bar 11 of Fig. 2.9 is a trivial gesture that I've been playing since I was a kid. I always start like that. Perhaps it's a way of opening a door into my childhood. Starting this way always makes me remember something. It puts me in a mood to create something new.

Coda

I only go to the piano after I've been composing to try things out—not to hear what they sound like. Music can take place fully in your head; it's something that you can think and hear in your imagination. The emotional truth of a great work of music is inextricably linked to the musician's inner world of imagination and discovery—or to what I call the mind's ear.

KARL H. PFENNINGER

The evolving brain

*All behavior is a reflection of brain function . . . The action of the brain
underlies not only relatively simple behavior such as walking and smiling,
but also elaborate affective and cognitive functions such as feeling, thinking, and writing a poem.*

E.R. Kandel, in Kandel and Schwartz, 1981

Understanding the mind as a concept

This chapter is designed, in part, to demystify the human brain, a uniquely
complex organ in terms of its anatomy, physiology and chemistry. We
will discuss the capacities of the nervous system, its building blocks,
their genetic roots and their plasticity, and then extrapolate from the emerging
concepts to higher brain function. In his chapter, Damasio approached the
same issue from the opposite direction, starting with the analysis of higher
brain function and relating it to our rapidly growing knowledge of the circuitry
of the human cerebral cortex. Both of these approaches are based on the study
of the physical substrate of the mind, but there are others. As Reeke and Sporns
(1993) wrote, 'it is not so widely agreed that one needs to study the nervous
system to understand behavior'.

Indeed, traditional psychology postpones (or denies?) the goal of relating
behavior to brain function. But the field is changing. Contemporary philosophers of psychology, such as Paul Churchland (1981), argue that in the not so
distant future, traditional psychology will be replaced completely by neuroscience. In the interim, modern psychologists, such as Steven Pinker (1994),
have begun to bridge the traditional gap between psychology and biology by
relating the development of cognitive functions in vertebrates to the evolution
of the brain. The result is 'evolutionary psychology,' as Pinker defines it—the
integration of psychology and anthropology into the rest of the natural
sciences, especially neuroscience and evolutionary biology. Darwin could not
have been more prescient.

*In the distant future I see open fields for far more important research.
Psychology will be based on a new foundation, that of the necessary*

acquirement of each mental power and capacity by gradation. Light will be thrown on the origin of man and his history.

Charles Darwin, 1859

Like the computer, the brain is an information processing system—or a vast array of such systems. However, the analogy stops there because the 'wiring' of the brain, unlike that of typical computers, can adapt to functional needs. This important concept is known as 'plasticity'. Only the most up-to-date recent computers are beginning to show signs of 'plasticity'. Nevertheless, modern electronic computing plays critical roles in our quest for understanding how the brain works. Perhaps most significantly, computing is at the heart of a relatively young branch of science, the generation and study of 'artificial life' and its subdisciplines, including computational neuroscience. These disciplines use the computer to model biological systems in such a way that they possess some of the key properties of their real-life counterparts. As David Marr (1982) said, this approach uses computational theory to look at a specific *process* (such as vision), whereby the focus is on the computational problem rather than the 'hardware' (i.e. the actual wiring of the brain). Such computer models may be based on properties of simple neuronal circuits that have been analyzed in detail. But they endeavor to explore the function of large neuron assemblies (Selverston, 1993)—or they may seek to elucidate complex behaviors, without knowledge of the relevant neuronal circuits. Thus, computational neuroscience is expected to contribute to our understanding of brain and mind by helping to fill the gap between the cellular/molecular and the behavioral levels of inquiry. Eventually, the link between computer modeling and biology will be provided by the answer to the question of how specific representations and algorithms deemed critical for a specific process are implemented in the neural machinery (see Marr, 1982).

The complexities of brain and behavior are so great that multiple approaches to study them are not only useful but actually necessary. This results in confusion and (apparent) conflict but, in time, these approaches will converge. The data obtained at all levels must be synthesized into a coherent set of concepts if we are ever to understand the mind and its creative powers.

Functions of the nervous system

The nervous system is designed to process and store information, and its function is to regulate the responses of the organism to its external environment and internal milieu. For example, the visual system of an animal recognizes its enemy. This information is processed in the brain and translated to result in a flight reaction. The running entailed by the flight reaction increases the animal's metabolism and, consequently, the organism responds by increasing its breathing and heart beat rates, again regulated by the nervous system.

With the progression of evolution, the nervous system has assumed functions of increasing complexity, so that we can now distinguish several different levels of operation in the most advanced animal species and humans (see also Damasio's chapter). This can be represented as a stratified hierarchy or ladder with vegetative functions at the base, followed by instincts, learned behavior, language, intelligence and creativity at the top (Table 2.2). As we will see later, this hierarchy is likely to reflect an evolutionary phenomenon. The lowest level of operation, essential for the integrity of the organism, is the control of *vegetative functions*, such as the regulation of blood pressure, heart beat rate, etc. This is all that the nervous system does in very primitive animals. Clearly a step up from there is behavior. There are two very different types of behavior. *Instinct*, a form of inherited behavior, is characterized by the lack of adaptation to specific circumstances, and the information necessary to perform these instincts is encoded in the genome. The spider does not learn from its parents how to construct the web; it's instinctive behavior. Another well-known example is the mating behavior of the stickleback fish, whose female will follow a crude, non-functional model of the male as long as it has the red belly characteristic of a male ready for mating; there is little or no adaptation of instinctive behavior.

Learned behavior and memory increasingly overshadow instincts in more highly developed species such as mammals or birds and enable the animal to adapt its behavior to particular circumstances. Canines, for example, can learn

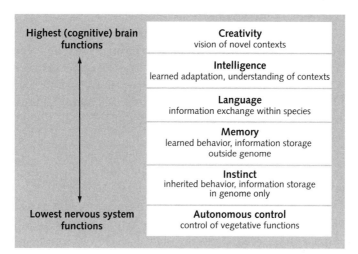

Highest (cognitive) brain functions	**Creativity** vision of novel contexts
	Intelligence learned adaptation, understanding of contexts
	Language information exchange within species
	Memory learned behavior, information storage outside genome
	Instinct inherited behavior, information storage in genome only
Lowest nervous system functions	**Autonomous control** control of vegetative functions

Table 2.2 Hierarchy of nervous system functions.

the sophisticated tasks of a guide dog. Learning and memory are momentous advances in nervous system function. Their development is a major break-through of nature that enables the organism to hold information outside the genome, in the nervous system. Prior to memory, the only place for an organism to store information was the genetic code—the DNA sequence. But by necessity, information storage in the genome is extraordinarily slow. It requires mutations, which are random, and natural selection over thousands and millions of years. An advanced nervous system, in contrast, can acquire, accumulate and use new information within a very short time.

Language, the capacity to exchange information between individuals of the same species, is a significant step up from simple memory because it enables members of a species to transmit the information they have acquired to their peers and to subsequent generations. The advantage is obvious: sharing one's experience verbally saves others from having to brave the same trials or to rediscover all knowledge. Thus, language must be tied closely to the advances of human society as a whole. *Intelligence*, near the top of our ladder of nervous system functions, goes beyond mere data storage. It can be defined as learned adaptation to unforeseen realities in the environment and understanding of the context and the relatedness between different realities in our environment. Intelligence thus necessitates processing and integration of large data sets.

Finally, *creativity* forms the top of our hierarchy. Creativity involves the vision or the determination of novel contexts between facts in our external or our internal worlds—contexts that had not been recognized previously. This requires the association in the mind of diverse and apparently unrelated images and, thus, represents a higher level yet of integrative capacity of the nervous system. How do these concepts relate to modern neuroscience?

A clue comes from the fact that the hierarchy of brain functions described in Table 2.2 could be redrawn on a time scale to reflect evolutionary advances. For example, fish exhibit primarily instinctive behavior, with a limited ability to learn. In contrast, birds and mammals, especially primates, have a far greater capacity to learn. The advances in brain function in vertebrates parallel the massive development of the cerebral cortex, which is a relatively minor part of the brain in fish and becomes the domineering structure in primates.

Pinker (1994) makes the case for the evolutionary basis of language. Linguists have come to the astonishing conclusion that languages may be mutually unintelligible but share a single computational design of their syntax. This finding, as well as studies on how children learn a (any) language, strongly suggest the innate (i.e. inherited) ability to recognize meaning in syntax and word morphology. Even though the different sounds and words of different languages must be learned, comprehension appears to be genetic and, thus, represents an evolutionary step.

How can this be? The process of evolution depends on four major biological principles: procreation of the species; heredity of properties (through the genome, the DNA); variance (i.e. mutations introduced into the genome); and natural selection (i.e. survival of those best adapted to a particular environment). We observed already that language comprehension appears to be inherited. Pinker (1994) argues, quite plausibly, that mutations in primates may have shifted the use of neuronal circuits originally not involved in vocal communication to a role in language. Mutations also may have caused the numerical expansion and refinement of these circuits. That the exchange of hard-won knowledge among members of the species offers a distinct advantage for survival (selection) has been mentioned already. So, it is not unreasonable to view language and intelligence as advanced steps, and creativity as the climax, of an evolutionary process.

How does this evolutionary concept, which emphasizes genetically predetermined features of brain function, relate to the fact stated earlier that the brain has the capacity to adapt to functional needs? In order to understand this important question, we must first examine the building blocks of the nervous system.

Elements of the nervous system

The extraordinary complexity of the human brain presented for a long time a formidable barrier to its investigation. However, over the last 25 years, the reductionist approach—the study of simple model systems that were amenable to detailed analysis—resulted in dramatic progress. The successes in this arena depended on the advances in ultra-sensitive technologies, which propelled cellular and molecular neuroscience forward to an unprecedented degree. Although much remains to be investigated, this knowledge explosion has provided us with a rather detailed understanding of how neurons form circuits, how they interact with one another and how they transmit information to one another.

The human brain is an enormous collection or network of circuits, formed by about 10 billion nerve cells or neurons and their countless processes. On average, these cells each form 10 000 synapses (specialized neuronal contacts at which signals can be transmitted from one neuron to the next). The signal flow in these circuits serves two purposes: one is to transfer information, for example, from a sensory organ to an effector organ, such as a muscle cell; a second purpose is information storage, as has been recognized in recent years. The pattern of signal flow seems to constitute at least an aspect of long-term memory. As a corollary, the circuits themselves—that is, the flow of information in these circuits—can be modulated, either functionally, by leaving the circuit intact but tuning it in one way or the other, or structurally, by forming or deleting specific synapses and loops in a circuit with the result of memorization. This modulation of the circuits is called *plasticity*. As I proposed in 1986 (Pfenninger, 1986), functional similarities between such plasticity or memory and development seem to be of paramount importance. Actually, we have started to understand how neuronal circuits are being established during development. The combination of the functional principles and the known structural elements into larger units enables us today, at least conceptually, to develop a mechanistic understanding of brain functions up to the level of memory. Higher levels of operation are largely the domain of extrapolation from what is known about the simpler systems. What follows is an attempt to lay out this extrapolation as it might apply to creativity.

Genetics, development and plasticity

During brain development, 10^{14} synaptic contacts (10^{10} neurons $\times$ 10^4 synapses each), thousands of miles of nerve fiber connecting them and the resulting circuits need to be formed. The constituent proteins that enable the neurons to form these circuits are genetically encoded, of course. In very simple species, such as the extensively studied worm *Caenorhabditis elegans* (which does not seem capable of learning), neuronal circuits are highly consistent from animal to animal or 'hard-wired'. In other words, the detailed circuitry of the worm's small nervous system is programmed genetically. In the more highly developed vertebrate brain, however, theoretical limits make this impossible. Estimates indicate that the human genome, for example, is not nearly large enough to encode all the molecules that would be required if all 10^{14} synaptic contacts in the brain were genetically predetermined. In addition to genetic programming, therefore, other functional principles must apply.

In recent years, numerous molecules have been identified that help establish the connectivity patterns in the circuits of the developing brain. Today's consensus is that the nerve fiber pathways and the wiring *principles* for different neuron populations are programmed genetically. The detailed synaptic connections for each neuron, however, clearly are not. This latter point was demonstrated in numerous studies, especially the work of Hubel and Wiesel and their colleagues, for which they were awarded the Nobel Prize in 1981 ('For discovering how sight stimulation in infancy is tied to future vision and how the brain interprets signals from the eye'). The main message of this work is that normal usage and function of the developing nervous system is a prerequisite for the establishment of normal neuronal circuitry and normal nervous system function in the adult. In other words, in more highly developed nervous systems, function 'validates' the correct circuitry, or neurons have invented a mechanism to adapt their connectivity to function. The resulting circuits are not 'hard-wired', they are malleable or 'plastic'.

A good example is strabismus, or cross-eyedness. Malalignment of the eyes means that the two sets of signals that reach the brain from the two eyes are not in tune (see Stevens' chapter 'Line versus color', Part 4); they are not complementary and, therefore, three-dimensional vision cannot be established. If this state persists past a critical stage in childhood, normal three-dimensional vision will never occur even if the deficit in eye alignment is corrected later on. The disturbance in the development of visual system circuitry resulting from strabismus is so severe that it is anatomically quite obvious in experimental animals with this defect. However, if eye alignment in the strabismic child is corrected early enough, the brain starts to receive complementary images (i.e. complementary sets of signals from the two eyes) and the circuitry that produces three-dimensional vision is adjusted to establish normal function. Numerous other examples exist, and they all indicate this important feature of the nervous system—the shaping of neuronal circuitry in the developing organism by normal nervous system activity.

Nervous system plasticity does not stop with development, however. The remodelling of circuits and the formation, modification and deletion of synapses continue in adulthood in numerous brain structures, especially those known to be involved in learning and memory. Memory thus appears to be very similar to the events that take place during development. This forms the basis for the concept that learning, in fact, is an extension of a developmental process. How do we go from here to intelligence and creativity? This is where we have to rely on generalizations and extrapolation.

Extrapolation to higher brain function

> [There] . . . is a new natural philosophy, founded on the realization of the import of complexity, of evolution. Very complex systems—whether organisms, brains, the biosphere, or the universe itself—were not constructed by design; all have evolved.
>
> John Brockman, 1995

The visual system may again prove useful as an example. As illustrated in Fig. 2.10a; two sets of visual signals, two-dimensional data each, enter the brain from the left and right eyes. Processing at different levels of the brain and integration of this information leads to three-dimensional or spatial vision (cf. Stevens' chapter). Thus, this is an excellent example of the brain's capacity to generate literally and figuratively a new dimension based on incoming signals. Taking this one step further, and relating it to our earlier discussion of the highest brain functions, one can argue that the understanding of known contexts and the vision and establishment of novel contexts involved in intelligence and creativity, respectively, depend on the development of additional dimensions by the brain. As shown in Fig. 2.10b, complex sets of data stored in many different circuits in the cerebral cortex may become integrated, perhaps in a novel way, in a particularly capable brain, and this may result in a new vision of, or the discovery of a new causal relationship between these data sets. Such a process would constitute creativity.

As Damasio explained in his chapter, the higher-vertebrate brain, and especially that of humans, has an elaborately developed, so-called 'association cortex'—a structure characterized by extensive connections with other areas of the cerebral cortex and specialized for holding 'mental images'. This is where the extrapolation from simple neuronal systems meets the direct analysis of higher brain functions.

What next?

If the concepts presented here are correct, their ramifications are momentous: the influence of a child's environment on the development of his or her intelligence and creativity is likely to be highly significant. If the circuits important for data integration at the highest levels and involved in intelligence and creativity resemble those studied in the visual system, as seems likely, then these circuits are probably subject to the same plasticity observed in the visual and other systems. In that case, an environment that stimulates the use of these circuits during childhood would be expected to promote the intellectual and creative powers of the brain. Janina Galler will address this issue directly, but from a different angle, in the next chapter.

Where does creativity come from? That the cells, synapses and molecules of the nervous system as we know them are simple building blocks for the construction of the brain is beyond question. Also, we have quite detailed neuroanatomical and physiological knowledge that identifies the nature and major streams of signals as they travel from one brain region to another. For example, the flow of visual data through the optic nerve to the lateral geniculate nucleus, a central region in the brain, and from there to a specific part of the cerebral cortex is well understood (cf. Stevens' chapter). However, we are far from understanding the detailed blueprints for the processing circuits in the cerebral cortex, and the complexity of these arrays of circuits is daunting.

Through the reductionist approach (i.e. through the study of simple neuronal systems) we have obtained a wealth of cellular and molecular information. Are these data suitable as brick and mortar for the construction of the

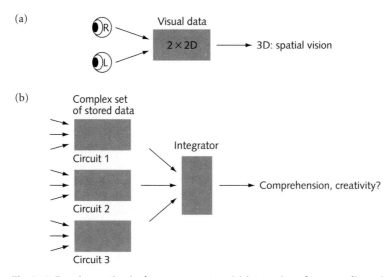

Fig. 2.10 Data integration in the nervous system: (a) integration of two two-dimensional images of the same object recreates the third dimension in the brain; (b) integration of different but related data sets also may generate new 'dimensions' or the vision of novel contexts.

immensely complex edifice representing the brain and performing cognitive functions? Surely not by themselves. The solution to this problem is likely to come from several different directions, especially:

(1) the exciting recent developments in cognitive neuroscience discussed by Damasio in his chapter (i.e. the amalgamation of neurological and psychological testing with neuroanatomy and, especially, modern imaging techniques);

(2) chaos theory and one of its key tools, fractal mathematics, which can be used to decipher highly complex sets of interdependent natural phenomena (see Mandelbrot's chapter and the book's concluding chapter);

(3) computational neuroscience, which will help to define the nature of data processing, the algorithms, necessary to achieve a particular brain function.

The synthesis of the data generated by these diverse approaches will eventually result in a comprehensive image of how the brain produces a mind that can perform creative functions.

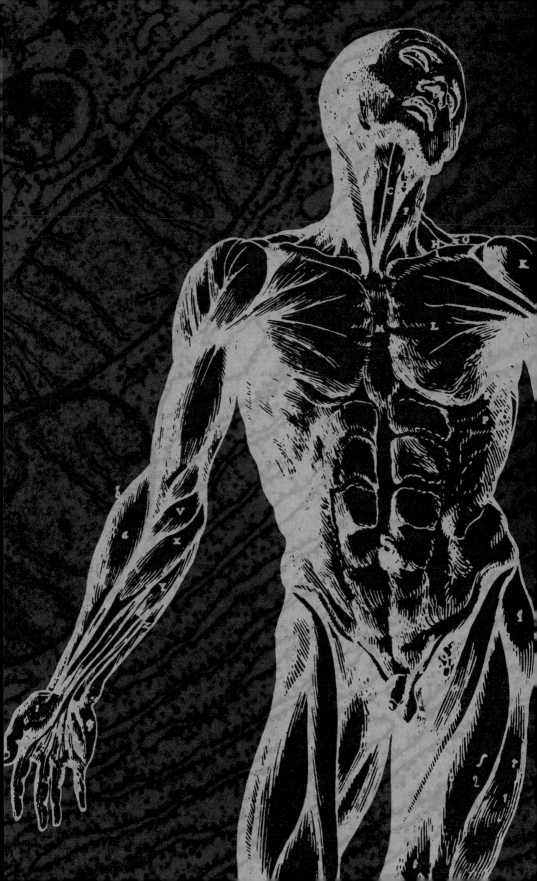

PART THREE

The adaptive mind: deprivation versus rich stimulation

JANINA R. GALLER

The early experience

Creativity comes from a person's inner being. If that person lacks confidence and hope, the act of raising a child can become difficult, even intolerable.

D. Goleman, P. Kaufman, and M. Ray, 1992

The effects of nutrients on behavior, whether short-term or permanent, are of more concern in children than adults. This is because it is well established that the developing organism is more vulnerable to nutritional insult than the mature organism.

L.S. Crnic, 1990

It is now well accepted that the level of growth and development attained by the children of a community is the best index of the general level of cultural and economic development of the community and of the country as a whole.

L. Sinisterra, 1987

Environmental factors and their influence on the development of brain and behavior

For over 25 years, I have been studying the combination of poverty and malnutrition in children who grow up primarily in disadvantaged environments. My work has allowed me to see, through a developmental window, how the brain, behavior, and children operate within the context of different environments, and how these environments modify children's behavioral plasticity (or their ability to adapt). It has also given me great insight into how early malnutrition affects learning and how these early childhood experiences have a long-lasting and profound impact on mental development.

In past days, the vast majority of the world's children who were subjected to serious malnutrition did not survive. Typically, they either died or suffered grave consequences from which recovery was rare. With gradual advances in public health and medicine, a new group of children began to emerge—survivors of malnutrition and its concomitant social and economic problems. Currently, approximately 40–60 per cent of the world's children have been impacted by malnutrition. Even in the United States, a very high number of children in inner cities and rural areas are afflicted with this particular problem. Childhood malnutrition is not only found in developing countries; it affects societies on a global scale.

Three to seven per cent of all cases of malnutrition are severe. However, the most prevalent form of malnutrition is mild and not always obvious to the human eye. The *critical period*—the time of maximum impact—for nutritional deficits to affect a child is from the second trimester of pregnancy through the first two years of life. Investigators, such as Bill Greenough (see chapter by Pfenninger, Part 2), have demonstrated that the brain has a tremendous capacity to evolve and change throughout most of life—in fact, well into old age. Yet, my studies demonstrate it is at this tender and early age, when brain growth and development are most accelerated, that environmental factors have the greatest impact, with consequences and deficits that can be permanent.

To demonstrate and explain the problems of childhood malnutrition, and how one can try to overcome them, I will discuss a series of three different studies I have been involved in over the last three decades. I will then discuss aspects of intervention and the early experience.

A rat model

Animal models are routinely employed to study human problems such as childhood malnutrition. Malnutrition, by itself, is quite difficult to isolate in the human condition since it coexists with poverty, other environmental deprivation, and infection. The combination of these factors complicates the picture. With animal models, however, one is able to control experimentally for these factors.

> Even the most sophisticated multifactorial analysis is no substitute for the experimental testing of hypotheses, and this can only be done with animals. It should be self-evident that experimental animal and human field studies must interdigitate if any conclusions are to be reached before the end of the present interglacial period.
>
> J. Dobbing, 1968

Approximately 30 years ago, I first began working with an important colony of rats that originated with R.J.C. Stewart at the London School of Tropical Hygiene. When Reg Stewart was forced to retire at age 65, I inherited the colony. The rats were then in their thirteenth generation of malnutrition, and I had the privilege of bringing the colony from England to the United States. This animal model was particularly relevant to human populations where malnutrition is usually not a one-time event, but rather a chronic, insidious process present throughout the life span and across generations.

Physical vs. behavioral recovery after early malnourishment

It is clear that programmes of nutritional supplementation alone will not solve the problems of poor development in chronically undernourished deprived children to any great extent.

S. Grantham–McGregor, 1987

The differences between a malnourished rat pup and a well-nourished pup are readily apparent. One of the most striking characteristics is the milk line on the belly of the well-nourished animal, which is absent in a malnourished pup. For our study, we took the malnourished animals at birth and fostered them onto healthy foster mothers who had no history of malnutrition. The malnourished pups regained normal physical size almost immediately. However, physical growth and size are the *least* sensitive outcomes of malnutrition.

We were therefore especially interested in evaluating the animals' behavioral parameters and their ability to adapt to the demands of their environment—their plasticity. In the 1930s, T.C. Schneirla was one of the first researchers to utilize this term, defining it in a manner that is somewhat different from its common use today (Aronson et al., 1972). He looked at plasticity more broadly, from the perspective of adaptive function, which is how I am employing it. Schneirla's view was that the plastic process is the ability of the organism to respond to the demands of its environment. If an animal or human is challenged, its survival depends upon its ability to respond, or to adapt.

One of the early tests of adaptive function, known as the *home orientation test*, involves placing the young pups at a distance from the nest and their mother on postnatal day 5. We then wait to see if the pups can find their way back home. Animals with a history of previous malnutrition, even though they had been fostered to a healthy mother, were not able to find her—unlike their well-fed counterparts. The previously malnourished pups showed a clear-cut delay in their response to the changed environmental condition. By the time postnatal day 11 had arrived, both groups of rats—the control rats and the previously malnourished rats—were performing at similar levels. I present the interpretation that, when damage occurs early in life, the result is not only the immediate physical effect on the organism—there are also long-lasting neural consequences. An animal, or a human, may spend a significant amount of time unable to learn from its environment. The animal that cannot find its way back home cannot function as normal animals do, and it is not maximally absorbing or learning from its environment during the observed delay period.

Effects on rat adaptive behavior: swimming in an indoor pool decorated with travel posters

Another of the many tests we conducted on the animals was first detailed in the 1930s by Karl Lashley. Prior to Lashley, research dating from the early 1900s described the rat as a very stupid animal, and the period literature on animal behavior commented repeatedly that the rat is an inappropriate organism for the study of cognitive and behavioral functions. Lashley felt that current testing procedures incorporated too many distracting stimuli and thus, the rats were overwhelmed. To test his theory, he first put the rats on a stand in front of two windows (Fig. 3.1). The rats did not like being on the stand and this, along with a puff of air at the appropriate time, motivated them to jump through the window. In response to a sequence of visual cues, one of the windows would be locked. Each rat had to learn to recognize the correct sequence of stimuli in order to correctly jump through the unlocked window. By allowing the rat to focus its attention on the task at hand, the 'dumb animal' suddenly became an intelligent one (Lashley, 1963).

The rat is now routinely used to study learning and the impact of early damage. This example shows that the interpretation of higher brain function is likely to be in the eye of the beholder. Sometimes, creativity lies in *how* we test an organism or how we test children, not necessarily what we are looking for as the outcome.

How did our rats perform in the Lashley test? There were two very interesting findings. First, when previously malnourished animals were challenged with simple stimuli, they performed at exactly the same level as their healthy counterparts. It was only when they were challenged with more difficult tasks, requiring the discrimination of more complex stimuli, that they began to fall behind. The second finding—an important part of our observations—was to assess *how* these animals failed. The previously malnourished animals made more errors because they *perseverated*; in other words, they would fixate on a particular side. For example, a 'right-dominant' rat would pick the window on the right and would keep jumping to that side, although the stimulus had shifted. This tendency to be more recalcitrant to change, to perseverate, and thus be non-adaptive, was much more striking in the animals with histories of previous malnutrition.

An interesting observation we have made in our recent studies, using an animal model of prenatal malnutrition, is that behavior falls apart under certain circumstances. We employed the Morris Maze Test, in which we placed the animals in a large swim tank, approximately six feet in diameter. A platform

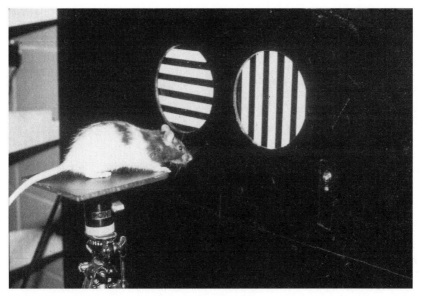

Fig. 3.1 Rat learning to jump through unlocked window.

was submerged in the water. The water was opaque, a small amount of milk having been added to prevent the animal from seeing the platform. The rats had no orienting clues to rely on except brightly colored travel posters on the ceiling and surrounding walls; they had to determine the position of the platform relative to the orienting stimuli. When introduced into the tank from different directions, an animal had to depend on those spatial markers to locate the platform. We found that the healthy control animals, who had always been well nourished, swam directly to the platform when challenged by different starting positions. When the previously malnourished animals were put through the same tests, they tended to go around the pool repeatedly, passing the areas where the platform had been randomly placed. Again, they apparently perseverated with their original idea about where the platform would be, instead of responding to the need to locate the platform in space and thus exhibit adaptive behavior.

The damage of early malnutrition crosses generations

After bringing the rat colony to the Massachusetts Institute of Technology (MIT), we followed the animals for 25 generations. In the course of these long-term studies, we made two very interesting observations. First, males had a harder time overcoming the deficits than did females. This is not unusual, and it has been recognized that the male fetus is generally more vulnerable to prenatal damage. Second, it took from two to three generations to overcome some of the deficits that we observed. We concluded that the early malnutrition effects lasted generationally; this led us to a series of other considerations.

Physiological changes in the brain: damage or compensation?

[There are] two alternative hypotheses concerning the nature of the effect of early malnutrition on cognitive development. We shall call these two positions the 'Hardware' and the 'Software' hypotheses. The hardware hypothesis, which Galler maintains, holds that malnutrition occurring during critical times in early development causes irreversible damage to those brain structures (Hardware) that are responsible for optimal cognitive functioning. Alternatively, the Software hypothesis rejects the brain damage position and maintains that during the period of malnutrition the organism may be 'distracted' from learning those aspects of its environment that are important for optimal cognitive functioning later in life.

D.A. Levitsky and B.J. Strupp, 1987

I would like to describe a set of experiments that is very different from the more recent animal investigations. Due to the availability of new technology, we have been able to expand our analysis of the animals beyond behavior to their neurobiological underpinnings. In this series of studies, we exposed female rats to five weeks of malnutrition prior to pregnancy, and continued to malnourish each female until the birth of her pups. At birth, pups were fostered to healthy mothers so that they were nutritionally rehabilitated from that point on. We could then approach an understanding of the effects of malnutrition on the central nervous system from a broad perspective, studying behavior, neurophysiology, neuroanatomy, and molecular neurobiology.

In these studies, we focused on a specific region of the brain, the hippocampus. It got this name because of its sea horse-like shape. The hippocampus is particularly meaningful for our work because it is important for learning and memory. It is also a simple structure compared to other parts of the brain. Additionally, we were interested in the hippocampus because it lends itself particularly well to interdisciplinary research in our animal model.

Studies on the hippocampus do not tell us what is going on in the whole brain; they simply open a window on an encapsulated structure of the brain, enabling us to address questions of interest. A broad spectrum of data on the hippocampus already exists in many disciplines, and the hippocampus has been shown to be vulnerable to a wide range of perinatal insults. Finally, the hippocampus grows predominantly postnatally. Because we are studying pre-natally malnourished animals that are raised by normal foster mothers, we are thus able to capture the effect of a prenatal insult on functions that may not even emerge until after birth, when the hippocampus develops fully.

With the hippocampus as the locus, we studied neuronal systems electro-physiologically. For example, we looked at 'long-term potentiation'—the enduring modifications of synaptic transmission of ion currents considered to be involved in learning and memory (see Pfenninger's previous chapter in Part 2). There were profound, persistent alterations of long-term potentiation in developing animals that had been exposed to malnutrition only during the prenatal period. We analyzed other properties of the neurons, such as den-dritic arborization and receptor distribution, and found them to be very distorted relative to control animals.

Most remarkably, however, despite these clear signs of distortion in 'neu-ronal wiring,' the *behavior* of these rats was relatively unaffected. Let me refer again to my friend, Karl Lashley, who was the first to use adequate tests for studying rat behavior, thus demonstrating the rat's remarkable intelligence. Lashley conducted an experiment in the 1930s in which he removed a large portion of a rat's brain and found that the rat retained the ability to learn. Does this mean the brain is redundant? Does it mean one can be creative with only a small part of one's brain? Damasio would be quite offended if I said that was the case. It is not. But I think we are beginning to see a very interesting phenomenon. There appears to be a discrepancy between the fundamental neurobiological findings and the results at the behavioral level. However, thought about at greater length, it may make sense: the changes may be adap-tive. Why should the animal completely lose its ability to adapt? I now think that a lot of the 'wiring' changes we observed in the experimental animals were not deficits or damage resulting directly from malnutrition; rather, these changes may be the brain's 'efforts' to compensate for, or adapt to, the malnutrition insult.

An example of compensation may involve neurotransmitters. In his chapter, Damasio spoke about certain neurotransmitters, such as dopamine. With the exception of dopamine, we observed that every other neurotransmitter in the brain was elevated in response to malnutrition. Dopamine was not. Although it is not clear what this means, I think we should consider the possibility that there is an elevated discharge of these neurochemicals to perhaps compensate for a reduced number of interconnections of synapses between neurons. What may look like a problem of enhanced transmitter release may be the brain's attempt to compensate for an intrinsic difficulty. Thus, there may be an intrinsic mechanism of the brain—a built-in *desire*—to right itself. This concept is of great interest, although it is only hypothetical at this time.

The link to child malnutrition and behavior

Animal studies are quite interesting, but they must be viewed from a larger perspective. The application of what we learn from animal investigations to the context of the child and the human being as a whole becomes extremely important. However, a shortcoming in the field of malnutrition research with children was that most studies, prior to 1970, were short term and had used small numbers of children. I used a small grant, received from the Ford Foundation in 1973, to visit a number of developing countries, seeking a setting that would make a long-term study of many children possible. We determined that Barbados would provide an extremely suitable environment in which to apply some of the questions we had investigated in our animal studies to a population of children with histories of childhood malnutrition.

Barbados, an independent country, is 15 by 20 miles in size, very easily accessible, with approximately 250 000 inhabitants. The most important factors for selecting Barbados were: (1) Excellent school and health records provided an enormous, readily available amount of data. Maximum use of this record-keeping system could be made. (2) Barbados' *National Nutrition Centre* (NNC), shown in Fig. 3.2, under the direction of Dr Frank Ramsey, had records on 2100 children who were either malnourished or at risk of malnutrition. This is quite important because, in many studies of clinical populations, your subject population comes to you from a hospital setting. In Barbados, there was obligatory reporting of malnutrition with compensation for referrals. Therefore, this group of children was representative of the population of study and not subject to selection bias. (3) The stability and economic status of the population was relatively homogeneous. Barbadians are of a lower middle class, and the extreme poverty in many other developing countries of the world is not present there. In fact, according to world economic indicators, Barbados is one of the wealthiest of developing countries. Consequently, the outcomes of this particular study should be more relevant to the United States and other developed countries. Figure 3.3 shows a typical home in Barbados.

Why did children become malnourished? When we began our study, the main source of revenue on the island was sugar cane. When the sugar market was low, the economy declined, and malnutrition was present. When the sugar market rose, however, there was very little malnutrition. Consequently, the affliction was very dependent on the island economy. We have data on every child born between 1967 and 1972 on the island of Barbados who had one episode of malnutrition. They had either protein-energy malnutrition (PEM) or kwashiorkor. (The African term 'Kwashiorkor' means dissatisfied or displeased child because this condition most often occurs when a baby is weaned off the breast—usually because of a secondary occurrence, such as another

Fig. 3.2 Barbados' *National Nutrition Centre* (NNC).

Fig. 3.3 Typical Barbados home.

Fig. 3.4 Children with protein-energy malnutrition (left) and kwashiorkor (right).

pregnancy—and becomes profoundly unhappy and subsequently malnourished.) They were matched to healthy classmates by age, gender, and handed-
ness. Control children also came from a similar socio-economic background. I
chose to use classmates as a control, rather than siblings, because not all
siblings had the same parents.

Following these children for up to 30 years enabled us to look at a wide range
of variables. As with our rat studies, we were especially interested in the adaptive functioning of these individuals. In the 1960s, the only interest of scientists
and the lay community was whether children with malnutrition were mentally
retarded. In the course of our studies, we have concluded that IQ deficits may
only be a small part of the picture. What is much more interesting is how these
children respond to other demands created by their environments.

Figure 3.4 shows examples of malnourished children. The child on the left is
afflicted with PEM, while the child depicted on the right has kwashiorkor. Both
of these children were ill at a mean age of six months, and they were sick, in
hospital, for about four weeks. In Barbados, these two conditions occur at the
same ages, when children are less than one year old.

What happens with treatment? Physical recovery following reversal from malnutrition occurs readily, resembling what we found in the animal studies. If you
provide the child with an adequate diet, there is apparently complete recovery in
physical growth (see Fig. 3.5). Tanner, who wrote extensively on physical growth

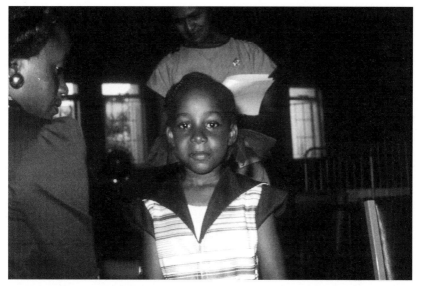

Fig. 3.5 Physical recovery after malnutrition.

and development, had predicted that physical growth would catch up completely in these underprivileged populations (Tanner and Preece, 1989). We have documented that by mid-adolescence, catch-up is virtually complete. In contrast, mental functions show permanent deficits, as was also seen in the rat studies.

Early malnutrition, attention deficit disorder, and school performance

> *Even after children had physically recovered, it was relatively easy to see that they suffered emotional, psychological, and social retardation. Children of 5 and 6 years behaved like toddlers of 2 or 3.* Colombiharina a, *a food supplement, repeatedly proved to be excellent for physical recuperation, but useless in the face of the mental impact of malnutrition and chronic depression.*
>
> L. Sinisterra, 1987 (commenting on the results of
> intervention programs for the poor in Cali, Colombia)

When we first went to Barbados and found these wonderful school records from the NNC, we developed a list of 30 questions to give to the teachers. This turned out to be particularly informative because each teacher had a previously malnourished child as well as control children in her or his classroom. The teachers couldn't physically distinguish between them since the malnutrition hadn't been severe. This was a natural and ideal arrangement for determining how teachers evaluated these children. The questionnaires were distributed and the teachers answered them. A factor analysis was employed to analyze these data (teachers' answers), producing results which group related questions.

The results showed that 60 per cent of children (5–11 years of age) with previous malnutrition consistently exhibited a group of behaviors associated with *attention deficit disorder* (ADD), including short attention span. Prior to this study, ADD had not been documented in a developing country; the disorder had been considered a Western problem. In our healthy control group, only 15 per cent of the children exhibited the ADD-related group of behaviors. This figure is consistent with the diagnosis of attention deficits in 10 per cent of the children in a normal population in the United States. The most interesting finding was that an attention deficit in these children was associated with an early episode of malnutrition, specifically in the postnatal period. In summary, there was a fourfold increase in ADD symptomatology, from 15 per cent in the control group to 60 per cent in the previously malnourished children. (In the last 10 years, perinatal conditions such as hypoxia and lead poisoning have also been associated with attentional deficits.)

The cognitive function of the previously malnourished children was also studied. On the island of Barbados, and in other Commonwealth nations, all 11-year-old children are tested on the 11+ Examination. This test determines placement for high school. In Barbados, this is particularly important because the number of seats in academically oriented high schools is limited. We found that children with previous PEM or kwashiorkor performed substantially worse than children from the healthy comparison group. This finding was of interest to the Ministries of Education and Health of Barbados. These agencies have been participants in this research program from its incipience. Closer examination of the findings revealed that performance on the 11+ Examination was related to the presence or absence of attention deficit at earlier ages. We demonstrated that teacher assessment of attention deficits at 5–7 years of age significantly predicted scores on this examination.

Although IQ was reduced by about 10 points in the previously malnourished children, it did not have a strong relationship with 11+ scores. Socio-economic and home environmental conditions were also measured. These factors were not significant, probably because of the relatively homogeneous populace and the availability of health care.

Success of the studies in Barbados

As mentioned before, we worked very closely with the Ministries of Health and Education in Barbados. All children in our study were followed by the NNC until they were 11 years of age, and they participated in an informal intervention program that corrected their physical problems and attended to their overall nutritional status, growth, and development. As a part of Dr Ramsey's program at the NNC, there were additional measures for high-risk children which were helpful and effective in preventing further cases of malnutrition. In fact, one of the gratifying outcomes of our work in Barbados is that there is no longer any serious malnutrition on the island. In the last year of our study, there was only one admission to the hospital for malnutrition, and this was a child with a pre-existing medical condition.

We recently returned to Barbados to look at the offspring of our previously malnourished and comparison children. Since we have been following these individuals since 1973, many now have families of their own. And again, we find indications that problems continue into the next generation, as we observed in the rat model, and also recur in the context of intervention.

Intervention designed to mitigate the long-term effects of early malnutrition remained the issue needing a solution. Again, the early malnutrition experience itself may be of a very limited nature and duration. However, this was documented to have very profound and long-lasting effects in animals, as well as in humans. The types of intervention that are routinely provided by physicians (such as vitamins, diet, etc.) do not mitigate these long-term effects. Therefore, it was apparent that another approach was necessary, so we attempted to develop appropriate intervention programs.

Of devoted rat mothers and unfit human mothers

> *In the course of our field work, we came to know the families of the children we treated very well. In this way, we found that the children were as retarded as their parents. Not surprisingly, the child had a mental stature which matched his family and community environment. This observation was critically important for our future work.*
>
> L. Sinisterra, 1987

We made a number of very interesting observations in our studies of intergenerational malnutrition in the rat models. Early on, we saw that rat mothers rearing the previously malnourished pups spent extended amounts of time suckling those babies—almost twice as much, compared to the normal pups. We had little understanding of why this occurred. Malnutrition produced by several different methods had the same effect. It was an interesting problem because environmental factors could not readily be isolated from nutritional factors. In summary, altered mother–pup interaction, which may also have long-term effects on the offspring, accompanies postnatal malnutrition in animal models.

Viewing this finding from a broader perspective, looking at some of our findings from Barbados, and thinking about it in the context of children, we realized this altered maternal behavior was a compensatory response. These mothers were compensating for the diminished ability of the malnourished pups to find their way back to the nest, for the risk of heat loss, and for the previous nutritional deficit. Therefore, what initially appeared to be a confounding problem was actually an adaptation to improve the survival of the pups.

Although we did not directly observe the quality of parenting in the previously malnourished children, the early hospital records contained information on 'mother craft' at the time of hospitalization. There was no indication of aberrant behaviors at that time. Studies of 'failure-to-thrive' children in the United States have reported that mothers of these children are often inadequate in their maternal skills and overly stressed. A small number of mothers in our study (under 100) showed similar patterns of behavior; the majority appeared to adapt by *increasing* their involvement with their malnourished infant.

Early intervention: studies in Yucatan

Based on these observations, we hypothesized that the early experience of the child is intimately connected to the mother–infant bond or relationship, and that intervention programs would need to act at this level to be effective. We developed a program accordingly. We implemented it in Mexico because, as already mentioned, moderate to severe malnutrition was no longer present in Barbados. Therefore, the study was conducted in south-eastern Yucatan, where malnutrition was pervasive. We selected four Mayan villages. In two of the villages, we started the intervention program, and in the two others, we provided only a weekly medical consultant to address the health of the local population.

The four Mayan communities each had a population of about 800–1000 inhabitants. Most of the villages were engaged in agricultural activities. The villagers still follow the traditional Mayan way of life. The homes are single, large rooms with exterior cooking facilities. Running water is available, but sanitation problems persist. These communities were selected because we felt the impact of a successful early intervention program should be measurable there.

Mitigating the impact of early deprivation

In these Mayan communities we applied our intervention program to all women of child-bearing age. We worked specifically on the mother–infant relationship and tried to help mothers to respond appropriately to the needs of their children. A weekly educational program was instituted, including lectures on child health, nutrition, and development, so that women could learn ways of responding to the individual characteristics of their children, hopefully enabling them to escape the negative effects of a very deprived environment. The women themselves undertook responsibility for the program and the included activities.

We have followed the children to 36 months of age and measured their growth and a range of behavioral characteristics. Again, we believe that the caretaker–child interaction is of paramount importance in this particular type of setting.

We are in the process of analyzing these data. The physical growth of girls in the intervention villages was significantly better than that of boys or than that of girls from the two villages with no intervention. Socio-economic conditions in the villages were also very closely associated with the physical growth of the children. Thus, children from more traditional communities, in which the parents spoke Mayan, did not fare as well as children from more modernized communities where Spanish was the dominant language.

In a pilot study, we found that children with mild to moderate malnutrition had more 'difficult' temperaments than well-nourished children, independent of socio-economic conditions. For example, they were more irritable and difficult to console. Our continuing strategy involves evaluating and improving child health and nutritional status in combination with early intervention. It is our belief that this approach, even under conditions of severe poverty, will help to mitigate the long-term consequences of malnutrition and deprivation that we have documented over the past 25 years.

Concluding remarks: can we optimize a child's behavioral development, stimulate its creative potential?

> We concluded that children must develop a wide range of socially effective behaviors by the time they reach school if they are to become useful members of societies and participate fully in culturally valued aspects of contemporary urban life. Unfortunately little was known at that time about important, identifiable, and changeable components of the psychological ability of young children. It could have been that poor development of affective, attentional, social, and other noncognitive psychological characteristics were the most serious result of poor nutrition and environmental deprivation.
>
> L. Sinisterra, 1987

Throughout my years of study and observation, I have come to several conclusions. One is that a child's mental development starts before birth. I am referring to a very early process with an outcome that can be measured in an adult individual. The potential for impact on an individual's development is greatest in the earliest phases of development—even in the womb. This holds true for a number of characteristics, including creative behavior. As previously mentioned, recent work shows that the brain continues to evolve and to modify its circuits at later stages of life, including adulthood and aging. You are not excluded from influences and interventions as you grow older. However, the majority of neural development is complete by age two.

Another conclusion is that about 40 per cent of the previously malnourished and deprived individuals were able to overcome the early insult. It is perhaps as valuable to focus on the adaptive skills that spur individuals to overcome early adverse conditions as it is to focus on those who have suffered some deleterious outcome. In our series of studies, successful adaptation appears to include heightened parental responsiveness. In addition, changes in infant temperament may draw more attention to those children who need greater care.

HOWARD GARDNER

Creators: multiple intelligences

The difference between the artist and the non-artist is not a greater capacity for feeling. The secret is that the artist can objectify, can make apparent the feelings we all have.

Martha Graham
(Quoted by Gardner, 1993a)

All it takes to be creative, then, is an inner assurance that what I think or do is new and valuable. There is nothing wrong with defining creativity this way, as long as we realize that this is not at all what the term origi-nally was supposed to mean—namely, to bring into existence something genuinely new that is valued enough to be added to the culture. On the other hand, if we decide that social confirmation is necessary for some-thing to be called creative, the definition must encompass more than the individual. What counts then is whether the inner certitude is validated by the appropriate experts.

Mihaly Csikszentmihalyi, 1996

Who is creative? A creative individual is one who affects others' lives. Since I am a social scientist—with an emphasis that is largely cognitive—my studies take the form of a search for patterns. In this chapter, I am going to focus on what we might call the top of Pfenninger's hierarchy (see page 91), or the highest level of creative behavior.

Each of the seven innovators pictured in Figs. 3.6–12 merits the epithet 'creative.' Not all seven were recognized as highly creative individuals early in their lives, nor were they all universally acclaimed throughout their lives. As many researchers have shown, creativity and IQ are not necessarily linked. However, although everyone can raise the issue of the isolated genius who is ignored, misunderstood and overlooked, my claim is simply the following: in the absence of a judgement by a competent field, one simply cannot determine whether an individual is creative. Thus, an important creative triangle exists which consists of three nodes—the *domain*, the *field* and the *individual*.

The superstructure for my analysis of creativity

This creative triangle, based on pioneering work by Mihaly Csikszentmihalyi, involves the relationship between:

1. the child and the master;

2. an individual and the work in which he or she is engaged;

3. an individual and other persons in his or her world.

These three points or 'nodes' form the basis of the triangle (Table 3.1); this creative triangle forms the superstructure of my chapter. By introducing these elements at the outset, I wish to stress that all creative activity grows, first, out of the relationships between an individual and the objective world of work and, second, out of the ties between an individual and other human beings.

I begin with the *individual*, then focus both on the *domain* (the work) and the *field* (other persons). In order to keep my thoughts as jargon-free as possible, I will define the terms I am using. By *domain* I mean the symbol system within which the individual works. What is a symbol system? Picasso was an artist; he dealt with colors, textures, lines and forms, which were the traditional symbol systems of his discipline. Every individual works in one discipline in which he or she masters and uses the current language, or changes that language and/or contrives a new one. Thus, the *domain* is the body of knowledge and practices to be mastered by the next generation. The other term I use is *field*. By *field* I mean the judges and institutions that decide who is an outstanding talent in a discipline, or the group of knowledgeable individuals who judge the quality of new work in the *domain*. For example, in visual art it is the *field*—the gallery owners, agents, individuals who work in art departments, critics and fellow artists—who select a few individuals as worthy of attention. Thus, Pablo Picasso was widely acknowledged as a master in his *domain* by gallery owners, fellow artists like Matisse and critics (who constitute the *field*).

Creativity, and the highly creative individual, can be understood only by analyzing the dynamic interaction of the individual within the three points of the triangle that define the individual as 'creative'. This complex interaction is the basis of my analysis of the phenomenon of creativity.

Seven innovators: shapers of the modern world

The actual subject of my discussion is a case study of seven individuals whose highly innovative ideas have shaped the modern era. After more than twenty-five years of background analysis, I recently completed this study. Not only have the individuals in this study mastered their discipline or *domain*—they have changed it. In some cases, they have created their own domain.

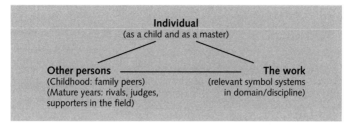

Table 3.1 The creative triangle.

Just in case you can't recognize the seven, their pictures might help. They come in pairs so you can see these people when they were young, comparatively unknown and 'doing their thing', and again when they were old and had already 'done their thing'—although some of them kept on doing it.

Figure 3.6 shows the most important theoretical physicist of the century, Albert Einstein (1879–1955), who certainly changed the way that we think about the physical world. Figure 3.6(a) shows a young man named Albert; Fig. 3.6(b) shows the physicist after he had already become Einstein, the twentieth-century genius whose ideas challenged some of our most fundamental questions about existence. By his own testimony, Einstein was a person interested in the phenomena of the physical world as expressed in mathematical terms. When he was young, he was at odds with conventional formal education. By the end of his life, however, he was adulated by the field and as revered as Newton, whose picture he kept on the wall above his bed. He had also become an ardent pacifist.

Figure 3.7(a) shows Picasso (1881–1973) just at the end of adolescence. Picasso is an example of the phenomenon of the prodigy. The term *prodigiousness* connotes a gift that borders on the miraculous. As a child, Pablo Picasso's drawing surpassed that of his father, an academic painter of modest talent. Figure 3.7(b)—much more immediately identifiable—was taken when Picasso was older. By this point, he had developed cubism (together with Georges Braque), painted the highly controversial *Les Demoiselles d'Avignon* and gone beyond the limitations of his field to create *Guernica*, which is a new-style masterpiece. When the photograph in Fig. 3.7(b) was taken, Picasso was the most famous artist in the world.

Igor Stravinsky (1882–1971), who composed some of the most expressive music of the twentieth century, is shown as a young man in 1920 in Fig. 3.8(a). The musician once explained his own composing activity: 'I compose because I am made for that and cannot do otherwise . . . I am far from saying that there is no such thing as inspiration . . . Work brings inspiration if inspiration is not

Fig. 3.6 (a) Einstein at his desk at the patent office in Bern, 1905 (courtesy of the Albert Einstein Archives, the Hebrew University of Jerusalem, Israel); (b) portrait of Einstein early 1950s (courtesy of Hulton Getty).

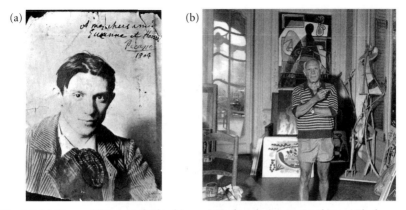

Fig. 3.7 (a) Picasso, 1904. Inscribed to his musician friends, Suzanne and Henri Block
(courtesy of Musée Picasso, Paris © RMN) (b) Pablo Picasso, 1955 (courtesy of Hulton Getty.)

discernible in the beginning.' And the familiar photograph in Fig. 3.8(b) is the mature artist whose skill in conducting his own music was renowned.

Figure 3.9(a) shows T.S. Eliot when he was a student at Harvard College and already writing poetry. Thomas Stearns Eliot (1888–1965), a St. Louis-born poet who settled in Europe, is well known as the author of *The Waste Land*— arguably the most influential poem written in the English language in the twentieth century. The photograph in Fig. 3.9(b) is the more familiar image of T.S. Eliot—older and sterner.

My children think the next man is Ben Kingsley, the actor who starred in the movie version of Gandhi's life, but actually it's Mahatma Gandhi himself (1869–1948), whose vision led India to independence. A single-minded man, who was a relatively successful young lawyer, his life followed a reasonably conventional pattern until around 1905 (Fig. 3.10(a)). After reading the writings of Ruskin, Tolstoy and Thoreau, he moved his young family to an 1100-acre development, 20 miles from Johannesburg. Then his life took a different direction, which eventually affected the course of the twentieth century (Fig. 3.10(b)).

Figure 3.11(a) is a photograph of Martha Graham, who was forming her dance company in the early 1930s. Figure 3.11(b) shows Martha Graham (1894–1991) at a somewhat older age—but certainly not the elderly Martha Graham who continued to dance till she was seventy. She was choreographing and developing styles until her death in 1991, when she was over ninety.

Perhaps because I am a psychologist, I have to talk about at least one psychologist. If the name that first springs to mind is the physician turned psychologist, Sigmund Freud (1856–1939), you would be right. The first photograph

(a)

(b)

Fig. 3.8 (a) Stravinsky as a young man in 1920; (b) photograph by Erich Auerbach of Stravinsky rehearsing with the BBC Symphony Orchestra on 8 December 1958 at the Maida Vale Studios (courtesy of Hulton Getty).

Fig. 3.9 (a) T.S. Eliot, aged nineteen (1907), as a student at Harvard; (b) the older Eliot (courtesy of Hulton Getty).

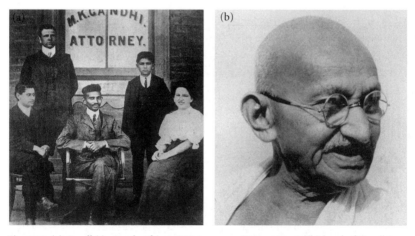

Fig. 3.10 (a) Gandhi in South Africa, 1903 (courtesy of Hulton Getty); (b) head of Gandhi (courtesy of Hulton Getty).

(Fig. 3.12(a)) is the young Sigismund (his given name, which he retained until early adulthood). The one in Fig. 3.12(b) is of Sigmund Freud, the father of the psychoanalytic movement, who worried about the survival of an inherently destructive human society.

The major part of my discussion will center around the study which I describe in greater detail in my book, *Creating Minds: An Anatomy of Creativity Seen Through the Lives of Freud, Einstein, Picasso, Stravinsky, Eliot, Graham and Gandhi.*

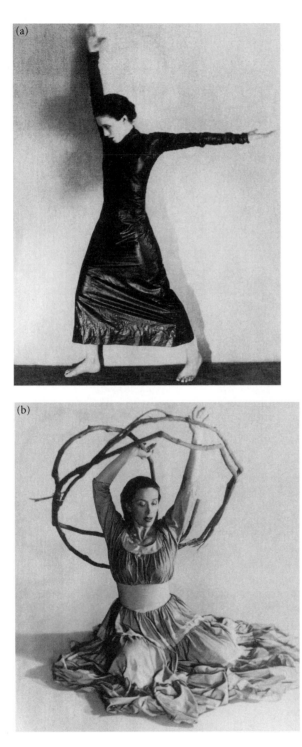

Fig. 3.11 (a) The young Martha Graham dancing in *Strike*; (b) the older Martha Graham, dancing in *Salem Shore* (courtesy of Hulton Getty).

Fig. 3.12 (a) The young Sigismund Freud; (b) the older Sigmund Freud. (Courtesy of the Freud Museum, London.)

> *In comparing Picasso with Freud, I was deliberately contrasting people who exemplify different intelligences: linguistic and logical in Freud's case, spatial and bodily in Picasso's . . . I wondered how creativity played out in the different intelligences, and from this puzzlement arose the idea of a comparative study of a small number of individuals, each exemplifying a different human intelligence.*
>
> *Howard Gardner, 1993a*

I am interested in understanding the nature of the creative process in these, I think indisputable instances of high creativity, and my discussion falls naturally into several parts. The first part, '*All previous thought*' highlights what past psychologists have had to say about creativity—unfortunately not particularly illuminating. Then, I devote an equal amount of time to what I modestly call '*Our view*'—although really, it's mostly my view, which is basically a conceptualization of creativity. As you get more and more into the social and behavioral sciences, conceptualization becomes more important, more of what the enterprise is about at the present time. Then, before I finish, I promise to answer two questions I am sure are foremost in your own minds. Number one is, 'How can you be creative?' And the next one is, 'Are you creative?' So stay tuned!

All previous thought

Actually, there are two areas in psychology which have focused on creativity. One is *psychometrics*, or the measurement concept, and that is just as unsatisfactory as the attempts at measuring intelligence. Janina Galler does a good job of deriding IQ tests, so I don't have to do the same thing. Unfortunately, IQ tests are wonderful compared to creativity tests. The basic question in a creativity test is, 'How many uses can you come up with for a brick?' If you come up with a list of uses, and they are unusual, you are creative. If not, no prizes. Creativity tests are now little used because they don't really correlate with being creative in the real world; they're not very valid. Yet, in most psychology textbooks, if the word 'creativity' appears in the index at all, it would actually refer you to tests like this.

A psychometrician, Joy P. Guildford, developed the tests to show that creativity could be measured independently of intelligence. Psychometricians think that there is a polymorphous, perverse quality called 'creativity,' and that if you can name lots of uses for a brick or a paperclip you can do anything that is creative. These tests are supposed to measure which individuals have the potential to be creative. I think there is an intrinsic fallacy in that view. Sadly, the creativity test still has lots of influence with psychologists.

The second area to focus on creativity, and one which I think most of us find more interesting, is the *psychoanalytic perspective*. Freud was very interested in creativity, particularly in the arts, and he thought that creative individuals had certain kinds of personalities, certain kinds of motivations. They were sublimators: what they were interested in they couldn't have, and so they created works of art or works of science. In general, Freud thought those of us who liked their works also were sublimators: we could not have what we really wanted and instead preferred to look at more distanced objects that contained, for example, an unconscious sexual motivation:

> *Having demonstrated the importance of sexuality in motivating human behavior in general, Freud called attention to the sexual factors that undergird a creative life. In Freud's view, creative individuals are inclined (or compelled) to sublimate much of their libidinal energy into 'secondary' pursuits, such as writing, drawing, composing, or investigating scientific puzzles.*
>
> Howard Gardner, 1993a

Freud was also impressed by the parallels between the creative artist and the child at play. I believe that there is a vein of truth in the Freudian view, whereas I do not feel there is one in the psychometric perspective; however, while Freud's characteristics may apply to some creative people, they also apply to non-creative individuals. There really isn't any simple way to distinguish between those people who achieve high levels of creativity and those individuals who are just neurotic or 'hung-up'. So, Freud's views on creativity have attracted much attention—and a considerable amount of criticism.

A more recent and fruitful approach is the *cognitive approach*. This sees creativity very much as a mental phenomenon: either a problem-solving phenomenon, or sometimes a problem-finding phenomenon. The general view among cognitivists is that creative people aren't really any different than the rest of us. They have the same basic machinery, the same basic mechanism, the same basic memory, and so on. But some individuals have attained expertise after a long period of hard work, which means their machinery is better tuned and perhaps can work more quickly. Cognitivists spend a lot of time trying to figure out the actual mechanisms involved in creative activity. They talk a lot about the way in which creative individuals identify problems and solution 'spaces'. For example, some cognitive researchers have shown these principles at work in specific *domains*, such as jazz improvisation or imaginative writing. Others look at the strategic 'bets' that creative people make, or how creative individuals determine when to probe further and when to cut their losses and move on. But I think this point of view falls down because it is not clear which of the people who work very hard are actually going to be able to do things that others denote as creative, and which ones are just going to be, so to speak, highly tuned experts.

Moving from the work that I find less interesting to more recent work that I find most promising, I come to two individuals whose names may well not be known to you, but who I think are really on to good work. One is Howard Gruber, a student of Jean Piaget. He has exploited an approach in which he works intensively on individual cases. The Gruber team has uncovered a number of principles that seem to characterize the work of major scientists, like Charles Darwin:

> Gruber speaks of an 'evolving systems' approach to the study of creativity: that is, one monitors simultaneously the organization of knowledge in a domain, the purpose(s) pursued by the creator, and the affective experiences he or she undergoes. While these systems are only 'loosely coupled,' their interaction over time helps one understand the ebb and flow of creative activity over the course of a productive human life.
>
> Howard Gardner, 1993b

Gruber spent twenty years studying the notebooks of Darwin covering only a short period of time (1837–8), to try to trace Darwin's thinking on an almost hour-by-hour basis. Twenty years on Darwin, twenty years on Piaget—the span of Gruber's career. It is very labor intensive.

The psychologist, Dean Keith Simonton, who is at the Davis Campus of the

University of California, has taken the exact opposite approach, which is called in good Greek fashion, *historiometric*. Any question that you could possibly think of about creativity, Simonton tries to quantify. He simply assembles the facts and tries to come up with the law which best answers that particular question:

> *In a typical approach, historiometric investigators like Simonton review large bodies of data to determine the decade of life in which creative individuals are most productive. Such studies have led to the findings that maximal productivity typically occurs between ages thirty-five and thirty-nine, but those profiles differ appreciably across disparate domains of knowledge: thus, poets and mathematicians reach an apogee in their twenties or thirties, while historians or philosophers may peak decades later.*
>
> Howard Gardner, 1993b

So, if you want to know at what age poets do their best work, he'll look at 20 000 poets and tell you that, on the average, it is 32.6 years.

My work, such as it is, is an effort to bridge the gulf between Gruber's detailed views of individual creators and Simonton's large-scale quantitative studies undertaken with broad bodies of data. Traditionally, these stances have been labeled *idiographic* and *nomothetic*. I begin with individual case studies, but I do so quickly, or even superficially, in the hope that I can extrapolate some modest laws about the creative process. What I am doing here, in talking about seven people, is to suggest some of the laws which might begin to emerge if we went from 7 to 70 to 700—though we will probably never get to Simonton's 70 000. Nor will I stop with two creative individuals who are minutely analyzed.

So much for all previous thought.

Our view: a new way of thinking about creativity

> *Creativity results from the interaction of a system composed of three elements: a culture that contains symbolic rules, a person who brings novelty into the symbolic domain, and a field of experts who recognize and validate the innovation. All three are necessary for a creative idea, product, or discovery to take place.*
>
> Mihaly Csikszentmihalyi, 1996

> *Thus, creativity lies not in the head (or hand) of the artist or in the domain of practices or in the set of judges: rather, the phenomenon of*

*creativity can only—or, at any rate, more fully—be understood as a
function of interactions among these three nodes.*

Howard Gardner, 1993a

What I want to do next is to describe a point of view which has been developed over the past 10 or 15 years in collaboration with two colleagues: David Feldman at Tufts University, and Mihaly Csikszentmihalyi, then at the University of Chicago. There are interesting data that have emerged from this view; however, I think it is primarily conceptual. Our view is a way of thinking about creativity and ought to be analyzed initially on those terms. In that sense, this approach is quite different from the bulk of the presentations in this book.

The definition of the *creative individual* that I use is—an individual, or talent, who regularly solves problems or fashions products in a *domain* in a way that is initially novel, but ultimately becomes acceptable in at least one cultural setting.

Let's unpack that definition. First point: the creative act is something that is done regularly. As Antonio Damasio says, creative people don't do something once in their life—it's a way of being—and it's very important to understand that. Creative individuals solve problems, everybody agrees about that; they also find problems and fashion products. Unfortunately, the latter two are more difficult for psychologists to study because to isolate a problem, to create a great symphony, to build an organization takes months or years or a life-time—and psychologists are not very good at looking at those kinds of phenomena.

Probably the most important word in my definition is *domain*. We've discussed the term before, but just to briefly recap, a *domain* means an organized activity in a society where there are levels of expertise, stages of development and, generally speaking, symbol systems with which people in that discipline work. Individuals who want to be creative, who are judged to be creative, work in *domains.*

Finally, the last part of the definition: initially, the problem solving is a novel or strange approach, and yet, ultimately, it catches on. This part of the definition is half accepted by everybody. However, when you add cultural setting to the definition it becomes very insidious because it basically says that judgments of creativity are culturally relative. The creative individual is recognized by communities which I will call at any given moment, *fields.* So, this seemingly innocent definition is a mine field, and my students and others have had fun detecting the mines.

I am going to pass over this next point quickly because it comes up in almost every other chapter: creativity never will be understood from the perspective of a single discipline, and the more we learn from different disciplines, the better and more chances we will have to understand at least the big 'C', creativity, that I am interested in. That involves at least four levels of analysis. Analysis by Pfenninger and Damasio was sub-personal (genetics and neurobiology) and personal (psychological, cognitive, personality, motivation). Two levels which have not been talked about in any depth are distinctive in what I shall refer to as the Feldman/Csikszentmihalyi/Gardner perspective. In this perspective, one focuses on those organized structures within society which are called *domains*. For example, what is known about physics, what it is that is done in physics, what it is that is known or done in maths, what it is that is known or done in dance or music or painting is all part of a *domain*. People work in *domains* or disciplines; people master the elements of their disciplines and go on to challenge or change these *domains* or disciplines within which they work.

Finally, the work of creative thinkers within domains is judged by communities of individuals, which I call *fields*. Judges, editors, tenure committees, fellowship committees, gallery owners, newspaper critics, institutions all render judgment on the quality and appropriateness of the contribution at hand.

In the late 1980s, Mihaly Csikszentmihalyi made a significant conceptual advance in the area of creativity. He suggested that the question to ask is not *what* is creativity, but *where* is creativity? And he said (contrary to what you may have thought before) creativity does not exist in the head, nor does it exist in the brain. As a number of people have commented in passing, you could know every bit of neurocircuitry in somebody's head and you still would not know whether or not that person was creative—although you could probably judge that he or she was not creative if there wasn't any circuitry there!

Let us go back over the 'creative triangle'. Creative thinkers have individual talents; they are people with brains and minds and souls and so on who are taught these talents by experts in the *domain* (that is, the teachers, the masters and so on). The talents allow creative thinkers to do things—to make products, to perform, to solve problems or to lead people. All of this activity is—for the sake of this discussion—evaluated by the judges, the *field*.

The *field*, over a short or a long period of time, selects certain individuals and their works as being worthy of attention. A very few people actually fashion the *domain*, which means that—10, 20, 30 or 100 years later—when a new generation studies the discipline, it is a different *domain*. Physics is different because of Einstein; music is different because of Stravinsky; dance is different because of Martha Graham; painting is different because of Picasso; the world as we know it is different because of Gandhi. So, the question is no longer 'What is creativity?' Instead we must ask, 'Where is creativity?' And creativity inheres in the dialectic or the dialogue among the *field*, the *domain* and the individual. I submit to you a conceptual advance.

The analysis: the big 'C' creators

The study I carried out was selected with two primary considerations in mind. One, I selected people who came from the same general era—the modern era—who were largely influenced by the culture of Western Europe. And two, each of the seven individuals chosen was supposed to reflect what I call a different kind of intelligence. I will spare you a discussion of the theory of multiple intelligences, but basically, as a species, human beings have gradually evolved to be able to think about a number of different kinds of content in the world, so to speak (Gardner, 1983 and 1993b). Just to run through my seven individuals again: Eliot was supposed to epitomize the linguistic; Einstein, the logical/mathematical; Stravinsky, the musical; Picasso, the spatial; Graham, the bodily/kinesthetic; Gandhi, the interpersonal; and Freud, the intrapersonal. Even if you think the whole theory does not make complete sense, at least you will agree that these are people who did different kinds of things.

So, if we begin with the thought that each creator represents a different kind of intelligence, it is important to know how dissimilar or similar the various talents were judged on other kinds of dimensions. In my effort to span the distance between the two different approaches—the Gruber intensive individual studies, and the Simonton large-scale databases—I ask, which generalizations apply to all seven big 'C' creators? Which apply to some? And which generalizations seem to apply to more than one?

The foundation of my study is the story of the lives of these seven highly creative individuals. This constitutes my effort to draw out some kind of a theory of creativity and the creative process. I studied these people as intensively as I could; I used a lot of secondary sources. When I had to, I used primary sources. Of course primary sources are more interesting, but it is much more time consuming to go over notebooks and things like that—and I did want to finish while I was still alive!

I particularly examined what I call breakthroughs—the times when these seven individuals discovered something or created something new which ultimately affected the discipline they worked in (or even created a new kind of discipline, for example, Freud's discovery of the psychoanalytical method). My organizing principle was the general conceptual framework I have given you— looking at the individual cognitively, personality-wise and so on; looking at the domain in which the individual worked; and finally, looking at the operation of the field, or the group of individuals by which they were judged. And I will summarize my results basically along those terms. But actually, as Galler says, the most exciting aspect of doing any kind of research is the observation of the unexpected. And so, I am going to share with you four or five surprises which, in a sense, made this study of highly creative minds doubly worthwhile.

Portrait of a creator: common themes

> *I am greatly honored and flattered by your kind letter of February 14th—*
> *for I have admired you and your work for many years, and I have learned*
> *much from it. But, my dear Professor Csikszentmihalyi, I am afraid I*
> *have to disappoint you. I could not possibly answer your questions, I am*
> *told I am creative—I don't know what that means . . . I just keep on plod-*
> *ding . . . I hope you will not think me presumptuous or rude if I say that*
> *one of the secrets of productivity (in which I believe whereas I do not*
> *believe in creativity) is to have a VERY BIG waste paper basket to take*
> *care of ALL invitations such as yours—productivity in my experience*
> *consists of NOT doing anything that helps the work of other people but to*
> *spend all one's time on the work the Good Lord has fitted one to do, and*
> *to do well.*
>
> Peter Drucker, quoted in Csikszentmihalyi, 1996

A not-so-unusual childhood

I want to give you a general picture of these seven creative individuals because, to my surprise, biographically, they were similar. And of course, all seven form a very dramatic contrast to Galler's undernourished children. These people came from bourgeois homes (that is the best single word)—homes that were reasonably comfortable and relatively intact. These creative talents were born not in big cities, but at the periphery, the boondocks; but at the same time, the families were not living so far away that they were essentially ignorant of what was going on elsewhere. And the major lesson in each house was hard work. These were homes where the families believed in the 'Puritan ethic' and the 'Protestant ethic,' or were Jewish homes that were upwardly mobile. There was love and warmth, but it was often directed toward doing work.

By and large, it was more important that you worked, and worked well, than that you worked in one specific discipline. Most of the parents did not push their kids to be a certain kind of person in terms of what career they would choose, but did push them to be a certain kind of person in terms of work habits and discipline. The creators were not always close to both of their parents; in fact, most of them had nannies whom they loved much more than their parents. So, all of these creative individuals shared a strong work ethic, a comfortable home (in neither a big city nor a ghetto), love and affection.

Uncharted waters: the breakthrough

All the big Cs had apprenticeships of one sort or another; Antonio Damasio in his chapter also refers to that. And what is quite interesting to me is that they all migrated to the big city; they were drawn there as if by magic. When they were young, they found other people who were like them. They went to the same place; their lives followed a similar pattern. They were the young turks; and they had the sense that together they were going to create a revolution.

At the moment of the actual breakthrough, however, these creative individuals were isolated (with one exception, which I will talk about later), alone and struggling to come up with a new way of thinking about the discipline they were in:

> *This is a highly charged moment. At this point, the Exemplary Creator becomes isolated from her peers and must work mostly on her own. She senses that she is on the verge of a breakthrough that is as yet little understood, even by her.*
>
> Howard Gardner, 1993a

I was reminded of this very strongly when hearing about Benoit Mandelbrot's early experiences.

Ultimately, the novel insights may be propositional or linguistic, but when the creators are struggling toward their breakthrough, the thoughts are very amorphous and hard to get a hold on. The creators are isolated while they search for some kind of a new language or symbol system adequate for the problem at hand. For example, after Picasso parted company with Braque and made his first unique breakthrough, he used familiar symbols in a new way (colors that clashed; forms that crashed), and at that moment neither artists nor critics understood what he had done, nor did they follow his lead.

So much for the surprising similarity in the biographies of the seven big Cs. One last, very minor point: because of my manner of selection, they all lived around the same time and were influenced by the same cultural pocket.

More than one intelligence

My assumption has been that these seven creators differ from one another in the kinds of intelligences they exhibit. I chose these people because each was thought to exemplify one of the seven intelligences I detailed in my earlier book, *Frames of Mind* (Gardner, 1983). However, I studied them enough to see that all of these talents had more than one intelligence that was quite highly developed, and quite frequently the contribution or achievement depended upon a melding together of more than one intelligence. A rough summary of their intellectual profiles follows in Table 3.2.

All of these highly creative individuals had areas of weakness—except possibly Stravinsky. Freud's weakness was that he hated music; he loved to collect artifacts and he loved drama, but when his sister's piano practicing annoyed him,

	Strength	Weakness
Freud	linguistic, personal	spatial, musical
Einstein	logical-spatial	personal
Picasso	spatial, personal, bodily	scholastic
Stravinsky	musical, other artistic	
Eliot	linguistic, scholastic	musical, bodily
Graham	bodily, linguistic	logical-mathematical
Gandhi	personal, linguistic	artistic

Table 3.2 Intellectual profiles of seven great creators.

his doting family had the piano removed from the house. This says something about Freud, but it also says something about the era. In this era, it was much, much harder for women to get what Virginia Wolf called 'a room of her own'. Certainly Freud's sister, like Shakespeare's sister, never really had a fair crack at being a great intellectual. This is a very important point, and it explains why six of my seven creative individuals are men.

Ten-year periods

I do not have the time or space here to run through the detail that I charted in my study. To summarize, I was able to look at the life patterns of the big C folk in my study and trace the trajectory of their creativity across the decades. I found that things happened in approximately ten-year intervals from the point where those individuals began to work in their chosen *domain*.

Now, there are two footnotes to that. One is that in certain areas, particularly the arts, creators seem to go on forever; poets—think of Shelley and Keats—might be the exception. However, in mathematics and science, it seems much more difficult to keep going on in ten-year periods. The other interesting, but purely speculative footnote relates to neural networks and connectivity and what it takes for there to be a structure that is, so to speak, in equilibrium or settled. A new kind of settling or organization cannot happen overnight; it might occur in ten-year intervals (which is, of course, just a speculation). But, after creating enough chaos, it is going to take time to get settled. And that is why I think the breakthroughs seem to take longer periods of time, even though the big Cs are being creative all along.

Focus on personality

I love my work with a love that is frantic and perverted, as an ascetic loves the hair shirt that scratches his belly.

Gustave Flaubert
(quoted by Gardner, 1993a)

Let me now discuss the personalities of these seven individuals, and their motivation, both conscious and unconscious. As different as they were cognitively—and we have discussed the fact that each of the seven had very different kinds of minds—all seven were surprisingly similar when they were looked at from the point of view of personality.

All seven highly creative individuals were incredibly ambitious and hard-working, and they became tougher and tougher-skinned as they got older. As mature creators, they were almost impervious to what other people said, except when there was criticism. And they basically had personality configurations that were surprisingly similar and difficult.

A related discussion concerns the degree of effort attached to self-promotion. All seven creators recognized the importance of bringing their work to the attention of others in their *field* (to use our term). These people spent a lot of time making sure that the *field* knew what they were doing; they made sure that their activities were brought to the attention of that group of individuals who evaluated others—those who were judges, critics, and so forth. Their efforts ranged from an ordinary degree of self-promotion to really extraordinary measures. I would range our creators in the approximate order shown in Table 3.3.

Einstein was at the lowest end of the spectrum, while Freud was at the top. Some were lucky enough to have somebody else (a parent, spouse, an aide) who would promote them; otherwise, they found someone to help them. They might have been detached or isolated, but they needed other people to promote them.

As these creative individuals (the big Cs) got older, they became people who were—to put it politely—not very nice. Picasso, I think, was the most extreme. He seems to have taken sadistic pleasure, if not creative inspiration, from

Ordinary self-promotion			Extraordinary self-promotion		
Einstein	Picasso	Eliot Graham	Stravinsky	Gandhi	Freud

Table 3.3 Range of self-promotion.

inducing discomfort in others. But even people like Gandhi, who were in love with mankind *en masse*, were very, very difficult for the people around them. *The Guardian* reduced my theory to a headline that read 'Einstein equals genius minus niceness'. They had quite a lot of fatalities in their own families; in fact, suicides surrounded all of these people. The 'heat' around them was exciting so that people were attracted to come close, and then they got singed or burnt.

Now Einstein, I think, was benevolent in certain ways. However, he was highly self-absorbed. If Einstein did not see other people, it was fine with him—and he never really had a relationship with his family; he was just very, very distanced. If you want to raise a creative child, you might wish to calculate how likely he or she is to come to visit you in the hospital when you are sick!

So anyway, these people turned out to have surprisingly similar kinds of personalities.

Creativity: expanded and new domains

Let me say just another word about *domain* and *field*, and then finish up with the things I found quite surprising. First, in the area of *domain*, these creative people had quite different experiences. Some people, like Picasso, worked in a *domain*, namely art, which existed long before they began. Picasso changed the *domain*, but he never had to consider doing something in a new *domain*. Picasso dealt with colors, textures, lines and forms and so did the artists who followed him.

In contrast, Freud created his own discipline. He went from one domain to another over about a twenty-year period. He never got the acceptance he wanted; he never did something that fulfilled his notion of making a great contribution. In the end, he created a new *domain* called psychoanalysis, which had never existed before. He also created a *field*—namely his psychoanalytic colleagues who judged not only who was good but who could become a psychoanalyst. So, in this respect Freud was the opposite of Picasso.

In the case of Martha Graham, what happened was quite interesting. Of course, dance already existed, but modern dance did not. It was a kind of movement formed by Graham and a small group of committed dancers—and a group of critics working for New York newspapers who said that something new was going on, and that they had to write about it:

> *While Graham and her associates were charting the domain, a small*
> *group of influential viewers comprised a self-styled field to judge the new*
> *forms. Rarely if ever has the action of a small group of critics proved as*

decisive in the course of a particular art form. (The closest analogy is
perhaps the circle that had promoted cubism two decades before)

Howard Gardner, 1993a

John Martin began to write regularly about dance for *The New York Times* and Mary Watkins became the new dance critic for *The New York Herald Tribune*. Watkins declared that 'dancing is no longer a step child of the arts', and Martin singled out Martha Graham for special praise when he wrote that, 'no other dancer has yet touched the borders to which she has extended the compass of movement' (Howard Gardner, 1993a).

Freud created his own new *domain*, and Picasso and Martha Graham extended the borders of their *domains* by adding new dimensions to established disciplines.

Revolutionizing the field

A couple of comments about *field*. When I was a child, one of the baseball cards I collected said that Einstein's theory of relativity was only understood by twelve people—and I think that it probably listed all twelve people. In fact, it was not important that only a few people understood what Einstein was doing; the *field* was tiny. If the venerated physicist Max Planck and a few other physicists said Einstein's general theory of relativity was good, that was enough.

The case of Picasso and cubism (which I referred to briefly in my comments about Martha Graham) is interesting because when he painted *Les Demoiselles d'Avignon*—the large oil painting that was his first really adventurous work—it evoked such a negative reaction in the *field* that he hid the painting and would not let people see it. This is an example of the judges essentially expunging something for a time. The art dealer Daniel-Henry Kahnweiler recalled:

> *What I'd like to make you realize at once is the incredible heroism of a man like Picasso, whose moral loneliness was, at the time, quite horrifying, for none of his painter friends had followed him. Everyone found that picture crazy or monstrous.*
>
> Quoted in Howard Gardner, 1993a

For a time Picasso refused to exhibit the painting, but he never lost faith in his breakthrough. He felt that it was important to take risks and to revolutionize the way that the *field* saw, by creating unacceptable new images.

Einstein, Picasso and Martha Graham were in elite kinds of *fields* and *domains*. What happens when you are trying to affect millions of people the way that Gandhi did? It raises interesting questions. Should political innovation be considered in the same terms as the creation of a scientific theory or new manipulations of art or dance symbols, or indeed as the creation of a piece of music? My answer is 'on balance, yes'.

> ... on balance, this study is enriched, rather than compromised, by the inclusion of Gandhi in this sample ... Gandhi is a prototypically creative master ... in his chosen domain (the moral domain) ... he shared fundamental insights that were both simple and revolutionary; no racial or ethnic group is inherently superior to any other, conflicts need not be settled with violence, compromise can strengthen both parties. Perhaps most revealingly, the experiences surrounding the strike and fast at Ahmedabad have the familiar ring of core components of a creative breakthrough ... the tentative working out of a new language.
>
> Howard Gardner, 1993a

Gandhi's insights into human beings had parallels with Einstein's insights into the natural order. And yet, questions remain.

Some surprises

Types of creativity

When I began the study in earnest in the 1980s, unreflectively, I assumed that in some way all creative work was the same. But in the seven highly creative individuals whom I studied, I found seven creators doing five quite different kinds of things. So, now when I think of creativity, I think not only about different intelligences, but also about different kinds of creative endeavors.

James Watson and Francis Crick are probably the best examples of scientists using creativity to solve one particular problem. In their case, the problem was, 'What is the structure of genetic material?' Einstein did some of that too. But both Einstein and Freud were people whose thinking went beyond trying to solve one particular problem. They were highly creative individuals who were trying to formulate general conceptual schemes which they, and others, could subsequently use. A lot of science occurs in these two categories.

What artists are doing is slightly different. They are creating permanent works within a genre—in most cases a genre which already exists, for example, dance or symphonic music. Sometimes, as in the case of modern dance or performance art, the genre changes radically. It becomes something new, and criteria have to be established to deal with new kinds of symbol systems or a new artistic language.

But what I found most surprising—and I never would have come up with this if I hadn't decided to study Graham and Gandhi—is the kind of creativity inextricably linked with performances. For Martha Graham, all that mattered was her dance at the historical moment it was danced; everything else was commentary. That is why she tried to dance forever. And it is the reason why she felt dead when she finally stopped dancing at the age of seventy, even though she continued to choreograph for her company until virtually the time of her death. It was typical of dancers of her generation that they did not want any video or film recordings done. So, there were no motion pictures taken of her until she was too old to dance. She believed that an 'autographic' work does not exist apart from the images inherent in the given moments of a performance in front of a specific audience. She wanted only that one image at that one live performance to linger in people's minds. Nowadays, with the dependence on the National Endowment of the Arts and other funding agencies you have to videotape everything—but that is not the impulse of the individual creator.

It is important to distinguish between the ritualistic dancer or dramatic artist, whose performance can get better or worse and can be done again the next day, and the high-stakes performer who is risking security, health and even life in the service of a mission which might be a military campaign or presidential debate or, in Gandhi's case, a highly charged political performance. When Gandhi confronted people naked, without weapons, or whilst fasting, he basically had to do this in such a way that he could survive. He developed the concept of *satyagraha* so that his goals of changing people's minds and behaviors could be achieved. He developed new principles and became a high-stakes performer:

> Gandhi may have had brilliant or scatterbrained ideas; but in the end it was his capacity to appear credible to his followers, and to the rest of the world, by virtue of his example at specific historical moments, that constituted the central aspects of his creation . . . In Clifford Geertz's famous phrase, it's a form of very 'deep play'.
>
> Howard Gardner, 1993a

This form of creativity is far removed from what most of us do. Scientists are not called upon to be performers; their work is more distanced. When I am lecturing I am, in a way, performing, but it is not really the essence of what I do, and I certainly do not give the kind of care to it that a stage performer would, let alone a high-stakes performer.

So, one surprise was this taxonomy of different kinds of creative activities.

Prodigies versus mature creators

Another surprise was the answer to the question: 'What's the relationship between being a prodigy and being creative as an adult?' If you had asked me before I had completed this study, I would have answered, 'Well, these people were probably all child prodigies, or close to it', and I would have been wrong. Picasso was the only one of these seven highly creative individuals who could have been called a prodigy in any sense. Einstein spoke relatively late; Martha Graham did not become a dancer until she was twenty. In fact, at age twenty you probably could not have predicted what most of the seven were going to become. You knew Einstein was going to be a scientist, but most people did not think he was a creative genius—they just thought he was weird! And the others weren't much different. As a young man, Gandhi had been an indifferent student and might well have sunk into oblivion. Instead, he embarked on a journey that was to change his life and the life of our times.

Most of us are neither prodigious nor highly creative; a few people, like Picasso and Mozart, score on both counts. The more common picture is people who are prodigious but don't do anything particularly interesting as adults. On the other hand, most of my big Cs were individuals who were not prodigious but did eventually become high-level creators. The way I have expressed that is that the prodigy knows the *domain*, because it is usually given to him or her by a parent, but to become a highly creative individual, needs to construct a personality that is challenging rather than docile. There is a wonderful line from Guillaume Apollinaire, who became Picasso's first friend and biographer. He said that the most difficult transition ever in human nature was Picasso having to go from being a prodigy to being a challenger or some-body who could reflect about what he was doing:

> *The prodigy tends to work in ignorance of what is going on at the fore-front of the domain and, while often extremely gifted in mimicry, cannot be expected to go beyond conventional practices. Indeed, the prodigy will focus on his or her own interests, on pleasing 'significant others,' or on mastering the common code of the domain, rather than engaging in a genuine dialogue with leading innovators of the time, or with exemplary figures drawn from history.*
>
> Howard Gardner, 1993a

Mozart had to go through the same kind of change. Those who were not prodigies became hard workers, diligent, ambitious. They had to select their own *domain*, but they did not do so randomly; they selected the *domain* from constrained options. For example, of all the people I studied, Freud, who was the best student, had the largest range of domains from which to select. However, only when he created his own *domain* did he accomplish something most people think of as highly creative.

The creator's environment: dependence and isolation

I mentioned that these people—particularly when at the point of a break-through—were pretty much isolated from others. But paradoxically, and unpredictably for me, at this time they all needed to have somebody reassuring them, holding their hand (affectively), saying 'You're okay', and holding their hand (cognitively), saying 'These ideas are not crazy. I may not understand exactly what you're saying, but you're not totally nuts.' And sometimes it was just one person who provided both the cognitive and affective support. In the case of Martha Graham, this person was a man named Louis Horst, an American of German heritage who had long been an accompanist, composer and informal mentor for another dance group. He composed for Graham and, while the relationship was not always smooth, effectively became Graham's *alter ego*. Sigmund Freud got cognitive support from a man named Fliess, to whom he confided, 'Not a leaf has stirred to show that *The Interpretation of Dreams* meant anything to anyone.' But Fliess was not his only source of support; Freud received affective support from his family.

So, there is this need for other people to embrace you when you are looking at the precipice and asking yourself: 'Am I wacko?' This was a surprising find-ing. It was one which was reminiscent in some sense—and this is as psycho-analytic as I ever get—of the initial relationships which children have with their parents or their peers, when they are trying to communicate something that has not been communicated before, to create a new language other people can understand. In a way, I think it is the essence of the creative endeavor and the link between art and science. In both of these realms, the people are struggling to create a language which does not exist yet. In one important sense, they have to do this alone, but in another sense they must have help. That portrays a very interesting kind of balance.

Finally, and perhaps slightly melodramatically, all seven of these creative individuals lived for their work: Unless you have been around such people or studied them, it is hard perhaps to understand the extent to which they were obsessed with their work. Increasingly, with age, nothing else mattered. I think this is why there were a lot of casualties around them and why often, in the end, there were frustrations in being that kind of an individual.

Summary: the basic findings

These individuals—each representative of a different kind of intelligence—were engaged in many kinds of creative activities, which ranged from problem solving and problem finding to creating works of genre, to developing theories or frameworks, and also included performing. Against this background, I found it interesting how similar all seven creators became as human beings, or how similar their personalities were. They all doubtless had good minds, and I suspect good brains—whatever that means. But ultimately, I do not think you can really understand the creative activity in which they were involved, unless you look at the interactions between who they were as people, the *domains* they chose to work in or created and the *fields* that made judgements about their work and exchanged signals with them.

> *Where is creativity? The essential burden of the 'triangle of creativity' has been to investigate the dialectics among the individual person, or talent; the domain in which the individual is working; and the field of knowledgeable experts who evaluate works in the domain.*
>
> Howard Gardner, 1993a

I began by introducing the framework of the 'triangle of creativity,' or the three 'nodes' which interact and form the basis of an individual's level of creativity. In this study, it becomes apparent that the most important question is not 'Who is creative?' but 'Where is creativity?'—and that cannot be evaluated. Nor can an ultimate decision about an individual's creativity be made without some kind of evaluation of the rapprochement between individual, *domain* and *field*. Only occasionally is there an almost perfect fit. What seems to be defining in the creative individual is the capacity to be able to exploit an apparent misfit. Thus, this study shows it is not feasible to look only at the individual.

Finally, I would stress the importance of other people (or the matrix of support) at the time of the creator's greatest breakthrough, and the great focus all seven individuals had on their work, which increasingly led to the exclusion of everything else:

> *If one feels in possession of (or possessed by) an enormous talent, one may well feel that the talent comes with a price; and one may seek to make that covenant as explicit and unmistakable as possible. By the same token, when one is working at the edge of one's creative powers, invading territories never touched before, the need for help and support is unprecedentedly great.*
>
> Howard Gardner, 1993a

There is a fundamentally superstitious or compulsive aspect to their nature that all seven creators believed was necessary in order to maintain their gifts. And as I mentioned earlier, even though some of these individuals led fairly wild lives in certain respects, they all remained very bourgeois in their working life. None of these big Cs totally rejected tradition. This perhaps trite statement may be very important.

Before I finish, let me mention some obvious limitations of the study; I am sure you will have no trouble coming up with others. All seven creators lived in one era (the modern era), and although they were not all Western Europeans, they were in a sense all formed by or in reaction to the culture of Western Europe, and this includes Gandhi. They were almost all men—six men and one woman. And the kind of creativity they represent is what I call revolutionary creativity because their creative breakthroughs produced very sharp breaks with the *domain* in which they worked. That's why I selected these seven individuals.

Our Western European culture is based on revolutionary ideas. Certainly in other cultures—for example, China—revolutionary creativity is not even known. It is only in the political realm, and not until very recently, that individual Chinese are singled out as highly creative individuals. Their breakthroughs are evolutionary, not revolutionary.

Did I select the right people? I hope the study will be judged on its ability to explain the work of these seven individuals, rather than on the costs of not including subjects who represent other populations. And what about the *domains*? Or has my focus been too cognitive? I know the cognitive story is not the whole story. Of course, there are many other meritorious individuals who have been missed by the *field*, or by this study.

Two final questions

First, how can *you* be creative? To answer this, I want to return to the list of the four different levels of analysis: the sub-personal (genetics and biology), the personal (personality), the impersonal (domain) and the multipersonal (field). Of course, there is not much you can do about your brain, nor about your personality, nor about your intelligence—they are sort of fixed. Thus, there is no point in going back over the sub-personal and the personal. However, by studying the *domain* (to see what it is like, where it might be going, where the gaps are) and by examining the *field* (how it works, how it makes judgments, how it can be addressed or not addressed), there is—I think—a window of opportunity for those individuals who want to reach for the big C.

My final question is this: '*Are* you creative?' The answer to this question is more complex because the actual judgement of whether you are creative can take a long time. People like Emily Dickinson, Herman Melville and Gregor Mendel were only judged creative after they died. So, the bad news is that the *field* can work very slowly, and you might actually die before knowing that you are creative. But the good news is that because the *field* is so slow, you will never know for sure you are not creative.

Plate 1 *Rebirth of a Tree,*
1997
180 × 97 cm
oil on canvas,
by Françoise Gilot.

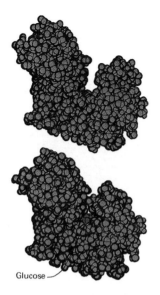

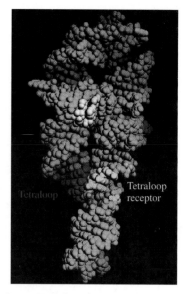

Plate 2 Molecular structure of the protein hexokinase, an enzyme, without and with its substrate molecule, glucose (red), inserted. (Courtesy Professor Thomas Steitz, Yale University; copyright W.H. Freeman and Company)

Plate 3 Complex molecular structure of a ribozyme, a catalytic form of RNA, which is more reminiscent of a protein molecule than of the double helix of DNA.

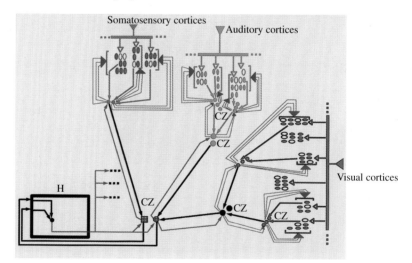

Plate 4 Simplified model of some aspects of brain function. From each of the visual, auditory, and somatosensory sectors, there are both forward projections (black lines) from functional regions (open and filled dots) toward convergence zones (CZ), and backward projections (red lines). H depicts the hippocampal system – one of the structures where signals related to a large number of activity sites can converge. Forward and backward pathways are not rigid channels; they become active when concurrent firing in cortices or CZs takes place.

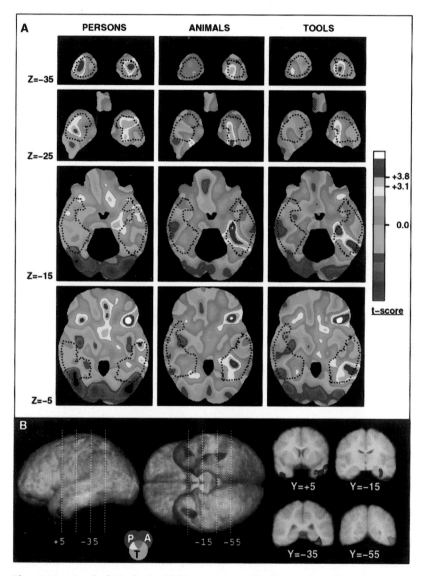

Plate 5 Mapping the living brain. (a) Three columns of PET scans show distinct regions of activity (enclosed by black dotted lines) for each of three naming tasks. (b) PET data for the regions of activity are superimposed on 3D MR data. Areas of overlap are displayed on the Venn diagram (P = person naming; A = animal naming; T tool naming).

Plate 6 *(left)* *Chandelier* by Dale Chihuly, Mediterranean Court, Honolulu Academy of Arts. (Photo: Russell Johnson)

Plate 7 *(right)* *Bright Yellow Soft Cylinder with Blue Lip Wrap*, 1990, by Dale Chihuly. (Photo: Roger Schreiber)

Plate 8 *Niijima Floats* by Dale Chihuly, Central Courtyard, Honolulu Academy of Arts. (The Mediterranean Court with *Chandelier* can be seen in the back.) (Photo: Russell Johnson)

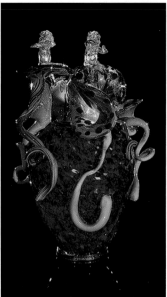

Plate 9 *Venturi Window* (installation of Persian wall pieces) by Dale Chihuly, Seattle Art Museum. (Photo: Eduardo Calderon)

Plate 10 *Mottled Red Venetian with Two Putti*, 1991, by Dale Chihuly. (Photo: Claire Garoutte)

Plate 11 *Macchia Forest*, 1994, by Dale Chihuly, Santa Barbara Museum of Art. (Photo: Scott Hagar)

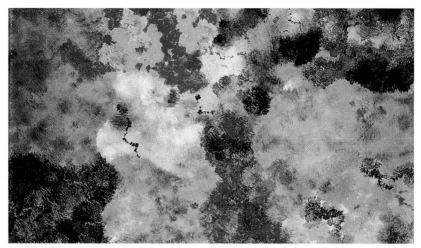

Plate 12 *Erinnerung an Italienische Primitive II [Memory of Italian Primitives II]*, oil and gold bronze on canvas (115 × 66.5 cm), 1927, by Augusto Giacometti. Bündner Kunstmuseum, Chur, Switzerland.

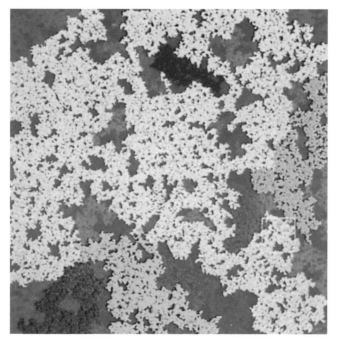

Plate 13 Percolation cluster.

Plate 14 *(above)* A fractal landscape that never was, reminiscent of full synthesis of a complicated chemical from the elements. (Art by R.F. Voss)

Plate 15 *(right)* *Fractal Planet Rise.* Another fractal landscape that never was. (Art by R.F. Voss)

Plate 16 *Nightfall on Red Island.* Yet another fractal landscape. (Art by F.K. Musgrave)

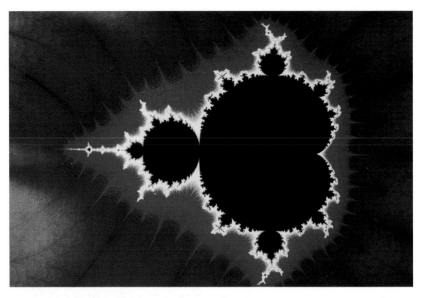

Plate 17 The Mandelbrot set. Some writers describe it as 'the most complicated object in mathematics'. Why? Because simple observations made by eye have, for twenty years, defeated the best minds' efforts at mathematical proof.

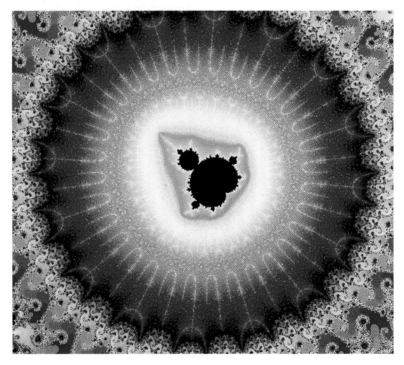

Plate 18 A very small piece of the Mandelbrot set.

GEORGE E. PALADE

Tides of genius

Looking back, over the past 50 years, each agonist, each participant in this amazing experience can say, 'Et in Arcadia ego'—I, too, was there when the Golden Flower was blooming in full splendor.

George E. Palade, 1993

One of the most significant, unique characteristics of the species *Homo sapiens* is undoubtedly its creativity, meaning the ability of the human brain to figure out solutions to all kinds of problems, from the oldest and apparently simplest (like verbal communication and tool making) to the most recent and most elaborate (like the fission and fusion of atoms or genetic engineering or the control of membrane and protein traffic in the cell).

Creativity is expressed very unevenly in the human population. We are interested primarily in the highest levels of creativity because these affect the development of human civilizations the most. In addition to *solving* problems, the creative mind *recognizes* new problems as the result of a continual dialogue with the world around it. If this is the definition of creativity, then creativity is essentially limited to the human species.

Creativity is in the genes.

Creativity is a genetic, human condition

As in other creatures that came out of the shop of evolution—the worms, the flies and the mice—a substantial fraction of the human genome must be involved in building the body plan during development. The total number of genes in the human genome is still unknown; estimates run from 50 000 to 100 000. The genes mapped, identified and sequenced to date account for only a few thousand, and most of them encode 'housekeeping' proteins found essentially in all cells of the body or proteins of some specialized (differentiated) cells, such as those in muscles or glands. Humans, like worms, flies and mice, have their own so-called 'homeotic' genes—genes which direct complex patterning events in the formation of the early embryo. Beyond these earliest stages in development, we may assume that many other genes are required for the proper construction of each of the human organs; we may wonder how many genes are needed to control the development of the human brain—a process that involves so many neurons, so many specific cell–cell interactions and so much functionally important or critical circuitry (see chapters by Pfenninger and Stevens).

High creativity probably is a multifactorial genetic condition (comparable in a positive sense to a multifactorial inherited disease)—a condition involving the positive interaction of a large number of genes. We can imagine that because of the right combination of genes, a person acquires more synapses, a few more connections in the circuitry, and this may mean many subtle modifications in this circuitry (cf. Pfenninger's chapter in Part 2). The mind of such an individual, as a result of these changes, may attain a higher level of creativity.

Human adaptation and the golden flower of the Renaissance

Human creativity exhibits another, puzzling attribute. The historical record shows clearly that creativity—especially creativity in the arts and the sciences—is most evident at specific times and in special places, in rather well-defined areas of human activity. The creative mind seems to have a large margin of adaptability to the condition of its environment, its economic condition and the ethos of the time. What follows is a discussion of the interactions between the arts and the sciences in the context of Western civilization, as a function of time in history.

In relatively recent history, we have the amazing example of the spectacular flourishing of the visual arts (i.e. painting, sculpture and architecture) in the Italian Renaissance during the fifteenth and sixteenth centuries. From Italy, the Renaissance reverberated over the entire Europe. In the seventeenth century, there was a remarkable concentration in Italy of great musicians—composers, instrumentalists, singers and instrument makers—and some of these left Italy for Madrid and Vienna, taking their music with them. Later on, there was another wave of outstanding musicians, this time in the German lands of the eighteenth and nineteenth centuries. And, in our times, the twentieth century witnessed an unprecedented concentration of creative minds working in experimental scientific research in the natural sciences. There have been two major waves of creative activity: one in physics (after the end of the First World War) and another in biological and biomedical sciences (after the Second World War).

It appears, therefore, that creative minds can adapt—epigenetically, so to say—to areas of activity, supported by the resources of their communities and appreciated by the spirit (ethos) of their times. It's as if the presumed 'creativity genes' goad their owner to unusual accomplishments that can surpass what is known or has been done already and lead to the opening of large new vistas into the future. Of course, good eyes and good hands help, but the urge of the creative mind towards excellence is a major factor. This means creative minds will converge to fields of interest of their social and intellectual environment, perhaps to the detriment of other fields of human endeavor. The Italian Renaissance, for instance, also witnessed a flourishing of the humanities; it had its great writers, poets, historians and philosophers; it also saw progress in applied sciences (civil and military engineering) and the beginning of modern sciences—but no other field reached the splendid prominence of the visual arts.

For centuries, the Italian Renaissance has fascinated the minds of the Western world, and the masterpieces it left behind are still reason for intellectual pilgrimage and sources of touristic revenue for many Italian cities today. Wealth invested pays back. The Count de Gobineau (1816–1882), a French writer and diplomat and a profound admirer of the Renaissance, wrote a series of short plays based on the history of the period. He prefaced them with comments in which he describes the Renaissance as a unique achievement of the human spirit—the equivalent of a *golden flower* that comes to bloom rarely, in special places at special times, but affects forever the history of the garden in which it blooms, as well as the history of the culture or civilization to which it belongs.

There is something uniquely powerful about the work of the great masters in the visual arts. In the images they created, they have distilled so much faithful depth, so much feeling and so much convincing detail. In a few moments— though a few minutes of reflection and a later, second look would help—the spectator is able to grasp the state of mind, the social position, the feeling of the subject or of the model, his or her joys or sufferings, his or her cruelty or kind- ness. In fact, a great master succeeds in expressing a whole story, a whole drama, in one image—in two dimensions as a painting or in three dimensions as a statue. To attain that communication level, the written arts need a few chapters, if not a whole book. Music can do it a little better, in a sonata or a movement of a symphony, perhaps with a richer emotional envelope. The sciences cannot perform such miracles, and it is doubtless they could ever, even in the distant future, match such performances.

The basic approach of the visual arts in the Renaissance was to concentrate on human beings—fellow men and women—and to tell an enchanting or powerful or moving story in one image. The surrounding nature, the land- scape, received much less attention. Yet the mastery and volume of artistic achievements were unprecedented. It is hard to believe the Renaissance period witnessed the contemporary or overlapping existence of Leonardo Da Vinci, Michelangelo Buonarroti, Raffaello Sanzio (Raphael), Sandro Botticelli, Andrea Del Vecchio, Piero Della Francesca, Luca and Andrea Della Robbia,

Fra Angelico, Paolo Uccello, Benozzo Gozzoli, Tiziano Vecellio, Lorenzo Ghiberti, Filippo Brunelleschi, Donato Bramante and others. Many of them were true 'Renaissance men'—painters, as well as sculptors, architects and civil or military engineers. Leonardo, moreover, was a producer of entertainment events at the court of the Dukes of Milan.

There was another noteworthy element in the social context of the period. The masterworks were known and appreciated not only by the courts and the intellectual elite, but also by the public, the rank and file of the population. This broad contact with the public is explained, in part, by the fact that the Church supported the arts generously by providing resources and themes (i.e. biblical scripts). The artists contributed, of course, their artistry and also the models, usually their girlfriends or wives, who might pose one day as the Madonna and the next as the Venus.

In 1311, in Siena, Duccio di Buoninsegna finished the painting of the Maestà, the central piece for the altar of the cathedral. When the work was taken from Duccio's shop to the cathedral, the entire population of the city marched in procession behind the Maestà and nobody complained about the fact that the city had paid the master the record fee of 3000 ducats for his masterpiece. Clearly the visual arts, especially the religious works, had the support of the public. Every church and every cathedral longed to have at least a painting signed by a great name.

Very little experimental science was being conducted during the Italian Renaissance, but there was a revival of the sciences of direct observation. This was in line with the general tenets of the period, which were asking for direct observation and personal original contributions rather than comments on classical texts. The masterpiece of the new science was a treatise of anatomy, *De Humani Corporis Fabrica*, published by a Belgian immigrant, Andrea Vesalius, professor at the University of Padua in 1543. Vesalius' truly original treatise shows clearly the pervasive influence of the Renaissance visual arts and their aesthetics. The book has an ornate front page. The skeletons seem to be thinking, and the dissected cadavers are engaged somehow in interesting or surprisingly graceful movements while every muscle is reproduced to perfection (Fig. 3.13). Vesalius' *Fabrica* was the best of the then-new science of human anatomy, and the presentation of his scientific findings was done in the context of the visual arts of the sixteenth century. The influence of art on science—though obvious—did not affect the substance of anatomy, only the way scientific findings were presented.

The Italian Renaissance had been in the making for at least a couple of centuries. Duccio's work, for instance, belongs to the fourteenth century. What made it possible was a convergence of factors of which the most important was affluence, economic prosperity—the result of a near monopoly of the trade with the Orient and, in part, of industries based on that trade.

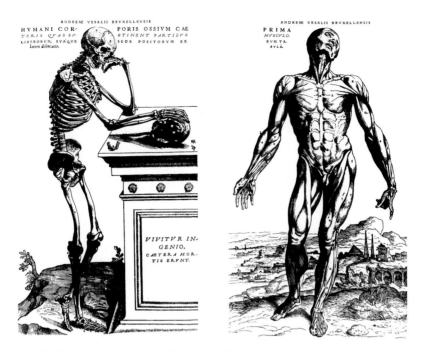

Fig. 3.13 Illustrations from Andrea Vesalius' *De Humani Corporis Fabrica*, 1543.

There was a multiplicity of support sources for the arts, since Italy was a conglomerate of sovereign states, principalities and republics—including the states of the Church (the papal states and the Vatican). Hence, every state and every city was in competition for artistic showpieces, palaces, cathedrals, statues and paintings of popes, princes and generals. Another important factor was the high and widely spread level of education, especially among the affluent classes (the Medici were businessmen). Finally, Italy was at that time the beneficiary of a brain drain at the expense of the crumbling and dying Byzantine empire on the one hand, and of northern countries (remember Vesalius) on the other hand.

Together, these factors were strong enough to compensate, for a while, for political instability and recurrent invasions by French and German imperial armies, and for the systematic looting of the wealth of the peninsula via war reparations or wedding dowries. Two Medici women, after all, became queens of France.

What finally led to the withering of the golden flower was the loss of affluence, not because Muslims were controlling parts of the trade routes, but because Portugal (and soon thereafter, Spain, England, France and Holland) traced—often with the help of Italian navigators such as Columbus—new routes around Africa or across the Atlantic Ocean. The monopoly had come to an end and with it, the prosperity that kept alive the whole social structure, from sailors, craftsmen and merchants to princes, cardinals and artists. If there is a lesson to be learned, it is that economic strength and local prosperity are of the essence, that multiplicity of resources helps, and that the movement of talent and brain power to more affluent regions is an unavoidable part of the process.

Post-Renaissance changes in the visual arts

With the advent of absolute monarchies in Europe, the visual arts adapted to the new conditions, which meant primarily a transition from multiple support sources to essentially a single source: the king and his court. Diego Velazquez painted his king, Philip IV, many times—not because he was a model of physical beauty or intellectual power but because, I presume, painting the king and other members of the royal family and court was part of his job description. Occasionally he escaped portraiture to show the full range of his creative genius. Examples of the resulting masterpieces are 'Las Lanzas', an epic to courteous military valor, and the ode to young life, 'Las Meniñas'. The little infanta in this latter work is the object of everybody's attention: the royal parents (seen only through a mirror), the nannies, the artist and the buffoons —all placed, of course, in courtly surroundings. The tradition holds.

It was only much later, in the democratic, bourgeois France of the end of the nineteenth century, that the emphasis in the visual arts shifted to ordinary men and women, who were neither royal nor aristocratic. Artists produced a series of amazing and enduring masterpieces that are odes to the beauty of young women, for example, 'Les Grandes Baigneuses' by Auguste Renoir, or to the joy of outside reunions among young friends, such as in 'Le Moulin de la Galette' and 'Déjeuner à Argenteuil' also by Auguste Renoir. These are, of course, only a couple of examples of a period of prodigious activity that also includes paintings of ever-changing nature for nature's own sake by Claude Monet. Impressionist painting spread throughout the world; it reached the American shores with Mary Cassatt. Was this another golden flower? Not exactly. One might say that it was the bud of a golden flower that withered away without reaching full bloom. Artists lost patience with tradition. The artistic community fragmented into small groups: radicals asked for a focus on the essence of forms rather than on details, as in the case of Brancusi, or demanded a complete liberation from the models of, and preoccupations with, the myths of the past. As artists turned away from realism, they moved toward abstraction, symbolism and surrealism. A final result was that, close to the beginning of the twentieth century, the human figure as it was known in the traditional visual arts lost its position of primacy and was replaced with a wide variety of abstractions.

At the same time, science was questioning, on the one hand, the direct divine paternity of man and, on the other hand, the validity (or reality) of all forms including those of man and nature. Forms were suspect—as perceived by the human eye, supposedly an imperfect optical instrument of low resolution, and as analyzed by the human brain which, in any case, could do no better than the eyes. Form as seen was regarded, therefore, as a distant echo of unseen thousands of molecular interactions that are better candidates for reality than a visual image (also see Stent's chapter in Part 1). Pablo Picasso, for instance, was saying, 'We should not paint only what we see on the surface, we should paint what we know to be there' (cf. Gilot's chapter in Part 4).

The primary mission of the visual artist is to convey his or her vision to fellow humans in an accessible form—a form that can have a direct, prompt impact. By giving up man and nature as seen, the visual artists risk abandoning their most efficient means of communication, they chance exiling themselves in an esoteric world, condemned to interact only with people of the same kind of conditioning and, hence, resigned to do little with their creative minds beyond the narrowing interests of their group. The fragmentation of the artistic community into quite dogmatic groups (cf. Stevens's chapter in Part 4) could be attributed to several critical developments. Among them we should include the senseless carnage of the First World War, the collapse after the War of the old order in so many parts of the world, especially in Europe, the emergence of the communist Soviet Union and the beginning of the policy of confrontation between East and West. But I believe that, beyond these destabilizing elements, there may be other, deeper reasons that led a creative mind to doubt the values of the past.

The emergence of modern science

Aboard a magic carpet, let us move into a new era of spectacular advances generated by creative human minds, this time in the natural sciences. As I mentioned already, there was first a series of momentous advances in physics which, over a few decades after the First World War, led to the elucidation of the structure of atoms and, in part, their nuclei, to the harnessing of atomic energy and to the production of atomic and nuclear weapons. In his reminiscences, Gamov, the physicist, refers to this period as the '30 years that shook the physics'. They also shook the world at the end of the Second World War and, in its aftermath, the Cold War. In fact, the world is slowly adapting to a non-shaking condition only now, after the demise of the Soviet Union as a world military power. Perhaps less spectacular, but more constructive and just as influential, were the more recent advances in laser technology and in solid state physics that led to the production of transistors and gave birth to computer science, automated instrumentation and the information age.

Spectacular advances in physics were followed by perhaps even more spectacular progress in basic biological sciences. I propose to concentrate on the latter because they occurred in a terrain in which I feel at home, and because I believe they will affect mankind even more profoundly than atomic physics.

At the beginning of the twentieth century, biological sciences appeared to be in a state of dormancy; there were only a few isolated areas of significant activity. The dormancy came after a period of intense activity towards the end of the nineteenth century, when immunity, antibodies and vaccines were discovered and used to treat or prevent infectious diseases, under the leadership of Pasteur and Koch. This was also the time when Abbé succeeded in improving the construction of light microscope lenses, a development that made it possible to describe in detail the structure of cells and tissues of many organisms and the changes they incur in different diseases, thereby establishing a useful and solid base for human diagnostic pathology that is still in use today.

The dormancy was broken in the late 1940s and early 1950s by the introduction of new instrumentation and new procedures in basic biological research (see also Pfenninger's chapter in Part 2). What followed was a period of spectacular advances that has continued at a sustained, if not increasing rate, to the present time, four or five decades later.

The golden flower blooms again

I should remind you that, in the early 1950s, the chemical nature of genes was still debated. The structure of DNA (the molecule of the genes) was unknown, and our ideas about the organization of cells were vague and incomplete. We did not know how and where proteins are synthesized, how cellular membranes are constructed or how genetic information is used by the cells and how it is transmitted from cell generation to cell generation at the molecular level.

Since my own career in scientific research started in the late 1940s, I could say I was there when the period of rapid developments started, and that I witnessed the entire course of these spectacular advances. First, cell structure was defined in detail by electron microscopy, and new structural elements, beyond the resolution limit reached by light microscopes, were discovered. However, the images obtained (Figs 3.14 and 3.15) were challenging, puzzling, at best suggestive, but not edifying: they did not tell what roles these new structures played in the life of cells. Then, newly discovered and already known subcellular components were isolated by cell fractionation procedures (separating

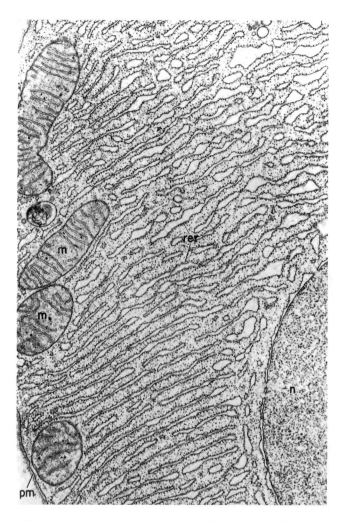

Fig. 3.14 Electron micrograph showing the structural organization of a cell (exocrine pancreas). The region of the cell between the nucleus (n) and the plasmalemma (pm) is occupied by numerous cellular organelles, such as cisternae of the rough endoplasmic reticulum (rer) and a few mitochondria (m). ($\times 9\,000$)

cells into their individual component parts) and their chemistries and functions defined. They proved to be highly differentiated, functionally specialized cell organs. Although constructed exclusively of perishable materials (lipids, proteins and nucleic acids), they were found to be tough and sturdily built.

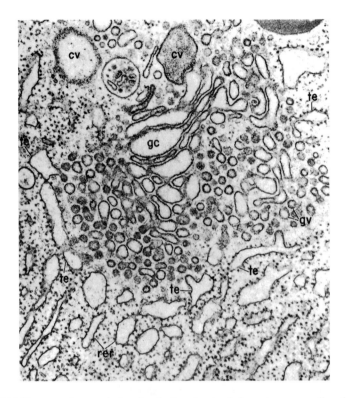

Fig. 3.15 Electron micrograph showing further structural elements or organelles of the cell (exocrine pancreas). Partial view of the Golgi complex, a cellular organelle. Cv, condensing vacuoles; gc, Golgi cisternae; gv, Golgi vesicles; te, transitional elements; rer, rough endoplasmic reticulum. (×20 000)

Since their functions survived cell disruption and lengthy isolation procedures, it became possible to reconstitute complex cellular functions—such as protein synthesis and protein transport from cellular compartment to cellular compartment—in the test tube.

During the last decades, it was also discovered that the cells operate an efficient protein and membrane traffic control system, much more reliable than any mail service. Every parcel, which means every protein and every membrane 'bubble' or vesicle in the cell, is delivered at the right address. As a result of these advances, we can now understand to a large extent what is going on in the cell.

In the early 1950s, an American post-doctoral fellow, James Watson, and a British graduate student who was not in a hurry to graduate, Francis Crick, were working together at the University of Cambridge, England. They figured out the structure of DNA molecules—the molecules of the genes of essentially all living systems. DNA consists of two complementary nucleotide strands twisted along each other in a double helix. It became evident, in a short while, that the hereditary transmission of genetic information was built into the structure of this molecule (see also Cech's chapter in Part 1). What the cells have to do is to separate the two strands and use each of them as a template to synthesize a complementary strand. The process starts with one molecule (or one gene) and ends with the production of two identical molecules, two identical genes, one for each daughter cell at the time of cell division.

In his youthful excitement, Jim Watson felt that little else was needed beyond discovering the double helix and wrote, 'the rest is engineering'. It proved to be elaborate and subtle engineering. An army of enzymes was found to be involved in DNA replication and still another army in the transcription of genetic information into RNA molecules that function as messengers (mRNAs) from the genes to the protein-synthesizing machinery of the cell (cf. Cech's chapter in Part 1). Yet another army of enzymes and factors was found to be needed to translate into proteins the information encoded in mRNAs, to modify these proteins after translation and direct them to their proper location within the cell's structural framework.

Obviously, we are already far beyond our starting base of the early 1950s. In the meantime, it became possible to identify specific genes and to introduce them (by 'transfection') into host cells—which results in the production of foreign proteins. The discovery of bacterial enzymes that cleave DNA molecules at multiple, specific sites made possible the construction of man-made genes, with all kinds of alterations that amounted to man-made mutations. All these manipulations became genetic engineering, led to the emergence of molecular genetics and created modern biotechnology, which is now producing human proteins in bacteria for therapy as well as experimental use.

We learned how to introduce foreign genes into fertilized mouse eggs to produce 'transgenic' animals in which to study the role of specific genes (expressed in excess) in the development and function of an organism. More recently, we also learned how to remove genes from developing organisms, so as to create 'knock-out' flies or 'knock-out' mice in which one can investigate the effects of a missing gene on the development and eventually the function of a mature organism. Finally, we have essentially completed the sequencing of the human genome, and we have arrived at a stage today at which we can start human gene therapy to correct genetic disorders. I should point out that many of these advances were made possible by concomitant progress in chemistry, which provided effective separation procedures, sensitive assays and improved methods for characterizing large and small molecules.

Now, if we go back first to the early 1950s and consider the level of knowledge (or rather, lack of knowledge) we had at that time, and then turn the clock back all the way to Aristotle, Hippocrates, Galen, Vesalius and Pasteur, we realize right away that no comparable period has occurred before in the long history of the life sciences. What we have gained in these last 50 years goes beyond the accumulation of a huge mountain of new information. It gives us a new understanding of basic cell functions; it allows us to perceive the logic of the different systems at work within the cell context and to understand why primeval cells were born with certain servitudes—like fluid membranes—and how solutions have evolved over time to cope with these servitudes.

To stress the rapidity of these advances and their profound impact, we can say that the last five decades have witnessed a true revolution in basic biological and biomedical sciences. The word 'revolution' is dramatic and occasionally fashionable. But to acknowledge the unique accomplishments of this period, we should go back to the fifteenth and sixteenth centuries of the Italian Renaissance and to Count de Gobineau, who described it as one of the rare golden flowers of human creativity that comes to bloom only once in a few centuries. What we have witnessed in recent decades has been the blooming of another golden flower of human creativity, this time in the natural sciences, and especially in the life sciences.

Tending the garden of the golden flower

For quite a while, the blooming of this new golden flower was an American phenomenon explained in large measure by the decision taken by President Roosevelt to accept and implement the recommendations of Vanevar Bush, the coordinator of the American scientific war effort during the Second World War. In his report to the President, published in 1945 under the title, 'Science, the endless frontier,' Vanevar Bush proposed that the federal government should support basic scientific research in essentially all natural sciences including biomedical sciences, as a first, necessary step towards a healthy economy. Basic laboratory findings should be the first step in the development of marketable products for civilian use, as it had been the first step in the development of effective weapons during the war. The industry was assumed to take care of the next step in the process—the development itself. The immediate result was the organization of the National Science Foundation, followed shortly thereafter by the organization of the National Institutes of Health (NIH), the two federal agencies which became rapidly the main sources of support for American basic scientific research.

Two other elements played major roles in the subsequent developments of the federal support system. The first was the decision to relegate research initiative to the periphery represented by universities and research institutions throughout the country. And the second was the introduction of the peer review system. The combined effect of these critical moves was the emergence of a new, uniquely American institution, the Research-Intensive University, which, in the process, became the primary driving force for the spectacular advances already described. Some of these new moves were partly adopted abroad.

Besides supporting basic research, the federal government also funded a series of programs for training new investigators so as to ensure the continuity of the research effort. As a result of all these developments, we have opened up vast opportunities for further advances that may extend the revolution or the blooming of the golden flower by at least three or four more decades. And we also have a large number of well-trained young investigators ready to man laboratory benches. Therefore, until a few years ago, we felt the future of basic research was secure, that the golden flower had what it needed (the equivalent of strong fertilizer and good, young gardeners) to keep blooming into the following century. But then, the level of federal support started declining, and this makes the immediate future uncertain.

If we look back over our shoulders, it becomes clear that the factors involved in the blooming of the golden flower of our time were the same as in the Italian Renaissance: prosperity based on trade and industry; widespread education, including professional training; multiplicity of support sources; and mass movement of talent (brain drain). What we are now witnessing is a decline in real prosperity—as opposed to apparent prosperity generated over the last few years by governmental deficit spending. Recovery becomes now a high-priority task, because real prosperity is the cornerstone on which the entire construct is built. This does mean, however, that factors needed for recovery should be recognized and their support maintained—if not enhanced. Investing in research in basic natural sciences, as well as in the development phase of their new findings should be recognized as essential factors for recovery.

You may consider that I described the revolution in basic life sciences some-what unrealistically with pluses only, and no minuses. In fact, there are minuses that deserve attention. To begin with, the rapidity of the advances and the highly competitive nature of the support system re-enforce each other and often claim all the time and energy of those engaged in scientific research, thereby narrow-ing their vision. The focus sharpens the scientist's advance, but at the price of limiting his or her interests and diluting contacts with humanities and the practicalities of political life. Some scientists developed the mentality of gold-miners, determined that the fellow next to them would not find the bigger gold nugget.

Many scientists consider themselves precious and special and expect society to treat them accordingly. But our society is a conglomerate of groups of diverse interests, not all of them necessarily rational. Some lose patience because the AIDS problem is not yet solved; some worry about the rights of their cats; and still others like the final product, but do not like the price tag. The problem is that the public at large appreciates the final products of scientific research, especially if they make work easier, life healthier and more fun. But the value of the initial findings and the long and expensive process that leads from the laboratory to the final product are rarely understood or appreciated.

There was a popular procession behind Duccio's 'Maestà' in Siena in 1311, but no procession, not even one of scientists, followed the double helix model of DNA of Watson and Crick in 1953 in Cambridge. A major scientific finding cannot have the same direct, immediate and broad impact on the public at large as an image created by a master of the visual arts. Perhaps the current extensive use of diagrams and cartoons to present scientific facts and interpretations is an attempt to compensate for this inherent limitation. Scientists must educate the public—and themselves—on the art of effective communication.

The scientific revolutions of the twentieth century have profoundly influenced Western civilization. The results are obvious all around us: in communications, travel, entertainment, industrial processing, textiles, marketing, military operations, medical practice and agriculture. In this respect, the scientific revolutions of the century have more than fulfilled their promise. Does this mean there were no negative results? We may assume that competition for creative minds has worked against other kinds of human creative activity. Perhaps it's no accident that today's great names in the written arts are coming from the periphery of the Western world, from South America and South Africa, where sciences do not dominate the scene. Have visual arts flourished less than sciences over the last few decades of the twentieth century? If so, is it by coincidence or direct causal effect? Man and nature have lost their traditional, central position in the arts, as mentioned already. In the sixteenth century, the visual arts were affecting the presentation of scientific findings; in the twentieth century, the sciences affected the central themes of the visual arts.

The golden flower may continue to bloom or may wither away, depending to a critical extent on the prosperity of this country and of Western civilization. But irrespective of apprehensions about its future and of its negative side-effects, the past 50 years will remain for a very long time the 50 years that catapulted the life sciences to heights never dreamt of before. We should realize that regardless of excessive competition, funding difficulties, complications and setbacks, it's been a privilege to live and work through the excitement and agitation of this revolution—much better than doing little through one of those periods of dormancy preceding it.

PART FOUR

Patterns of perception

FRANÇOISE GILOT

A painter's perspective

We all know that art is not truth. Art is a lie that makes us realize truth;
at least the truth that is given us to understand. The artist must know the
manner in which to convince others of the truthfulness of his lies.

Pablo Picasso, 1947
(conversation between P. Picasso and F. Gilot)

'How can anyone know if he or she is a potentially original artist?' some of my students asked. I answered, 'I can tell you that it's very simple. How many hours can you remain alone during a day, a week, a month, a year, a lifetime? If you can remain alone almost all of the time you can be a painter.'

From the age of five, I knew that I wanted to be a painter. My father, an agronomist, told me, 'If you work eight hours at law, I allow you to work eight hours at painting.' I went to law school and I continued to paint. Even then, I believed if you want to be a painter, you must be a great painter, or nothing.

In 1941, I decided I wanted to be a painter. I was in Paris, living from one day to the next because it was wartime and every day anything could have happened. The German authorities checked the paintings for content, so that everything we wanted to express had to be symbolic. The 1940s were a tragic time, many of my best friends were killed. It was not exciting; it was tragic.

If I had met Picasso in normal times, our differences would have been insurmountable; he was at the zenith of his career and I was at the beginning of mine. I had an exhibition and went to dinner with a friend at a nearby restaurant. I was one of the great hopes of my generation, respected by others. Picasso sent a bowl of cherries to our table; *that* was his introduction. It was May 1943. Cherries became a symbol in his paintings, and next to the cherries, three glasses. Picasso searched for ways to reorder the way we see our world. He was not literal; he found ways to symbolize a person through colors and shapes. He stared at me until my image became a part of his thinking, and then he fragmented and rearranged. The elements were the same, but the order was different, more complex. Although the shadow of Picasso was on my paintings for a while, it is not true to say that I am of Picasso's family of painters.

His teaching was indirect. He critiqued and talked about paintings, but mostly he talked about the work of others—for example, Manet or Cézanne. He always said that he couldn't comment when the painting wasn't finished. From Pablo, I learned to concentrate and to think about nothing else.

I was caught up in Picasso's orbit; it was in a sense a continuation of my relationship with my father, who had taught me to discuss and to be strong. Lions mate with lions: everyone else said yes to Pablo; I said no once in a while. When I met him, he was 61. After two children, I told Pablo our relationship had to change. I couldn't understand why he didn't know that I wouldn't like his Don Juan behavior. Our relationship deteriorated; in late 1953, with my children, I took a taxi and caught the train to Paris and left everything behind me. From 1960 until 1964, I often painted in London and exhibited in Paris and London.

In May 1969, I had a show in Los Angeles, and I also went there to make lithographs, but I didn't finish, and so returned in September. I told a friend, 'I don't want to see any of your scientists because scientists and artists don't mix.' When I went to a lunch at which Dr Jonas Salk was present, I didn't say a word. I saw him again at a black-tie dinner; this time it was different. In June, we were married in Paris; we became a citadel for each other and were married for 25 years, until he died. We had such a marvelous dialogue; we had to search to find a common ground.

Gradually, we changed our perspective; for a few months, a study at the Salk Institute was transformed into a painting studio. Instead of being surrounded by Picasso's friends, or painters, I was working in the midst of eminent scientists who discussed DNA, RNA and proteins. The words of the British art critic, Herbert Read, came back to me:

> The work of art is just as much or as little an empirical fact as the structure of a molecule of carbon; the empirical facts of science are just as much a question of choice, or of chance, or inspiration as a work of art.
>
> Herbert Read, 1960

In my mind art and science became two ends of a continuum in which both rely on the elements of choice, serendipity and inspiration. I will address the end of the philosophical spectrum I know best, which is painting.

In the modern sense of the word, painting encompasses whatever a painter does. In this chapter I will talk about painting from my perspective, and I will try only to make a few points—little 'tidbits'—that I hope will stir controversy. Unfortunately, in a philosophical framework, whatever you say, you should have said something else. This is especially true when discussing the philosophy of painting because anything you say about painting with the voice can only be a hollow fiction: painting is a language that goes beyond words. The language of painting is cryptic, a metaphor. Painters do have dialogues, but with paintings, not speech.

Painting is the art of silence

Those who speak about the art of painting often mention a language, and that language of painting is no mere reflection of organized speech. Through the use of symbols, images and emotions, painting brings a message that exists on many levels.

To reveal the essence of the inner and outer worlds is the objective of a work of art. Painting goes from beauty to the naked truth; however, a painter's definition of beauty is the artist's own. It is vital to understand that when a painter talks about beauty, it doesn't have to be pleasant, attractive or pretty. The beauty painters address is not oriented toward harmony, but toward abstraction, drama, power and exaggeration of all kinds. I am not trying to please or displease. I do not want to say 'this is ugly', or 'this is pretty'. It does not concern me. From a painter's perspective, whether or not a painting is pleasing or displeasing is not the critical element. I think beauty is neither ornament, nor superficial. Instead, it is a true or fitting expression of the essential order of life, which may or may not be beautiful in the conventional sense of the word. All beauty and all art depend upon a sense of order.

Art is a silent language, but it is also a reflection of the order of the cosmos. A symbol is not something that *describes* reality. The wheel, for instance, can be a symbol of movement; you do not have to paint running feet to represent movement. A triangle can also be a symbol; there are different levels at which you can interpret it. I don't mean 'symbolism' in the literary sense, but rather the very simple shapes and colors that can evoke certain thoughts without describing them.

Both scientist and artist endeavor to find and assert a basic order that is an essential part of nature and the cosmos. Whatever images we produce are a result of the matrix that is producing the structures, or the brain. For the artist, the result is a series of picture images. These are a mode of communication that is not the same as, but complementary to, the logical method of definition and verification used by scientists and mathematicians.

Symbols: a new plastic reality

The word 'symbol' comes from the Greek—*syn*, which means with or together, and *bol*, which means to throw—to throw together. A painting should be able to move our senses, our sensibility and our minds. There are several levels in my painting, but I do not find it necessary that they all be understood rationally; they should be felt rather than comprehended.

The symbol doesn't have to resemble what it evokes; it can be anything. For example, when you want to evoke walking you can draw a circle (not a foot) because the circle will roll. So visually, the symbol does not have to be an accurate description of reality. If you look at African tribal art, the proportions of the figures are not anatomically correct (the head can be extremely large, the legs even smaller, etc.), even the postures are not anatomically accurate—but the impact is strong. Graphic reality can surpass literal reality because of the power and the expressiveness of the relationships. This power is an important key to the understanding of the work of modern painters.

The spirit of discovery: an equation with the unknown

What is the possible kinship between the art of painting and science? I would say it is the spirit of discovery, especially in the last century, when the artist no longer tried to describe the outside world. There are now other ways of doing that. Since the advent of the camera, the artist has not been obliged to copy reality; he or she now can be purely subjective and can be free to draw upon what is within.

I think the painter is someone who places himself or herself in an equation with the unknown, and I think the scientist is basically in the same posture. What is an equation? In an equation, you have certain quantities that are already known even though they are not quantified; the others are by definition unknown. And the resolution is to explore and discover what may allow us to see or to comprehend a little bit more. And this spirit of discovery takes both artists and scientists beyond that which is conventional, or stereotypical.

A synchronistic perspective

The world appears to us in the form of figures
Carnets de Léonardo da Vinci, Editions Gallimard, 1942

All laws of artistic form have a core of the simplest mathematics.
Herbert Read, 1960

Perspective is the vantage point that links different points of view. If you take a historical perspective of art, starting with the past and coming toward the present, you can see there is a parallel development between the art of a certain historical period and the science of that same approximate period of time. Geometry (one of the first sciences to be developed) coincided with the rise of an Egyptian and ancient Greek art form based on a system of proportions. For example, the human figure was drawn with a set mathematical relationship between the parts. In a human being, the height to the ankle, to the knee, to the shoulder, etc. was measured in ratios relative to the size of the whole. And all those numbers were in a mathematical progression. So those numbers were really discoveries that paralleled the scientific explorations made at approximately the same time in geometry and in ancient Egyptian and Greek art. In fact, in ancient times, the arts were expected to be a visual equivalent of all available knowledge.

Mathematics dominated Islamic art. Because of religious beliefs, absolutely no design or motif in Islamic art could be based on the human figure. Therefore, everything about Islamic art is purely mathematical. Numbers are the simplest and most primary forms of thought; they are the most abstract symbols.

The mathematical–optical principles of perspective discovered by Filippo Brunelleschi before 1420 enabled painters to use scientific principles to control the illusion of forms and colors in space. Artists experimented with the organization of space in accordance with new scientific discoveries and were able to create a powerful illusion of reality. By establishing a scale for the size of figures in space, and by shifting the viewpoint to the right or left along the horizon line, or by diminishing the contrast of color in the distance, the painters who followed the lead of the scientists experimenting with optics gained an important new optical tool—the perspective of space. At the beginning of the Renaissance, artists created space through precise geometrical calculations and created a stage-like perspective in their paintings.

Leonardo da Vinci is a good example of an artist possessed by the spirit of discovery. He was fascinated by anatomy. He even went out at night to find corpses and dissected them, although it was absolutely forbidden at that time. He didn't reject the tricks of illusionary space, but he challenged the 'truth' of an artificially flat perspective; his truth was the truth of observation. Not only was he a supreme draughtsman, but his drawings were based on a profound understanding of the science that was known at that time. Not only anatomy, but also geology interested the artist. In his drawings of landscapes, he tried to show the different periods at which some layers of the landscape were distinct from others, like alluvions from bedrock, for example.

The paintings created by Poussin in the seventeenth century are plastic rhetoric. His silent pictorial language is the exact mathematical equivalent of the Newtonian concept of space. The mathematical compositions of such paintings are obvious. Older artists, influenced by the science of their time, in turn became models for later painters. Poussin was an innovator in the classical French tradition. Cézanne declared his intention to 'do Poussin over again from nature'. The post-impressionist, who is the well-spring for many of the major directions in twentieth-century art, showed the way forward.

Much of contemporary art is based on an unconscious dialogue between artists and scientists. For example, Picasso knew the English scientist, Desmond Bernal, a founder of molecular biology. Bernal, a Cambridge

University professor, was fascinated by the way the modern artist paralleled scientific structures, even though the artist was not consciously aware of the relationship. So, you can think of Picasso's cubist figures as having something to do with crystallography. In her memoirs (Gardiner, 1988), Margaret Gardiner, the daughter of the distinguished Oxford Egyptologist who accompanied the Earl of Carnarvon for the opening of Tut'Ankhamun's tomb, remembered when Picasso came to London to visit Bernal: 'He had this flat, and Picasso went to see him there and drew a king on the wall. It was a plain white wall, and he drew a crowned king in chalk and then said, "He looks rather lonely", and so he gave him a queen.' (This painting is now part of the collection of the Institute of Contemporary Art in London.)

I think artists by and large are interested in, and are more or less aware of, the important advances that scientists of their time have made; they feel free to use what is of interest to them. When I was married to Jonas Salk, the Director of the Salk Institute, I sometimes, but not often, listened to the lectures of visiting and resident scientists. About 20 years ago, I was interested in the lectures of Hubel and Wiesel on experiments they had performed on the brains of monkeys (see the chapters by Pfenninger and Stevens). They would put electrodes on one cell—a specific brain cell that was linked to the retina in the eye—and they would record a signal when that specific cell was activated. Then the two scientists displayed on a screen in front of the monkey, for example, a white rectangle on a neutral background or a red circle or square or rectangle on a different background. At the moment when an individual shape or color appeared, specific brain cells showed the greatest level of response. The moment when the image (square, circle, rectangle) shifted from one form or color to another was another trigger that activated specific brain cells. It's interesting because you know that painters (and viewers) are influenced by biological responses that are beyond their control (see Stevens' chapter in Part 4). Artists are not only responding to their own inner demons!

The creative process: a process of crystallization

Que croyez-vous que soit un artiste? Un imbécile qui n'a que des yeux s'il est peintre, des oreilles s'il est musicien, ou une lyre à tous les étages du coeur s'il est poète, ou même, s'il est boxeur, seulement des muscles?

Picasso, 1945
(from a conversation between P. Picasso and F. Gilot)

[What do you think is an artist?—An imbecile who has nothing but eyes if he is a painter, nothing but ears if he is a musician, or just a muse at all levels of the heart if he is a poet, or even just muscles if he is a boxer?]

Art is not only for the stupid, for people who cannot do anything else, as many people think. But the language of art is one that is not well known. I remember that Picasso used to say, 'Well, because people do not read Chinese that doesn't prove that Mandarin Chinese is not a beautiful way of writing; it's ideo-grammatic. Unless you know the Chinese symbolic way of picture writing, then what can you say against it?'

Each artist wants to communicate his or her vision. Vision is an important word in an artist's vocabulary. Of course that vision is such that it is not a language, in the sense that artists do not use words. Nevertheless, artists and critics alike talk about the language of art. The syntax of art—the way that images, symbols, etc. in this picture writing are put together—is not at all arbitrary. Calligraphic marks have a complex interaction. For example, if you take one line, and that line is horizontal, it's at rest. Nobody can see that horizontal line as active. If you have a line that is vertical, then it becomes more interesting because your eye must travel up and down. If the line is diagonal or zigzag, it is even more active. Everybody would agree, but not everyone thinks about lines. They are so elementary that every artist includes them as a part of the basic vocabulary. Other elements are also fundamental—shape, form, size and color. Through color interaction, the modern artist creates space. In modern art, we have abandoned any diagonals suggesting perspective. It is strictly with color that we find ways of giving a sensation of coming toward or going away.

I am a colorist, but during the wartime, my paintings were dark. Red, for me, is intensity; blue is a minor key. Colors convey a mood as well as location of forms in space. Each artist manipulates the basic elements, as well as many others, as a visual vocabulary to make statements, because the painter wants to have an impact on the brain of the viewer in order to convey his or her own unique vision.

What the viewer brings to the work of art will have an influence on his or her reaction. Whether they really dislike the art depends on what cultural 'baggage' they bring to it. If I am knowledgeable about music, I might read the score before I go to hear the concert, but if I am not, I might just want to go to the concert and listen to the music. I will not get all the subtleties of whatever is there, but I will get enough of it for the music to have an effect on me. Visual art is much the same. The more knowledgeable the viewer is, the more the viewer receives.

Entering into a dialogue with the canvas

As an artist, I have developed through the exploration of space and form, color and light, line and texture. I have a great appreciation of how these elements tend to gravitate towards balance. When such an equilibrium is achieved, the work has what I call its own inner logic (Plate 1).

Art might come from the unconscious, but once marks are put on the canvas, the canvas takes on a life of its own. As long as you only elaborate on your thoughts or feelings, or what is within, and brood about them, this rapport with an external object just doesn't exist. So for the painter, the problem is that he or she must have everything come together in a way that is true to the inner self and yet enters into a dialogue with the canvas, which is an object that is wholly outside and has a phenomenal reality of its own. I determine the size of the canvas; but I don't have it under my complete control. Many things are there even before I start putting anything on the canvas, like the square or rectangle of the canvas. The geometry of the shape of the canvas is important—the relationship of its length to its width, for example.

Even if I have already a vision, a vision is a result, and starting painting is a process. I am here, I am not there, so I have to find a way to get there by starting somewhere. Once I have put the first color or form, everything will follow. After that, it is a dialogue with the canvas.

I think about another line, another form. Perhaps a triangle? Ah, that poses more problems. What type of a triangle should it be: a rectangular triangle or an equilateral triangle? Should it be textured? A color or black and white? Will the impact be different from that of the first circle, or should it be? Red is a primary color. Should the triangle be yellow or white or red? What size should it be and where should I put it?

I paint with my mind and my body

I start with my feelings and emotions and with a theme in my head, even though I am not aware of it intentionally or rationally. It springs from the unconscious, of its own accord. I introduce an unusual tone or a form, such as a purple circle; that in turn leads to something else. Often in the same day, I will work on three or four different paintings to multiply the possibilities of interaction in each and in one to the other.

In this process of creation I will use my mind and body both consciously and spontaneously. Often the artist doesn't create only for aesthetic purposes, or for catharsis, but paints to reveal himself or herself and his vision of the world and—I think—his or her ideas, beliefs and passions. The painter as a human being is a body–mind continuum.

Seeing through an artist's eye

Painting is a product of the imagination projected onto a continuous or discontinuous surface. When I say 'continuous surface,' I am thinking of the cave paintings at Lascaux, where the surface is part of the environment. You have a stone, you start marking. Even gorillas in the zoo make marks; it must have been in our DNA for quite some time. About 30 000 years ago, men and women—women were also cave painters—were living and leaving their marks in caves or on cliffs. Or the continuous space might be a space like the Villa of the Mysteries in Pompeii where the painting is incorporated into the room. There is no point where the painting begins; the four walls are a part of a process of initiation that must be experienced to become whole. Since cubism, painting is about space. Modern artists paint on a discontinuous surface which can be geometric (square, circular, triangular, etc.) or even three-dimensional. Rauschenberg and Jasper Johns are two contemporary artists who create in three dimensions. The puzzle is that their work is still painting, not sculpture. The work is physically in three dimensions, but the mind accepts the art as two-dimensional.

Seeing is more than a visual experience; perception is more than a function of just one sense. For example, Henri Matisse was one of the greatest modern painters, and he was extremely myopic; he really didn't see very well. Yet his canvases are full of light and color, and a conscious awareness of space and form. Visual perception is more than just seeing with the eyes. More through touching than through seeing, Henri Matisse saw the world around him. And in canvases like *Water Lilies* (1905), Claude Monet, one of the impressionists whose work preceded that of Matisse, broke up light and color to show that seeing is not a fixed perspective but the synthesis of visual experiences that are not frozen, but constantly changing. A painter sees with his whole body.

Perception is more than a purely physical visual experience. How the painter sees is also related to the moods and emotions of the artist as an individual and to the artist's relationship to society, nature, objects, ideas and beliefs. Positive feelings are: narcissism, introspection, love, altruism or participation. Negative feelings are: frustration, resentment, hate, social criticism, satire, even caricature. There also is positive energy: sex drive, power drive and cosmic energy. Negative energy is: conflict, aggression, decay. When I say positive or negative, I don't imply a moral judgment; strong work can arise from negative feelings like *The Disasters of War* by Goya or *Guernica* by Picasso. The artist's internal passions and power interact with cosmic forces to establish a new way of seeing that is different from—and yet fundamental to—the limited perspective of the ordinary world. To see a new way is to use the full continuum of mind and body. Feelings can lead the painter astray, but through his passions, the artist can break through his limitations and habits to reveal depths beyond the reach of his ordinary perceptions.

Towards an aesthetic theory of art

Here is an experiment I share with my students. I explain that when you think about art, it is like grabbing at a towel. You have to reach out for any part of the towel that you can grasp. You can start a painting either with something geometric, or something fairly mathematical. You can divide the space of the canvas into different sections. You can begin with a proposition of some kind which is fairly abstract and only in your head. That's fine. Or you can grab a certain amount of color and just throw it. That will result in chaos, but you can just as well start with chaos. I mean, there is no one way to start that is better or worse than any other way. Just start.

All the artist seeks is within that artist. That is why I say painting is a kind of a debate with the unknown. Nor am I the only artist to express these feelings. In a way, there is something more than being empirical or rational about art. A currently popular phrase, the art of the unconscious, is true.

Each time the painter begins a painting, even if the previous painting was the most beautiful painting, the painter standing before the empty canvas is again at zero, absolute zero. Serendipity plays an important role in art. I limit the number of elements that I introduce into my canvas, and aim to keep focused and within certain boundary lines. And even though I consciously try not to just drift away or drift along, the painting is not simply in the artist's head. Something also happens on the canvas which transforms the vision.

The eureka element

Painting is physical: it has a certain amount of thickness or transparency. In spite of keeping focused and trying to create within the boundary lines, there are all kinds of elements that cannot be quantified. The best solution does not only come from keeping within those bounds. Even a painter who is possessed— who has an idea in mind and who cannot allow any other idea to get in his way—can look at his canvas and acknowledge that suddenly something unexpected has happened. It is possible to remain focused and still combine elements in a way that is new, but you must always expect the unexpected. The unknown hides there, and when it appears, the painter ascends to a higher level.

So the painter begins at a level that is fairly pedestrian and uses a limited number of devices to get started. At a certain point, something *gels* and the painting is no longer just intellectual ideas, or just mathematical thoughts, or just the structure of a cell or crystal, or a tangential reference to your own knowledge of art of the past or present, or even an expression of your own will to create this or that. Something begins to be there and it is an unknown.

The old is familiar and comfortable. We should always be so pleased when we do something we have never seen before, but in fact the artist is not pleased. It is reassuring when a painting looks a bit like another painter's work because then it is easy. You can say: 'Well it can't be all bad, you know, if it looks something like—I don't know which other painter—but one that is familiar.' If that painter is recognized, then your painting will be praised. But when you have seen something new that has not ever been seen, not even in your own painting, the thing there is completely foreign. How can a painter make sense of this new creation? How can a painter or critic evaluate it? That is the dilemma, and the intensity and strength of a painter is measured by the artist's capacity to venture into that unknown region—beyond the conscious intellect and beyond that which is only in your head and beyond that which is barely a part of your previous paintings, something you can't recognize: re-cognize.

The integrity of the canvas

When I was a child, I often asked my mother, 'What is behind the canvas?' She would say, 'Aren't you stupid, it's the canvas itself.' I said, 'But I would like to see something there on the other side. What is there?' The history of painting is based on the illusion that the canvas itself is the starting point for the artist. Painting is about space, and all pictorial space has always begun with the surface of the canvas. Having said that, there is something very bizarre about Rembrandt's painting *The Anatomy Lesson* that hangs in Amsterdam. It's eerie. You have all those people around the corpse, and the corpse has an open wound. In one way, the wound in the body is also a wound in the canvas and the viewer can go through the layers of the canvas to something that is behind the surface of that canvas. So, I thought to myself that breaking the surface of the canvas in a traditional painting does not always destroy the pictorial illusion, especially not in Rembrandt's masterpiece.

There always has been a suggestion that, when a painting touches on something very important in human terms, the illusion of the canvas is pierced and goes beyond mere representation to incorporate a greater reality. I believe that is what Lucio Fontana did when he broke free from narrow aesthetic conventions that decreed that the canvas of a painting must be the starting point for the artist.

In 1949, Fontana slashed, slit, burned and tore his canvases to create a new dimension of space. I think when Lucio Fontana lacerated his canvases, he broke down long-established conventions and showed that painting is not just the surface of the canvas. That is just preconception, a convention—today, we can go right through the canvas and break down the artificial differences between painting and sculpture. By breaking away from conventional thinking, Fontana showed us more than a new way to paint—he opened up a new way of seeing.

> *Art is not decorative. It has to be existential—it is a way to understand oneself; and also to have a transforming effect on others. People rarely get in touch with the forces of the universe. That is what I attempt to do. I am not interested by the latest fad in art. I want to fulfill my own destiny as an artist and to do what comes to me as a global vision.*
>
> Françoise Gilot, 1993

The interactive viewer

> *'But what can a man 'create' if he doesn't happen to be a poet? . . . If you have nothing at all to create, then perhaps you create yourself.' And imagination is a true creative power from which destiny itself is bodied forth.*
>
> A.S. Huffington, 1993

Each viewer responds in his or her own individual way to a work of art. Naturally, the viewer will respond more positively to an artist who is in harmony with his or her perspective. For example, a viewer who is very sensuous will respond positively to a painter who is also very sensuous. A voluptuous, flesh-toned nude by Titian, like *Venus of Urbino* (1538)—which became the touchstone for Manet's brilliant portrayal of a nude in *Olympia* (1863)—will appeal to such viewers. However, a puritanical viewer might feel that his or her comfortable values were being threatened and would respond positively instead to a grey-toned, semi-abstract portrait by James McNeill Whistler, such as *The Artist's Mother*.

There are many different families of paintings—I call them families because I am a painter, not an art historian, even if I have been in some small way a part of art history. You can also say, as I do, that there are families of viewers. Expressionism is a family of painting, geometric abstraction is another family; there are as many different families of viewers as there are families of paintings. Not everybody is obliged to like Leonardo's *Mona Lisa*, nor equally must everyone be quick to admire Marcel Duchamp's irreverent Dadaist version *L.H.O.O.Q.* (phonetically 'elle a chaud au cul' [she is in heat]), which is a reproduction of the *Mona Lisa* with an Inspector Poirot-like mustache and beard added in pencil. I think it is very important to understand that not every individual has to empathize with each individual work of art, or even with all artists. Each work of art is a message in a bottle that the painter sends to sea, and it will be received by certain individuals and not by others.

In the nineteenth century, the viewer became extremely lazy because the over-refined sophistication of nineteenth-century painting had robbed him or her of the need to be active. Everything was finished ad nauseum; the viewer became a mere spectator, given all answers without any effort on his part. So, what does the painter do now? Like a writer in a detective story, the painter gives the viewer a few clues, and if he is clever enough the viewer will use his imagination to understand the result. I will give you 50 per cent of what I have to say, and you will find the rest. Now, it's much more interesting because in the process of viewing the painting, the viewer also has created something. The artist has created the capacity to find out what the painting is all about. So, the viewers should be capable of being attentive. If not attentive, they will probably miss everything that is important.

There are people who go to see contemporary art knowing in advance they won't like it: their minds are closed. They are not going to empathize with the painting, and they will see nothing there. Of course, if they tell themselves that before they go, certainly they are not going to enjoy anything! If they go with an open mind, they might have either a negative or a positive reaction—perhaps that reaction will be elaborated upon later—but what they perceive energizes them as a viewer, and their participation becomes their own creation. I believe this point is quite important. The painter is not operating in a vacuum; the artist is operating in society. And that is true even if a painter is not recognized in his or her own time.

Today, in the Vincent Van Gogh Museum in Amsterdam, young artists are translating paintings such as *The Potato Eaters* (1885) into three-dimensional constructions. His sunflowers are modern icons; his paintings can cost millions. But when he painted *Bedroom at Arles*, certainly he was not recognized. Nevertheless, some women in Arles sat for him and had their portraits made—and so did the postman and the soldier in the spahi uniform. The expressive genius of painters like Van Gogh was not possible without that minimum of consensus, that little complicity between other people and the artists who capture their image in paint. When the artists' models are simple folks, they are more capable of giving credit to the artist; perhaps they believe when they look at what the artist has painted, they *might* be that way.

So, art will advance only if those who are not artists are open-minded enough to think art might have a purpose, might show something never seen before and might also add to their knowledge of society, the human being, the great myth or whatever. Today, painting is simpler, but the role of the viewer is ever more complex.

The viewer as co-creator

Painting has become a performing art. Today, everything the painter does is only the beginning. Once the painting is finished, the painter can be dismissed—and then what happens? Well, the painting might sit in the attic for a while (but I'm not talking about that), or it might go to an art gallery, a public space or a museum where other people are going to select that painting rather than another. Then people are going to write about it, talk about it, redefine it in their own terms. Their opinions are added to whatever was initially there on the canvas. When the painting achieves immortality, it is apt to become an image on a T-shirt, or a part of another artist's painting. Nowadays, art becomes redefined, re-viewed and part of an ongoing public performance.

The philosopher, Heidegger (who speaks of human understanding), says that when we look at a sculpture from ancient Greece, what we are looking at is not at all an individual piece of marble or an individual work of art. What we are looking at is all the history that went on from then until now; we are looking at all the opinions we have about that culture as we know it. So, the inevitable meanings that are added to the object the artist created are endless multiples and re-evaluations of the original. Perhaps (and this is my thought, not Heidegger's), science has become speculative and art, empirical, because art is no longer what the artist discovers, but the creation of artist and viewer.

Perhaps it is an illusion that the human mind can have any direct access to a greater understanding. As we discussed earlier, an artist's perceptions are based on each artist's insights into the advances made by scientists, on the whole spectrum of the artist's mind and body, on a synthesis of the rational and intuitive, and on a symbolic form of communication which is a unique language that—like all languages—is ever evolving. The art of painting—which incorporates a tradition dating back to the fourteenth century—is an activity which is extremely, essentially human. Even though the artist must be alone to create, he or she must remain part of society because, first of all, as Marcel Proust said, 'There is no art without neurosis.' If we were all well-balanced, why should we spend hours doing crazy things? But the artist resolves all those inner conflicts.

Aware of the advances made by scientists, aware of their own emotions, artists bring a new perspective that is not a decoration, not just an ornamental guilding of received knowledge, and not just a little something you can have if time permits. No, no! It's very essential because it has to do with the basic aspects of human nature—both physiologically and psychologically—as well as the many different social ramifications. And it's a kind of mediation between the individual, nature and society, so to speak, through which we can find an order that will enrich the imagination and lead to new, more complex truths.

CHARLES F. STEVENS

Line versus color: the brain and the language of visual arts

Because we perceive and appreciate art with our brain, its structure and function naturally define the boundaries of the aesthetic experience.

Charles Stevens, 1993

When neuroscientists began to study the visual system with modern techniques—ones that permit us to monitor the responses of single neurons embedded in the brain—they discovered that the brain handles information about the edges in an image separately and quite differently from that about color and texture. The goal of this chapter is to explain how the mechanisms used by the brain to process images, such as the representation of an image in terms of edges and color, can determine the pictorial language of the visual arts. To explain what I mean by this, I will describe the building blocks of the nervous system, summarize how visual images are represented in the brain, and briefly explore the implication for artists and the way that they construct their images.

Much of art involves abstracting reality. The images created by even the most representational artists are not literal copies of the world, but rather these images are an abstraction that makes use of selected qualities of the subject. At least some of the ways in which this abstraction is carried out is not the product of free choice; instead, our abstraction of reality is determined by the way that our brain transforms the world that we see, or the sorts of transformations our brain applies to the world we perceive. For example, painters have always realized that how we see strongly influences what we see.

A key component of creativity in art (or science) involves the skillful handling of a number of formal elements, such as line and color. However, because of the way the brain processes visual images, the artist is not free to define the formal elements to be used; this choice is made from among a range of elements that are 'natural'. To explain this further I will begin with a few specific examples.

Seeing faces

Figure 4.1 shows a famous self-portrait of Rembrandt done toward the end of his life. If you have seen it before, you will recognize Rembrandt instantly. Figure 4.2 is a very simple line drawing of the same image. Although the drawing bears almost no literal resemblance to the painting, you can again instantly recognize Rembrandt and tell that the line drawing is 'the same' image as the painting. We so easily and effortlessly recognize line drawings that we are not even aware of how different they are from the original image, nor can we appreciate how difficult it is for a computer to tell that the self-portrait and the line drawing are 'the same'. My claim is that our instant recognition of line drawings reveals a fundamental aspect of the way images are represented by the brain.

For us to recognize a face, it is enough that the face be abstracted to just a few special lines such as those defining the eyes, the mouth, and the nose. But our visual system also makes use of other types of image processing, which is revealed by the fact that we can recognize a face represented in an image devoid of any lines. Figure 4.3 is an image, constructed by Leon Harmon in the 1970s, defined by equal-sized boxes and with no lines at all (except the edges of the boxes), and yet we instantly recognize this as a picture of Abraham Lincoln (although you might have to squint or move farther away to see the face most clearly). More recently, Chuck Close has very effectively exploited this type of abstracted representation by creating portraits in which a face is constructed of pixels made from his fingerprints, with different degrees of lightness and darkness (Fig. 4.4). Again, we are so good at recognizing highly abstracted images of faces that we do not ever know that this is hard to do—at least for a computer.

Line versus color: the great debate

About a quarter of a century after the Rembrandt self-portrait was painted, late in the seventeenth century, the French Academy was founded. The Academy provided a forum for an ongoing debate about the superiority of line versus color (see Gilot's chapter). This argument raged through to the end of the nineteenth century and beyond. 'The eternal battle between drawing and color' was how Matisse referred to this long-lasting dispute. The paintings by Rubens were taken to exemplify the importance of color, and those by Poussin the superiority of the use of lines. Although these two artists were silent proponents of the two opposing schools of thought, by the nineteenth century, the painters themselves were noisily involved in the debate. For example, Ingres believed that line was superior, and Delacroix championed color.

The line/color debate took on moral and philosophical overtones as it became involved with other issues such as notions about rationality and

Fig. 4.1 Rembrandt, self-portrait (detail), 1669. (National Gallery, London.)

Fig. 4.2 Line drawing of Rembrandt's self-portrait.

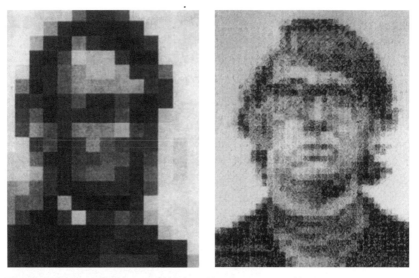

Fig. 4.3 *(Left)* Large-pixel image of Abraham Lincoln, constructed by Leon Harmon. (Courtesy Leon Harmon; copyright Scientific American.)

Fig. 4.4 *(Right)* Chuck Close, No. 6 in *Keith Series*, 1979. (Reynolda House, Museum of American Art, Winston–Salem.)

irrationality, coolness and emotionality, and so forth. The line, always recognized as an element difficult to master, was linked with the intellect, while color—with its evocative quality, its mysterious qualia—was coupled with the emotions. Thus, line was thought to be cool and rational, while color was viewed as passionate and irrational.

Modern art has extended and embellished this debate by selecting one element or another, and focusing mainly on the manipulation of this one dominant element. Mark Rothko, for example, produced beautiful large-scale canvases that are devoid of almost everything except huge patches of color. In works after the late 1940s, his floating, colored rectangles are compellingly beautiful in their simplicity and their juxtaposition of glorious colors. Lines are essentially eliminated from these paintings, and even the edges of the rectangles are blurred or indistinct. Rothko, then, worked with fields of pure color and explored the aesthetic limits of what could be achieved through the manipulation of this one formal element. Conversely, Franz Klein came to prominence in the 1950s with his large paintings dominated by black calligraphic brush strokes on a white canvas. Fascinated by drawing, he enlarged small sketches until they filled the canvas with abstract images that, in a sense, represent a limiting case of the line-is-superior position while simultaneously negating it through the use of linear elements that have become massive objects.

I claim that artists did not choose to manipulate those two formal elements —line and color (among others, of course)—by chance. Quite the contrary. Their choice was determined by physiology, by the processes our brains use to analyze the images that are presented to us.

How we see: some general principles

In order to explain how brain mechanisms limit the formal elements that can be used by artists to abstract images, I need to describe the primary steps in the transmission of visual information to the nervous system.

One of the most important organizing principles of the brain is encapsulated in the doctrine of localization of function. This doctrine is the modern counterpart of nineteenth-century phrenology and holds that each function carried out by the brain has its own distinct anatomical site. Thus, the nerve cells devoted to processing visual information are grouped together, as are the nerve cells for processing sounds or smells. We have visual parts of the brain, auditory parts, emotional parts, etc.

The localization of function exists on many different levels. That is, distinct parts of the brain are devoted to visual information processing, but within these large visual areas are many subareas that carry out particular jobs, and within these subareas are still smaller subareas, each with its specific computation role in image analysis. Visual information is processed simultaneously by at least three dozen anatomically distinct brain regions. For example, one particular region is concerned with processing information about motion, and another with the recognition of faces. If the face recognition region is damaged on both sides of the brain—as happens very occasionally with strokes or other injuries—the injured person can still identify an object as a face and can tell the parts of the face (nose, mouth, etc), but has no idea whose face it is, even if it is their own.

Figure 4.5a presents a highly simplified view of the anatomy of the initial stages of the visual system. The visual world is shown as a screen with the letter 'A' on it. That visual world, in turn, gets mapped onto another surface at the back of the eye, the *retina* (shown in Fig. 4.5a). Because of the optics of the eye, the 'A' appears turned upside down; everything in the visual world is projected onto the retina like an image onto camera film. In the retina, light falls on a two-dimensional array of specialized nerve cells (called *photoreceptor cells*) that detect the light and resolve the image into individual points. Each photo-receptor cell passes information about the light intensity it receives on to other nerve cells in the retina and then along nerve fibers (axons) to the cerebral cortex, in the form of electrical signals. In other words, sending visual infor-mation from the retina to the cortex necessitates that the images be encoded as a spatial and temporal pattern of nerve impulses.

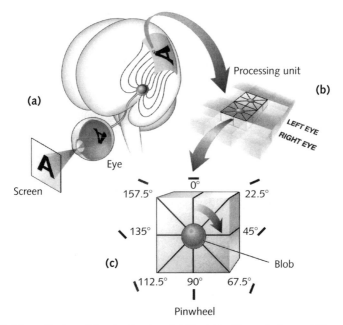

Fig. 4.5 Schematic view of the visual system. (a) The letter 'A' seen in the world is projected upside-down onto the eye's retina. Corresponding visual signals reach the brain via the optic nerve for further processing. Mapping of responding neurons in the primary visual cortex again reveals the shape of the 'A'. (b) Cortical processing units separate right-eye and left-eye neurons. (c) Pinwheel arrangement of neurons that respond to line orientations.

Structures and mechanisms: how the retina works

The eye is not just a camera. That is, the brain does not receive a 'raw' image from the eyes, but rather a highly filtered version of the image that is broken down into component parts. In the following, I describe briefly the first steps in the filtering of visual information by the nervous system. Our understanding begins with the eye's light-sensitive structure, the retina.

When light falls on the photoreceptors, special pigments absorb it so that the image is resolved into its color components. The mechanisms involved in color vision are now well understood. Three different kinds of visual pigment molecules—one type for each class of photoreceptor cell—are each designed to absorb best the light of one particular color. Due to differences in the chemical structure of these pigment molecules, one class of the photoreceptors is especially sensitive to red light, another to green light, and the third to blue light. These different pigment molecules enable the photoreceptors to transform the light signals into chemical signals—how much chemical tells how bright the light, and which cell contains the chemical tells where the light is and how much of a particular color it contains (how red, for example). Such chemical signals are then transformed into nerve impulses and transmitted to subsequent neurons in the visual pathway.

Because the photoreceptors form an ordered, two-dimensional array, the image projected onto the retina is resolved into component points (or picture elements, 'pixels'). Each point is broken down further into colors. For each pixel, the incoming photons are absorbed, as already described, by the pigments of specific color photoreceptor cells ('cones'): the red components of the image are best absorbed by the red cones, the green by the green cones, and the blue by the blue cones. Therefore, during transformation into chemical signals, the image is resolved into component points and each point into its three component colors. Although the image is no longer intact, the brain does get information on the light intensities, divided into three color signals, at all of its points. If you have those three color signals, you can recombine them and figure out what the color of the incoming light was. Basically, how the nervous system resolves and encodes the colors of an image is a concept familiar to us from color television with its closely spaced red, green, and blue dots.

The density of photoreceptor cells is not constant over the retina but rather highest in the center and progressively lower towards the retina's edges. Because of this arrangement, we have the sharpest vision in the middle of the retina and center of our visual image, and vision becomes progressively less sharp towards the edges of the visual field. The size of our optic nerve—the bundle of nerve fibers that carries visual information back to the brain—limits the amount of information that can be transmitted (sets the band width, in the modern terminology), and so the eye compromises by providing more information about the center of our visual field and much less about the periphery.

These mechanisms explain how a visual image is broken down into a very large number of picture elements and how, for each one of these elements, information about the light intensity and color—encoded as electrical pulses—is relayed from the eye to the brain.

The primary visual cortex: how visual information is processed

> . . . in the visual system, there is complex transformation of neural information at all levels in the system and progressively greater abstraction as information ascends into the higher centers. Thus, whereas aspects of tactile perception literally reside in the hand of the perceiver, visual

perception resides largely in the abstracting capabilities of the neurons of the brain.

Kandel, 1981

The signals from the retina go first to a special brain region—a 'relay nucleus', called the 'lateral geniculate body'—and then are passed on to the visual cortex (see Fig. 4.5a). Throughout this process of relaying visual information, the neighbor relations between retinal cells are preserved all the way back to cortex, so that a version of the retinal image is formed, as nerve impulse activity, on the visual cortex; this is indicated by the letter 'A' on the cortex in Fig. 4.5a. The primary visual cortex lies at the back of the brain, as illustrated in Fig. 4.5a, and receives visual information from the eye. This first visual cortex then relays processed visual information to the three dozen other specialized cortical visual areas.

The retinal image (in our case an 'A') is 'projected' onto the primary visual cortex, like onto a screen, as a pattern of nerve cell activity. 'Projected' here means that nerve fibers or axons carrying information from the top of the 'A' in the retina, for example, can be traced anatomically and functionally to the corresponding part of the 'A' in the primary visual cortex. It follows that each nerve cell in the primary visual cortex is involved in analyzing data from one particular part of the retina, the cortical cell's *receptive field*.

Just how is the visual image represented on the visual cortex? Consider a piece of the cortex, about 2 by 2 millimeters wide on the surface and approximately 2.5 millimeters deep (or about 10 cubic millimeters in volume) that forms, as we shall see, the basic processing unit. (To picture the size of this elementary processing region in the cortex, consider that the volume of a grain of rice is just about 10 cubic millimeters). This unit receives information from one small region of the retina and thus from a small part of the visual world. A specific elementary cortical region might, for example, be responsible for the corner of the 'A' as shown in the detail in Fig. 4.5a. The entire visual cortex is made up of such elementary processing units.

In summary, the light from every little region of the visual world is encoded by nerve impulse signals in the retina, and each of these signals is sent to a specific processing unit in the primary visual cortex where it is analyzed as will now be described.

Let us now examine how the visual information is actually represented in the primary visual cortex. To do this, we need to review a little about the cellular organization of cortex. The 10-cubic-millimeter processing unit of the visual cortex contains about 2 million nerve cells. Those 2 million neurons are

hooked together in complex circuits. Only about 5 to 10 per cent of the signals
—the nerve impulses flowing in the circuits of this unit—are coming directly
from the retina; all the rest are generated in the cortex itself as part of the image
processing.

Information flows from one nerve cell to the next at a special point of contact
called a *synapse*. There are about 20 billion synapses in a 10-cubic-millimeter
processing unit, so each of the 2 million nerve cells contained in the unit is
receiving information from about 10 000 other nerve cells. Most of these
10 000 nerve cells that supply synapses to a particular neuron are within this
cortical unit, but a significant fraction reside in neighboring regions and, thus,
are farther away. Perhaps 5 to 10 per cent of the 20 billion synapses in the unit
are transmitting information which arrives directly from the retina, whereas all
the rest carry further processed information. The formation of neuronal
circuits requires nerve fibers or 'wires,' and there are about 40 miles of 'wire'
inside this 10-cubic-millimeter bit of cortex.

Organization of the visual cortex

Neuroscientists can record electrical signals from individual cortical nerve cells
in living, even awake, animals, as images are processed by the animal's visual
cortex. If one records from a neuron in the visual cortex and then shines a tiny
spot of light on the corresponding part of the retina, hardly any change in electrical activity of the nerve cell can be detected; neurons in the visual cortex
essentially ignore individual spots of light. Rather, they respond selectively to
particular aspects in the visual world.

To understand this lack of response to a spot of light more fully, we must consider the fact that each cortical processing unit is subdivided in three main ways
(see Figs. 4.5b and c). The *first* subdivision separates the left eye's input from
that of the right eye as follows: the visual world that falls on each retina is split
so that everything in the right half of the visual field (i.e. projected onto the left
half of the left- and right-eye retinas) goes to the left part of the brain, and
everything in the left half of the visual field is sent to the right part of the brain.
In this small cube of cortex, some cells respond only (or mostly) to signals from
the right eye, and others respond to signals from the left eye. The information
arriving in the visual cortex from the two eyes is kept separate so that we can
use the slight differences in the two images to extract information about the
three-dimensional nature of the world from the two-dimensional projections
on each retina. According to the localization of function, the right-eye and left-
eye neurons are separated into left-and right-eye stripes in the visual cortex as
shown in the detail of Fig. 4.5b.

Seeing lines versus seeing color

If an animal views a large red or green piece of paper, most cells in the cortical processing units already described ignore it totally; most of the neurons in the visual cortex are color blind. The circuits in the visual cortex are designed so that most of the cells there respond—that is, produce nerve impulses—only to an edge or line. And a particular cell will only respond if the line has a specific position and orientation in the visual world. That is, visual cortical neurons have the property of 'orientation tuning' which means that each cell responds selectively to a line or edge with a particular orientation (angle with respect to the perpendicular) at a particular location in the visual world. The cells are arranged in the cortex so that neighboring cortical neurons respond to the same orientation (localization of function, again), but all orientations are represented within each processing unit. Neurons that respond to line orientations are arranged as a 'pinwheel' with each vane of the pinwheel being devoted to a single orientation. As one proceeds around the pinwheel, one finds neurons that respond selectively to all line orientations as shown in Fig. 4.5c. Pinwheels constitute the *second* main organizational component of the visual cortex.

Overall then, what is happening to the visual information between the retina and the primary visual cortex? The signals from the left and the right eyes, which represent not exactly the same information because the eyes are slightly apart, are being kept separate so that different small regions of the cortex work on right-eye and left-eye information, respectively.

Returning to the line–color disputes that raged in the French Academy, the Ingres camp could argue today that line is superior because it is most natural: a line drawing is representing an image the way the brain does. That is, a line drawing 'works' because it taps directly into the way the cortex represents visual images. But where, then, does that leave the modern descendents of the Delacroix camp? How is color represented? The color information is not lost when it reaches the visual cortex, as might be thought from the preceding discussion; it is just processed separately, in anatomically distinct groups of cells that constitute the *third* component of each processing unit.

The area shown at the center of each pinwheel in Fig. 4.5c is called a 'blob'. 'Blobs' are clusters of nerve cells that stand out when treated with a special histological stain because they contain more of a specific metabolic enzyme than the other cells. The 'blobs' of the cortex are about a third of a millimeter across, and this is where color information is processed. The cells in these blobs represent orientation information in a less organized way than the pinwheel neurons, but they respond strongly to color, although in a rather complicated way. That is, they do not report colors as simply red, green, or blue as do photoreceptors in the retina, but usually respond to several colors at once in a way that is completely orderly but too complicated to discuss here. A detailed examination of the way in which these cells respond to combinations of colors provides insight into how neighboring colors influence one another perceptually, and give a physiological rationale for the formal manipulation of color relations by artists such as Albers. The main point to be made here is that color information is kept separate in the brain and processed by a separate pathway.

Joseph Albers, who is known for his formal manipulation of color relations in his series '*Homage to the Square*', taught a famous course in design when he was a member of the Yale Faculty. One of the Albers exercises was intended to develop facility in the manipulation of lines. Albers would decorate the studio with long strips of paper twisted in complicated spatial patterns and ask the students to represent the complex paper object by just drawing edges of the paper in a way that would capture the three-dimensional feeling of the object. In this exercise, he was exploiting the edge-detection cortical circuits and training the students to manipulate this 'natural' formal element. Another set of exercises required students to manipulate only color relations in order to teach facility with the formal element represented in the 'blob' region of their cortex. In saying, 'We do not see colors as they really are. In perception they alter one another,' Joseph Albers was describing properties of cells in the blob system.

> From experiences of one kind or another shapes and colors come to me very clearly—sometimes I start in a very realistic fashion and as I go on from one painting after another of the same thing, it becomes simplified till it can be nothing but abstract—but for me it is my reason for painting I suppose. At the moment, I am very annoyed. I have the shapes on yellow scratch paper in my mind for over a year and I cannot see the color for them, I've drawn them again—and again—it is from something I have heard again and again till I hear it in the wind but I cannot get the color for it—only shapes—None of this makes sense—but no matter.
>
> Georgia O'Keeffe (1957), in Cowart and Hamilton, 1987

Georgia O'Keeffe's inspiration comes from her drawings which are then abstracted to emphasize relations between formal elements of the original that can be understood in terms of line as well as color.

Higher-order processing of images in the visual cortex and the arts

To this point, I have described a little of what is known about the processing of visual images in the first of three dozen cortical regions devoted to vision. In these later visual areas, extensive interactions occur between the different types of visual information (e.g. color versus line). In some areas of the visual cortex, probably as a result of these extensive interactions, individual neurons respond selectively to image elements of remarkable complexity and of special, social importance.

Before considering this higher-order processing, let me recapitulate the main points made so far about the brain representation of images. Our eye breaks each small region of an image into three component colors. Then we encode the light intensities of those three colors as nerve impulses and send them to a structure in the middle of the brain, the lateral geniculate body. From there, the information gets relayed to the primary visual cortex. At this first level, the image is analyzed further in at least three ways:

(1) Edge or line orientation. Which cells are responding tells you which direction the edge or line is pointing and where that edge is located in the visual world.

(2) The image is also broken down into colors, but at this level in the cortex, the color representation is more complicated than just the basic red, green, and blue of the retinal photoreceptors.

(3) Finally, the image also is decomposed into left-eye and right-eye signals.

Then what happens? The information is sent from the primary visual cortex to many other regions. Each one of these regions is also sending information back to the primary visual cortex so that even the initial processing is influenced by later stages in the system. In these later regions, information about different aspects of the image continues to be processed separately, but at each stage of processing is informed by results of other computations on the image. In general, the higher visual regions are separated into two image-processing streams—one concerned more with 'what', and the other more with 'where'. Color, for example is most richly represented in the 'what' stream and motion in the 'where' stream.

As one progresses to higher visual analysis areas, the cortical neurons respond to ever more complex stimuli. For example, in a part of the brain called 'inferotemporal cortex,' the cells respond to neither line nor color, but to complicated stimuli such as faces or to elements of a face as noted earlier. Thus, some cells in these higher areas respond particularly well to a mouth or to eye-like images; others, to symmetric complex images (note the importance of symmetry in art).

It was not just by chance that I used the face in my initial examples. Had I used a colored picture of a very complicated, three-dimensional object that was totally unfamiliar, the representation of that complex object with three or four arbitrary lines would not have been so immediately recognizable. Instead, I used a familiar Rembrandt self-portrait and anticipated that it would be instantly recognizable. Nor was identifying the sketch of that painting difficult. Faces are special because they are enormously important to us socially. The differences between the very beautiful and especially ugly face are actually tiny—a couple of millimeters here, and a few millimeters there. The fact that we can distinguish a beautiful face from an ugly one, or a copy of a famous painting of a well-known face from an original, is a testimony to the great power of the visual processing mechanisms specialized for objects of great social significance.

In closing, I would like to observe that the French Academy was really ahead of its time with its 200-year debate on the superiority of line versus color, because it put its finger on formal elements that are expressions of fundamental brain mechanisms. When we look at the world (or listen to it—a similar analysis could be carried out for audition, speech, and music), the mind uses an analytical process that breaks down extremely complex objects into simpler components that are suitable for the job at hand. This is what the French Academicians sensed. Modern neuroscience shows this analytical process is defined by the brain's circuitry, and that the brain decomposes what we see or hear into biologically predetermined components we can recognize.

The brain image-processing mechanisms underlying how we see determine what we see when we look at art and, I would claim, the function of other specific brain areas would dictate how we listen to music or read poetry. In other words, the language of the arts reveals the nature of information processing in the brain, and the arts in turn depend on these brain mechanisms to determine the ways art can abstract the world.

BENOIT B. MANDELBROT

The fractal universe

Of course, history cannot explain the mystery of the unreasonable effectiveness of mathematics . . . The mystery merely moves on and changes character. How can it be that the mixture of information, observation, and search for introspectively satisfying structures . . . should repeatedly yield themes so potent that . . . they continue to inspire effective developments in both physics and mathematics?

Benoit Mandelbrot, 1983

The education of a mathematical maverick

The hero is a loner. Like certain painters, he might be called a naive or a visionary, but there is a better term in American English: maverick

Benoit Mandelbrot, 1983

Allow me to be autobiographical because otherwise, this discussion would not hold together. I happen to have had a very peculiar education. Generally, this does not matter, but in my case it does matter very much. First of all, I did not go to school for grades 1 and 2. This is important, because much of the time I played chess and looked at maps. I also learned how to read fast, but my basic activities were geometric. Chess is very visual—and so is reading maps.

After finishing high school in the middle of the Second World War, I had an adventurous and difficult time keeping body and soul together. But I traveled around with a collection of science books I had found in the libraries of the people I knew in Tulle, a little town in central France where I had lived. Some of those books were very obsolete and, therefore, had illustrations. So, I lived in a universe in which the means of communication was an illustration, while discourse explained it or provided a proof. Hardly ever was a proof presented in the absence of illustration. Proof and picture were given together and, quite obviously, the student was expected to acquire fluency in a language in which the objects were not words and formulas—but shapes. This was a language that Galileo praised, as we shall see. I became good at it—a whiz, in fact!

The war ended. Like everybody else in France, at age twenty or so, I took the entrance exams to École Polytechnique and École Normale Supérieure. Those are killer exams in which the student is tested for proficiency in the manipulation of language, including symbols and formulas. My skills in those areas were poor. However, for every problem the teacher would pose, I thought immediately of a number of very strong, highly visual and sensual images. I could reason from these images directly, without the intermediary of words and formulas. This is how I solved the most difficult exam problems. One involved a triple integral, which no human can find algebraically in three hours under conditions of examination. I had no difficulty in reducing this integral because I visualized it as the volume of a sphere in suitable but very strange coordinates. So, I started adult life with this ability to speak the old, forgotten, and obsolete visual language of mathematics.

Unfortunately, an uncle told me that geometry was dead, that my skill was worthless, and that I had to learn the modern way of thinking because, otherwise, I would not get anywhere. To make matters worse—and the story better— this young brother of my father was a very prominent mathematician and a professor at the Collège de France, the top of academia in France. As a result, I did not immediately become a mathematician. In fact, I did something scandalous: École Normale Supérieure is the elitist institution that produces France's university professors; I was accepted but, after two days, decided that I didn't fit and quit. This was something so terrible that next to my name, many people's books include a very big black mark.

I had no real teacher, only a mentor, a man called Paul Lévy (the French probabilist, 1886–1972). 'Lévy had been kept at arm's length by the Establishment' (Mandelbrot, 1983), but eventually became very famous and widely recognized. I knew his work very well, but ours was a long-distance relationship. I also greatly admired John von Neumann, the eminent mathematician, who took me as his post-doctoral associate. He was very kind, but at the time much too concerned with high diplomacy and a possible war against the Russians.

I spent several years doing all kinds of things and became, in a certain sense, a specialist of odd and isolated phenomena—problems that my uncle, the Professor of Mathematics, was not interested in. I did not know or care in which field I was playing. I wanted to find a place, a new field, where I could be the first person to introduce mathematics. Formalization had gone too far, for my taste, in the mathematics favored by the 'establishment', but elsewhere had not even started.

I should mention an interesting aside. My uncle was a weekday pure mathematician, but a Sunday painter; his son is a physicist, but better known as a painter. Therefore, we all show evidence of gifts for abstract mathematics as well as for shapes. However, my uncle saw art and mathematics as totally separate fields whereas, for me, they were always indistinguishable.

Of mathematical languages

Galileo Galilei (the Italian mathematician, 1564–1642) became one of the fathers of modern natural science, especially physics and astronomy. An Arabic translation of texts by Euclid (the Greek mathematician and founder of geometry, about 330–270 BC) was first translated into Tuscan. In a wonderful book, Samuel Edgerton (1991) tells us a non-canonical but striking story: the well-known immense influence of Euclid on Galileo's thinking was mediated by the most unexpected intermediary of painting and architecture. The curious devices of Giotto, the painter and architect (*c.* 1267–1337), nearly grasped the true rules of perspective but missed a critical aspect; Euclid provided the missing element. Separation of space and action became characteristic of a phase of Italian painting. We are all familiar with some early Renaissance paintings like the martyred Saint Sebastian by Piero della Francesca (1420–1492), in which perspective is perfect and the vanishing point is almost overwhelming. Space is an abstract vessel lined by big walls.

Edgerton claims, very convincingly, that this style of painting was an indispensable step toward modern science. For example, Galileo's idea of inertia required separating the existence of space from what happens in space. This separation was never performed earlier. Perhaps I find Edgerton's idea persuasive because it fits with my prejudices. Everybody likes what confirms one's prejudices! I always felt that geometry (in the sense of Euclid) and art were very, very strongly related. To me, geometry has a very powerful, of course visual, almost sensual character.

According to Edgerton, there was another unexpected reason why Galileo was the person whom fate, providence, or whatever, chose to become the first modern scientist. This was no mere accident. Galileo was an educated resident of Tuscany and therefore, necessarily, was himself a painter. Other persons in Holland and France, Germany and England simply did not know how to interpret pictures (cf. Palade's chapter in Part 3).

> *Philosophy is written in this great book—I mean universe—which stands continuously open to our gaze but cannot be understood unless one first learns to comprehend the language in which it is written. It is written in the language of mathematics and its characters are triangles, circles and other geometrical figures without which it is humanly impossible to understand a single word of it; without these, one is wandering about in a dark universe.*

> Galileo Galilei, Il Saggiatore *(1623)*

Shortly after Galileo, René Descartes (the French philosopher, 1596–1650) used analytic geometry to transform figures into numbers. However, it is very interesting that Isaac Newton (1642–1727) wrote about physics using extraordinarily complex and delicate geometric renderings, with actual circles, tangents, and so on riding up on one another. Obviously, these figures must have been very important for Newton. However, the British philosopher and mathematician, Bertrand Russell (1872–1970), believed Newton was actually thinking in terms of calculus, and therefore, of a mathematical language made up of letters and signs and formulas—and not in a figurative language made up of shapes like the ones Galileo used.

In the history of science after Newton, figures, triangles, and circles became less and less important. The Torino-born Joseph-Louis Lagrange (1736–1813) and the French mathematician Pierre-Simon Laplace (1748–1827) wanted them gone. It was their belief that geometry had run its course, and they advocated that mathematics and the sciences should be written in a common language like French or English with, naturally, the mathematical language of formulas interposed. The idea of using shapes as part of that language became less and less common. About fifteen years ago, a French high-school textbook of geometry came out with not a single illustration! To justify the lack of illustrations, the author argued in his preface that the artistic and sensual character of pictures would delude the reader. Therefore, he wanted students to think of geometry in purely linguistic terms. In other words, the mathematical language of geometry should be conceived of in terms of letters, words, and formulas—not shapes.

Beyond Euclidean geometry

> *Historically, the revolution (that brought about modern mathematics)*
> *was forced by the discovery of mathematical structures that did not fit the*
> *patterns of Euclid and Newton. These new structures were regarded by*
> *contemporary mathematicians as 'pathological' . . . as a 'gallery of*
> *monsters'.*

> F.J. Dyson, 1978

Usually, we think in terms of Euclidean space defined by three dimensions, but a brilliant German thinker, Felix Hausdorff (1868–1942) took a bold step beyond the classics. His was an interesting story. Until the age of thirty-five, he devoted most of his efforts to philosophy, literature, and theater. Not until the age of forty-one was he offered (on the basis of only three papers in mathematics) his first academic position at the University of Bonn. Somebody in

Bonn must have been truly far-seeing because Hausdorff was to become a great mathematician indeed. One of his lesser works—in fact, a work of rather borderline significance, often ignored—provided a generalized definition of dimension that could be a fraction. By a fluke, I knew this work well.

The practical significance of the Hausdorff dimension emerged when I did calculations on stock prices and turbulence. In both of these areas, Hausdorff's new concept of dimension was to play a critical role.

Finance, turbulence, and self-similarity

My first scientific publication came out on April 30, 1951. Over the years, it had seemed to many that each of my investigations was aimed in a different direction. But this apparent disorder was misleading: it hid a strong unity of purpose . . . Against odds, most of my works turn out to have been the birth pangs of a new scientific discipline.

Benoit Mandelbrot, 1983

After many false starts, the first field in which my talents led me somewhere was economics. The problem that I dealt with is as follows. For a long time, economists had thought the reason they could not make sense out of price fluctuations (for example, the changing price of commodities such as cotton) was that data were not abundant enough. Economists believed they had both the correct theory and the right tools to apply that theory. The theory was language-based; the tools were mathematical, statistical devices. They thought all that was lacking was adequate data. Then, primitive computers and data became available. So, finally economists could apply their theories and techniques. Instead of triumphing, they failed terribly.

One day (under amusing conditions too long to recount), a man, who soon became a friend, handed me a stack of computer cards, saying he couldn't make any sense out of them and challenging me to do better. Where did I look for a better way? I had heard it was very difficult to distinguish a record of prices plotted on a scale of days versus one plotted over months—unless one could read the figure caption. You may have seen such records—the wriggles printed in newspapers tracking the changes in stock prices during short or long periods. Prices may be shown on a scale of days, months, or even years. Most people cannot tell the scales apart except by looking at the fine print.

There are two attitudes one can take towards this phenomenon. The easiest is to think, 'This is an insignificant curiosity.' But I took the opposite tack and hypothesized that the interchangeable aspect of these scales was their most important characteristic. Which conditions, which kind of variation of prices would result in the extraordinary fact that records with different time scales could be confused? So, I cooked up the simplest possible mathematical formula I thought could explain this phenomenon. That simple formula included no assumptions about people, markets, or anything else in the real world. It was based simply on a 'principle of invariance',—the hypothesis that, somehow, economics is a world in which things are the same in the small as they are in the large except, of course, for a suitable change of scale.

What I had discovered was extraordinary. Harvard invited me to be a Visiting Professor of Economics, teaching in a field I had never studied! So, here I was expounding this mathematical device and a kind of white magic was unfolding in front of my eyes and those of my audience. My formula for the variation of prices can be described as linguistic in the sense of being written in words and mathematical symbols. This formula was simplicity itself, yet yielded output patterns of extraordinary complexity that resembled financial fluctuations to an extent that was absolutely incredible.

Have you ever had the misfortune of listening to a stockbroker trying to explain the ups and downs in stock prices by all kinds of market configurations? Yet, all of these complexities can be produced spontaneously by a stupid little formula, one line long, which is devoid of any knowledge of economics or psychology. However, some people would not view my discovery as a basic contribution and found it very disquieting. It is work with which they have not yet made peace.

Now let me go to the next problem—the turbulence of gases and liquids. When I was at Harvard, another Visiting Professor lectured on turbulence. As layers of memory dropped away, I remembered I had heard about this topic in 1948, as a student at the California Institute of Technology. I remembered a certain Lewis F. Richardson (1881–1953)—a very strange man of the kind that England used to pride itself in producing (even though it treated them poorly). Around 1920, he postulated that weather or wind or local turbulence were all the same phenomenon at different scales. In a sense, Richardson was simply formulating a kind of scientific dictum (to be verified, of course), a reality that painters have known forever. There are famous drawings, attributed to the Renaissance artist Leonardo da Vinci (1452–1519), of fountains in which one sees eddies upon eddies. Leonardo was captivated by all natural phenomena and basically copied these eddies from manuscripts written in the twelfth century. Practical engineers had always known that turbulence in a river or a fountain, large or small, is made of eddies riding upon other eddies, or an ever-expanding pattern of eddies. That was just common knowledge. Richardson formalized it, and Kolmogorov did fundamental additional work on it in 1941.

What I had found, in a certain sense, was a subterranean stream of (mostly

Fig. 4.6 Self-similarity in the cauliflower. A knife subdivides a cauliflower head into a collection of smaller cauliflowers, then increasingly fine cuts yield increasingly smaller cauliflowers. Not only the realm of plants but other parts of nature have known fractals since time immemorial.

inactive) thought that self-similarity or some related invariance is essential. Self-similarity means that each part of a structure is similar to the whole. Figure 4.6 shows an object of ordinary interest in which each part is the same: a cauliflower floret looks like the whole cauliflower, and so does a part of that floret. In this particular cauliflower variety, you can go on fifteen levels by using first your hands and the naked eye, and finally by using a magnifying glass and tweezers. The property of self-similarity is so obvious that the word is self-explanatory. But it seems I was the first to use the concept—except for an isolated instance someone later pointed out to me. The extraordinary New Englander, Ralph Waldo Emerson (1803–1882), who was a sharp observer of people and events, used the word, in passing, when describing trees as being self-similar. In his time, and long afterwards, self-similarity as a *concept* was not thought worthy of being described by a word, and certainly not worthy of being investigated by scientists!

Richardson or Emerson, however, were not the first to observe self-similarity. As a matter of fact, the concept was already present in a verse written by the English satirist, Jonathan Swift:

> *So, Nat'ralists observe, a Flea*
> *Hath Smaller Fleas that on him prey,*
> *And these have smaller Fleas to bit 'em,*
> *And so proceed ad infinitum.*

Jonathan Swift, 1773

Actually, Swift was repeating a saying by the German philosopher and mathematician Leibnitz (1646–1716), who in turn was borrowing from that well-known Greek philosopher, Aristotle (384–322 BC). So, there was a long line of thought on self-similarity, going back very far—but nobody wanted to listen to me.

One day, I saw in one of Richardson's articles a report of measurements of coastline length as precision increases. Imagine a big ship following a coastline and measuring its length, while avoiding the small islands and peninsulas. Next, imagine a small ship that follows the same coast, entering each small bay and inlet; the captain of this small ship will declare the coast to be much longer. Now a man walks along the coastline, then a mouse. The smaller the scale at which one looks at the coastline, the finer the detail included in the notion of coast and the longer the measurement. Now imagine that this realistic coastline is totally artificial and can be produced by one line of algorithm. This is what I did.

In the Euclidean environment, established by the Greek mathematician and father of geometry, the fact that the coastline has a complicated shape would mean that one needs a very complicated formula to specify it. In Euclid:

$$x^2 + y^2 = 1$$

is a simple formula representing a simple shape, a circle. However, to get complicated shapes in Euclidean geometry, you need complicated constructions. For something as complicated as a coastline, you would need a highly complex algebraic expression. You would need 1024 parameters or variables to get a crude approximation, and you would need even more parameters if you wanted to get a better fit. In other words, Euclidean geometry is totally unfit for the description of very complex shapes. But then there is this other world: the fractal world.

A new world: fractals

This new world, which I was in the process of exploring and whose wide applicability began to be recognized, required a name. So, in 1975, I coined a term for it—'fractal'. One reason was that its mathematical description involved fractional dimensions. Another reason was that, in Latin, 'fractus' means 'irregular and broken up'. In this fractal universe-to-be, every old rule is turned around; simple formulas generate complicated results, and when simple formulas are changed, complicated results change.

> *Fractals are a family of highly complex shapes. They consist of an infinite number of irregular component structures—fragments—that resemble one another at any scale. Fractals are defined by relatively simple mathematical equations containing as a major determinant a fractional dimension. Philosophical roots of fractional dimensions can be found in Leibnitz' Principle of Continuity, the belief that nature consists of an indivisible array of units without abrupt transitions. So, even the dimensions defining Euclidean space became a target for interpolation. We are thinking usually in terms of Euclidean space, determined by three dimensions that are integers: a line is defined by one dimension, a surface by two, and a space by three dimensions. The concept of fractional dimensions, developed by Hausdorff, is not readily intuitive. However, it can be visualized as follows: an increasingly irregular boundary line that is self-similar at all scales becomes infinitely long and begins to fill remaining open areas. The boundary thus starts to resemble a ribbon rather than a line. What started out as a one-dimensional line takes on properties of a two-dimensional surface, and its dimension is somewhere between 1.0 and 2.0—fractal characteristics.*

To see the results of the fractal formulas necessitates easy but extensive calculation. Theoretically, they could have been done with tables of logarithms if enough 'slaves' had been available to do them. But even though the computers were very unsophisticated in 1963–4, they proved handy.

It was in the course of these calculations that the 'Hausdorff dimension' or the 'fractal dimension' came up. It proved to be very important—an invaluable concept! For the financial studies I mentioned earlier, I had to describe somehow the volatility of a submarket because some stocks were inevitably more volatile than others. The usual measures of market activity did not work but, lo and behold, Hausdorff's dimension was the proper description of volatility. I also used Hausdorff's dimension for some work in turbulence. It worked, but nobody understood a word of what I was saying—total, total dismissal!

On being ignored

> *Instances where new concepts and techniques come into science through branches of low competitiveness are rare today, hence anomalous. Fractal geometry is a new example of such an historical anomaly.*
>
> Benoit Mandelbrot, 1983

Here I was again, being misunderstood or ignored, but in an odd way somehow I became very well known, perhaps because I was receiving visiting professorships at Harvard (in two different departments), at the Massachusetts Institute of Technology, and at other places. I was lecturing at many very distinguished meetings on the various things I had cooked up, and people came to listen. At the end of the lectures, I received compliments from people I admired greatly; some of them were my age, others were much older. Some who might have been my teachers said the work was very beautiful and should be developed. So, I would go to bed very happy that night; there was interest; somebody was going to pick up studies in the area—but nobody did. I was absolutely alone, absolutely without stimulation beyond kind words.

Gunther Stent's paper on prematurity in science leans heavily on the case of Avery, MacLeod, and McCarthy. These men made the basic discovery that laid the foundation for Watson and Crick's later work on the structure of DNA.

> *The bacteriologists O.T. Avery, C.M. MacLeod and M. McCarthy proved in 1944 that DNA is the hereditary substance. The discovery went almost unnoticed at the time. Its significance became clear only a decade later. Stent views this as a classic example of premature scientific discovery. He argues that 'A discovery is premature if its implications cannot be connected by a series of simple logical steps to canonical, or generally accepted, knowledge.'*
>
> Gunther Stent, 1972

The story of these three people bears a strong parallel with my own. Of course, Avery was far better established than I was, and of course all the people who might be, or might have been, or perhaps will be in that situation may not be so lucky. Avery was unlucky in the sense that he died before his work was recognized, but that is not really the fault of society.

I had a very comfortable position at IBM, and IBM was extraordinarily generous because they felt it was a gamble worth taking; besides, the gamble cost almost nothing. But each time I asked the National Science Foundation for money, they could not find referees to evaluate the proposal and therefore viewed it as totally without merit. Actually, I did not really need this money because I already had other sources of support, but, my situation was becoming irritating. I had a very strong idea which had triumphed in finance against the extraordinary competition of very shrewd and committed people; and in turbulence I had made sense of things that—to everybody else—were totally without sense and coherence. And all of this was accomplished by a very simple formula. How could I make it known?

The first fractal images

The mathematicians who created the monsters regarded them as important in showing that the world of pure mathematics contains a richness of possibilities going far beyond the simple structures that they saw in nature. Twentieth century mathematics flowered in the belief that it had transcended completely the limitations imposed by its natural origins . . . Now . . . nature has played a joke on the mathematicians . . . The same pathological structures that the mathematicians invented to break loose from 19th century naturalism turn out to be inherent in familiar objects all around us.

F.J. Dyson, 1978

Anyhow, exploring the consequences of self-similarity was proving full of extraordinary surprises, helping me to understand the fabric of nature.

Benoit Mandelbrot, 1983

Now, I would like to skip several stages of my life and present some fractal images, emphasizing the growth of what would become my central *modus operandi*. To introduce self-similarity, look at the triangle in Fig. 4.7 and take out the middle part. You get three new triangles; each is the same shape as the whole, but twice smaller. And you can repeat that process with each of the new triangles over and over again. I called this collection of triangles a Sierpinski Gasket. It was one of the shapes that mathematicians played with, around 1900, during the great revolution against 'Old Mathematics', which died, to be replaced by the 'New Mathematics', which has since also died (cf. Dyson's quote). The formula describing this shape was very simple. Well, perhaps not quite so simple. But there was very little that you could get out of it. To do something interesting with the formula you needed something more.

Figure 4.8 shows a collection of landscape pictures in which that additional element was introduced. To make the formula meaningful, you need to introduce one of two things—either randomness or non-linearity (that is, deterministic chaos). To obtain fractal landscapes, you need randomness. As you go from one panel to the next, all of these landscapes look very similar. This is an example of statistical self-similarity. Each landscape looks like a different segment along a single coastline; in reality, we follow a zoom that represents the piece seen in the first panel, but after it was magnified (three times in succession) to show increasing detail. So, self-similarity was embodied very strongly in this computer-generated picture. But I am jumping ahead in my argument because the computer graphics used for this picture came much later.

The first landscape picture that I could generate according to my fractal

Fig. 4.7 Sierpinski Gasket—a curve with a strange odyssey. This shape was long known and used as an attractive design, proving that visual artists have known fractals for a long time. Much later, around 1900, it was demoted into a so-called 'mathematical monster'. Then, around 1975, fractal geometry changed it into an indispensable tool of physics. Finally, this shape opened the gate to ever new examples of art.

formula was a matter of blood and tears! Twice, *Science* refused to publish the paper, and twice *Nature* refused. Finally, a friend got the paper accepted for publication in the *Proceedings of the National Academy of Science*, which might be a great journal in biology but is not much read in other fields. Today, I belong to the Academy, but I seldom open *PNAS*.

Figure 4.9 is a later and better view of that same structure. It was generated by piling up little pyramids on top of one another, at random. If the rules of piling are appropriate, you get these structures. This is the simplest possible landscape model. Those ridiculous randomly piled-up structures, which have nothing to do with reality, give a surprisingly realistic landscape picture. So then the question arises, do these pictures provide new insights beyond mathematics?

Richard F. Voss came to IBM weeks after we had produced our first, primitive landscape pictures. He became a very close friend and associate for many, many years. Like the zoom in Fig. 4.8, Plate 14 is a rendering by Dick Voss of the same

MAG 1.00E + 00   MAG 4.00E + 00

MAG 2.56E + 02   MAG 3.20E + 01

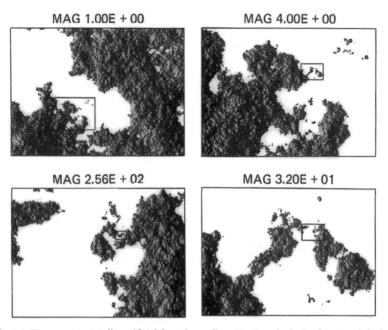

Fig. 4.8 Zoom onto a totally artificial fractal coastline. Starting clockwise from top left, the portion framed by a rectangle in one picture is blown to full size in the next. This is done three times. (Art by R.F. Voss)

Fig. 4.9 A fractal landscape that never was. This is neither a photograph nor a painting. This design was intended as a tool of pictorial rhetoric and indeed helps bring understanding and acceptance of fractal geometry. It also serves the needs and whims of geophysics and art. (Art by R.F. Voss)

idea. It looks like a landscape but is neither a painting nor a photograph; it tells nothing about the shape of the earth. What it does contain is the idea of self-similarity, or more precisely, self-affinity (which is a very closely related notion, the detail of which I will not go into here). The colors are those of actual land-scapes, not part of the fractal formula. Objections having been raised because the beautiful colors were obviously faked, we modified the same landscape by omitting the colors. Everybody identified the result as a mountain landscape in winter. Again, this was the product of a one-line formula. The fractal formula says the object is self-similar, that it is continuous. There are a few additional criteria—but the formula is very, very primitive.

In terms of progress in science, the rendering of these images involves an unusual step forward. The first step in testing the theory is performed in the language of shapes, in which it was written, and not in the language of symbols. In other words, if I gave you the formula that generated the image, and if you wanted to compare it with actual mountains, you would need to test it for two or three parameters. This used to be the sole goal of 'hard' science, in most cases it is still the main goal, and will remain a goal. Again, I emphasize that in each case you would be comparing only two or three parameters. With fractals something marvelous happens! You find the conditions for many more para-meters are satisfied.

And yet there is no implication of a replica of tectonic development in the formula; fractals have no reference to the study of the earth's crust or the forces that produce changes in it. At the same time as my deliberately phenomeno-logical (and you might say, arbitrary) formula was generating these mountain images, somebody else had developed a very elaborate model of tectonics. The man was very scornful of my images saying:

'Poof, this guy doesn't know anything about mountains and his formula con-tains no knowledge of the earth whatsoever. So, what can it mean? I have a much better formula which takes into account all the available knowledge of mountains.'

I replied: 'What about providing a picture of it?'

'Who needs a picture?' he responded. 'I fit the formula's 15 parameters from nature and the 15 measurements all check.'

I insisted: 'Please, do make the picture.'

He made a picture, and it did not at all look like a mountain; it was some kind of shape that came up accidentally in his effort to model mountains. That model was never heard of again.

The moment when we generated the first landscape figures was no key 'eureka!' moment, no dramatic revelation prompting me to say, 'I have found a key to the universe'. Instead, the application of the fractal concept to nature was a very gradual development, I did not realize immediately the full meaning of the landscape images and was to understand its full impact only later.

A simple formula: an endless diversity of shapes

Another very interesting feature turned up in the course of this work. The idea of roughness and hotness must be as old as humanity. Temperature was measured by Galileo, and hotness was given a perfect shape centuries ago—with the theory of heat (i.e. thermodynamics). But the concept of roughness remains elusive. People tried to grab the essence of roughness with all kinds of words and formulas, but failed. However, using fractals we can create computer images that are the same in every way, except for the roughness. Roughness can be controlled by a number in the program, and that number is the fractal dimension. Eureka!

In the *Fractal Planet Rise* (Plate 15) by Richard F. Voss, each part was created by using one simple formula, and then the two were put together. This introduces a new aspect of creativity. The formula was conceived with the down-to-earth desire to describe or fit some properties of an object. With this in mind, I always sought the simplest formula that fit. Between two formulas of equal fit or value, but with different degrees of complication, I always select the simpler one. So, I had this simple formula, and the shapes it generated were extraordinary.

I can show only a few of the shapes, but the possibilities are endless. Preserving the algorithm and program, but changing the 'seed' (the number you put in the computer program to stimulate randomness) generates diversity. For any computer, the number of different seeds is finite. Using 50 000 000 possible seeds, the program is equivalent to a virtual book of 50 000 000 pages, each showing the landscape obtained when the page number is taken as seed. The overwhelming variety of shapes this simple little formula allows was totally unexpected by me or by anybody else. I do not know how to describe this phenomenon. Is it the creativity of mathematics, or the creativity of a formula? How can a one-line mathematical formula generate shapes of such far-ranging variety and complexity? This is a phenomenon that begs to be discussed.

Computer graphics: seeing is believing

Everybody, including me, has this irresistible desire to fill in a gap and to explain why a certain advance was achieved by a particular person and not somebody else. One explanation is that I was working at IBM. As I said, this was an amazingly generous place at that time. In fact, it was the only, and therefore, the best place for doing my work. But IBM did not then believe in computer graphics, and did not stress scientific computation in some of the fields of mathematics and science that it supported. IBM did not expect me to make any money. Therefore, the computers we had were very cumbersome and it was almost impossible to do computer graphics (the place for this was Los Alamos). Our early graphics had to be generated with all kinds of bizarre computer arrangements.

As primitive as they were initially, our early images became very much a matter of salvation, perhaps a matter of rhetoric. I emphasize this point because of my earlier distinction between a language of letters and mathematical symbols versus a language which also includes shapes. In the present case, the second, 'figurative' language was introduced for rhetorical reasons: nobody understood my abstract formulas. Actually, those few who understood them had somehow convinced themselves that my formulas could not have any particular relation to reality and that, therefore, I was dead wrong in my thinking. And those who knew about reality could not imagine that an idiotically simple formula could embody as much of reality as I claimed it did. I was very well aware of these criticisms. Everybody reminded me that in reality, this idea of self-similarity was wrong.

These people reminded me of the old view that an atom was like the sun with its planets, with electrons spinning around the protons, which was just a very crude picture in the early papers of Niels Bohr, the Danish nuclear physicist who died in 1962. Of course the reality is very different. So, everybody kept telling me that new good ideas in science had to be abstract, and that there were no pictures in quantum mechanics because there *could not* be any pictures in it. Well, the situation isn't quite so clear. Much later, when I met the nuclear physicist R.P. Feynmann (1918–1988), the first words he used to greet me were that he recognized the geometer in me. He too never understood the formula until it had a good picture to go with it. At least I was not unique in my feelings about scientific language.

Now let me go on to a series of more recent pictures, bringing out the differences between the Heroic, Classical, and Romantic Ages. In the Heroic Age, the tools for computer graphics were miserable. That first picture of mountains (Fig. 4.9) was done on a laboratory oscilloscope and photographed. We worked day and night to get the formula on screen. The necessary tools did not exist at IBM; we found scrap instruments we could modify to accommodate to our needs (these things could not be bought off the shelf). The pictures by Richard Voss ushered in the Classical Age. At that time (around 1981–1982, when I was finishing *Fractal Geometry of Nature*), the system for computer graphics was almost workable; pictures took a couple of days. The necessary software did not exist; everything had to be developed from scratch. The work was still heroic in many ways, but one could express what the formula contained without even dreaming of adding any expression of oneself.

Richard Voss is a man of great culture and superb taste, a master programmer. I suggested the basic formulas; he found the best implementations. Everybody was saying how beautiful our pictures were, but we were adamant—their beauty was meant to enhance the rhetoric of words or formulas. Therefore, we agreed not to involve our feelings of taste or beauty, only reveal the formula.

This approach was very successful because it convinced everybody that there was very little in the pictures that was not in the formulas, except for the artificial colors. One of my Ph.D. students at Yale went further, towards the Romantic Age. At that stage, things can be done more loosely because the proof of what you can get has been established with strict minimal pictures. Let us look at this picture by Ken Musgrave (Plate 16). It illustrates an unfashionable face of pure mathematics. It is a composite: the ocean, the mountain, the lighting were put in place with shadows and everything computed. The principle of 'art photography' is that one never cleans up a corner to make a nicer effect; if you don't like something, you just do it again. In that respect, it is like high-quality photography. Y. Karsh, the famous photographer, never airbrushed his pictures. Instead, he would arrange the lighting differently and start over again.

Fractals—a 'new form of art'?

> . . . we do deal with a new form of the controversial but ancient theme
> that all graphical representations of mathematical concepts are a form of
> art, one that is best when it is simplest, when (to borrow a painter's term)
> it can be called 'minimal art' . . . The fractal 'new geometric art' shows
> surprising kinship to Old Masters paintings or Beaux Arts architecture.
> An obvious reason is that classical visual arts, like fractals, involve very
> many scales of length and favor self-similarity.
>
> Benoit Mandelbrot, 1981 and 1982

A moment ago, I called some of our earlier pictures 'minimal'. Let me dwell on that because I happen to have made a study of minimalist painting and sculpture. I hate minimal art. Consider Carl André (1935–) who, in the Sixties, laid the foundation for the American minimalist movement. One of his sculptures may consist of 17 aluminum beams, purchased from a supplier, a quarter-inch thick and one foot long, arranged in a very simple geometric shape. To describe this minimal sculpture so as to allow a fair reproduction would require many lines of mathematical formulas. The feeling is minimal—but not its source, description, or caption. In mathematical terms, only the implementation or sample is minimal.

For the fractals, however, the implementation is, if anything, baroque. I can show you an amazing variety of the most baroque structures, each of them obtained from simple formulas which take only one line. If this too is minimalist, it is minimalism in which the wealth of structure is not provided by a person or by human perception or ingenuity—it is provided by a mathematical formula.

Many fractal compositions are more satisfying to people than most of the art sold in galleries, and in fact we are paid more money for these pictures than some people get for their art (which is one criterion for art that some people believe in strongly). However, it is questionable whether or not fractals are indeed a new form of 'high art'.

Let me now briefly introduce a growth mechanism called DLA (acronym for diffusion-limited aggregation). The principle is as follows: you have little cells floating in the air; as they fall slowly to the ground they stick to it, or to other cells already attached to the ground, or to a branch already grown from an aggregation of cells. This phenomenon has been known for many years. People saw it, but they did not comprehend what they were seeing because they lacked the appropriate language to describe it. Figure 4.10 shows what this simple rule generates.

The discovery of DLA stimulated immense activity. Fifteen books and hundreds of papers were published—all of them without a proper picture, just formulas and words. Different authors published conflicting results that bothered everyone. I was working on something else, but eventually decided to look at the thing.

The first fractal pictures of DLA were in black and white and did not seem to be of much help. So, I was sitting in front of a computer with my assistant, telling him to color our pictures and to change the colors through what is called a 'color map'. Quite literally, I was acting not like a scientist but like a painter because I was choosing colors that would achieve a certain balance in the picture. The overall structure of the composition came from the fractal formula. In order to understand that structure better, we gave it different colors. As the colors were changing, something suddenly jumped out at me—the underlying rules that governed this lovely, complicated, and previously incomprehensible shape. At least to some people, this is beauty.

Another problem that was incomprehensible until proper pictures were available was a shape called a 'percolation cluster' (Plate 13). Compare a 'percolation cluster' with a painting by Augusto Giacometti (Plate 12). Alberto Giacometti is a sculptor whose thin, tall figures are in museums throughout the world, but Augusto Giacometti is relatively unknown. Almost all of his paintings are in Switzerland. I became a great fan, so I collect catalogs from his exhibitions. Before others turned to abstraction, this artist of extraordinary

Fig. 4.10 A diffusion-limited fractal aggregate. A childishly simple rule (see text) generates an exquisite image of increasingly life-like complexity that continues to baffle the mathematicians and the scientists. (Art by C. Evertsz)

imagination took a very real object—flowers in a meadow—and from it distilled a balanced pattern of color patches which you see in Plate 12.

Can I use the computer to produce a forgery of Giacometti? Of course not. However, one aspect of Giacometti's art is fundamental. Although his art is totally non-representational, or abstract, each painting contains elements of extraordinary balance and symmetry. It is this hidden, underlying order which is contained in the fractal formula.

Let us examine the relationship between this kind of abstract art and a classical composition by, for example, the French artist, Nicolas Poussin (1594–1665)—a painter I like very much. Poussin's paintings depict figures in landscapes. These figures themselves have nothing at all to do with fractals because the outer appearance of human bodies is not fractal. But even the classic art of Poussin is more than a translation of life. A painting lives or dies because of the spatial relationships that shape the overall composition. Some painters have an independent 'eye' and great imagination, and such artists create extraordinarily balanced and rich compositions of complicated underlying structure. To describe them accurately in traditional mathematical terms would take pages and pages. I know it because I have read many of these descriptions very carefully. However, many of these compositions follow fractal rules.

Basically, fractal images are independent of sentiment or any particular idea of beauty. Structures generated by a simple one-line fractal equation are complicated, unexpected, and their shapes vary from minimal to baroque. Many people find them beautiful. Because art begins where mere representation ends, a question arises: is this 'new geometric art' a form of art? The fact that many fractal plates, at least at first blush, could pass for high art, cannot be dismissed.

A different way of thinking

My uses of computer graphics provided an entirely new tool, generating a novel rhetoric and a different way of thinking and reasoning. This perspective was closer to the frame of mind of the eighteenth-century naturalists or the nineteenth-century geologists who examined the effect of shining polarized light on rocks, than to the world of pure mathematics.

The mathematician, Gaston Julia (1893–1978), was one of my professors in 1945. He was out of favor with the establishment. My uncle (the mathematics professor) did not like him as a person, but admired one of Julia's papers that had been shelved since 1917. He thought something great might be revealed by a second look, backed by a good new idea. Around 1947, I read the paper, which dealt with the iteration, or repeated application of mathematical transformations, but my thoughts were no better than anyone else's. Thirty years later, I decided to look again—this time more carefully and with a different perspective—at what Julia had been doing. Julia had a very strong feeling for geometry, but his theory had died because of the lack of depth of geometric imagination in the field. People had run out of questions to ask; the theory had been sitting dormant. Through the computer, however, I allowed the new tools to give rise to all kinds of conjectures that became wildly popular, leading to many books and thousands of pages of mathematics. Their authors could never have started without me, but I could not have gone anywhere without them. Computer-generated 'Julia sets' played a central role in the *implementation* and *acceptance* of fractal geometry.

The shapes in the 'Julia sets' have a hidden order. You can adjust the baroqueness of the shape by varying the terms of the mathematical formula in a controlled manner. Even though the formulas take one line, the complexity of the result is infinite. By choosing what to look at, you can either get this extraordinarily baroque, overwhelming, mannerist, late eighteenth-century kind of structure, or anything else you wish. None of the programmers were artists, but I think they were having fun with colors, and I think they had good taste. It's easy to see the relationship between this kind of 'art' and the conventional painter's image.

Fig. 4.11 A fractal design. Some wits perceive it as straining to be confused with a freshly discovered Stone Age cave painting. (Art by R.F. Voss)

As we near the end of this discussion, let me introduce you to the Mandelbrot set. I cannot explain how its formula works, but I want you to see how short it is. Here is the formula:

$$x' = x^2 - y^2 + C'$$
$$y' = 2xy + C''$$

Plate 17 shows an overall view and Plate 18, a higher magnification of one tiny area. Be warned: contemplation of the Mandelbrot set is one of the surest ways to let time pass without noticing!

Because of its boldness, complexity, and balance, Fig. 4.11 reminds many people of the paleolithic cave paintings in Lascaux or Altamira. However, the balance achieved in the formal elements of the image did not spring from someone's imagination nor lie in the colors. I can show this picture in fifteen sets of different colors; the effect is different, but equally strong. The balance of each composition is most remarkable, and so (in some cases, but not here) is the three-dimensional illusion of structures that actually are completely flat. (This 3D effect would take an hour to explain and is very amusing.) Fractals are superhuman (or non-human or anti-human—whatever you might want to call it), but they cannot be forgotten.

Let me return to 1300, to conclude with a story I hope is true. Because a king from a northern Iberian land found Euclid's text in Burgos, and Euclid was translated into Tuscan, Giotto's heritage led to Galileo and started a triumphant march to a science which became increasingly devoid of pictures as it became increasingly 'hard'. In 'hard science' I include, of course, molecular biology, but not botany or zoology, which are scorned today.

And now there is this different kind of visual rhetoric. Because of love for Euclid's world of geometry, because of the availability of increasingly elaborate computers with ever-expanding graphic capabilities, and because of increasingly skilled friends who program these computers, it has been my great privilege to discover this new way of generating extremely simple, truly minimal art of the most baroque or extravagant kind that one can imagine. This art can be altered in a predictable way by changing the parameters in the mathematical formula. Thus, the property of scaling order and self-similarity that characterizes fractals is not only present in nature, but in some of man's most carefully crafted creations. Are these images 'art'? Perhaps no more than simple circles are 'art' by themselves. Regardless, the concept of where man—with his artist's eye and his imagination—stands in relationship to high art is bound to change in view of this new universe of fractal images generated not by man, but by a simple one-line mathematical formula.

Acknowledgement. The figure credits suffice to show that a number of brilliant computer artists were fired by my dream and contributed mightily to its implementation.

Insights into the foundations of creativity: a synthesis

It is probably true quite generally that in the history of human thinking the most fruitful developments frequently take place at those points where two different lines of thought meet. These lines may have roots in quite different parts of human culture, in different times or different cultural environments or different religious traditions: hence if they actually meet, that is, if they are at least so much related to each other that a real inter-action can take place, then one may hope that new and interesting developments may follow.

Werner Heisenberg, 1958

The preceding pages illuminated questions of creativity and its origins from vastly different angles and broke through boundaries between traditional disciplines. Many of these issues now appear in a new light: the creative experience in art and science; the elusive entities of imagination, emotion and reason; the influence of the environment on creativity; and the mind's perceptions of our outer and inner worlds. To capture this light, i.e. to integrate both complementary and conflicting views, is the goal of this final chapter. This synthesis gives rise to a new and unifying concept that relates the generation of creative works and their evocative qualities to the way that our brains operate. This synthesis also endeavors to explain how we produce creative works of art and science, and why we respond to them.

On the nature of the creative experience and its biological basis

Science plays two totally different roles in this book. It is used as a tool to study the brain, the physical entity that generates creative behaviour; and, like art, science is being studied as the product of creative acts. Is science creative?

The question of cultures

Gunther Stent argues for a continuum between different forms of art and science, creative works that communicate novel insights about our inner and outer worlds. Stent also makes the important distinction between *works* of art and science and their *contents*. The creative work of science is characterized not really by the significance of the discovery it presents (its content), but by the elegance and conclusive nature of its experimentation and of its logical deductions—as exemplified by Cech and Mandelbrot. This relates directly to the controversy over discovery in science versus creation in art. Both art and science explore our worlds for new knowledge, but their creative qualities lie in the originality and power of the new contexts the creator generates to reveal the full depth of the novel insight (see the chapters by Adolphe, Chihuly and Gilot). So, Stent concludes that art and science are closely related areas of endeavor operating on a thematic continuum but expressed in different languages.

> *PICASSO: (Arguing) And what the hell do you know about it anyway . . . you're a scientist! You just want theories . . .*
> *EINSTEIN: Yes, and like you, the theories must be beautiful. You know why the sun doesn't revolve around the earth? Because the idea is not beautiful enough . . .*
> *PICASSO: So you're saying you bring a beautiful idea into being?*
> *EINSTEIN: Yes. We create a system and see if the facts can fit it.*
> *PICASSO: So you're not just describing the world as it is?*
> *EINSTEIN: No! We are creating a new way of looking at the world!*
> *PICASSO: So you're saying you dream the impossible and put it into effect?*
> *EINSTEIN: Exactly.*
> *PICASSO: Brother!*
> *EINSTEIN: Brother!*
>
> S. Martin, 1996

Stent's thesis of a continuum between art and science readily complements Gardner's concept of different intelligences. Gardner also sees a range of creative abilities that explore the spectrum from the non-linguistic, inner world to the linguistic, outer world, as represented by his choice of 'big C' creators: Stravinsky (non-linguistic)–Graham–Picasso–Eliot–Freud–Gandhi–Einstein (linguistic).

How many cultures are there if science and art are essentially similar? Science and art are perhaps more intertwined today than ever before, even though it may not appear that way. Tom Stoppard wrote a play (*Arcadia*) about chaos theory (see page 225), the composers Xenakis and Babbitt sought inspiration in mathematical formulas (see Adolphe's chapter), Gilot revealed her obvious interest in physics and biology, Mandelbrot discussed the fractal properties of paintings and sculptures and Rogers described the balancing act between his life in biomedical science and wood sculpture. Many artists and scientists, including those represented in this book, are bridging the apparent chasm—even with a degree of eagerness. Wouldn't simple curiosity drive any creative person's mind to explore the exciting advances in *both* modern art and science?

There are barriers, however. As creative thinkers explore new contexts in their inner and outer worlds, they often must break with tradition so that new creative works may be less familiar or even shocking. This is amply illustrated in this book (see the chapters by Adolphe, Cech, Chihuly, Gardner, Gilot, Mandelbrot and Stent). Abstract painting and sculpture are not amenable to the same literal interpretation as the realistic traditional works of art. Today's works of science present a similar problem; greatly increased knowledge and specialization are necessary to understand such works, and this renders them less accessible. Moreover, their potential consequences, for example, molecular cloning and nuclear technologies, may alienate the non-scientist. So, fragmentation results. Yet, as our understanding of the universe increases, fragmented or reductionist approaches prove to be less and less satisfactory. The desire for a higher-order understanding of natural phenomena and for a more scientific understanding of our inner world is growing rapidly. Only an alliance and, eventually, the merger between art and science into a single culture will satisfy this need.

A brain product

Where does the creative impulse come from? Robert W. Weisberg (1993), in his *Creativity: Beyond the Myth of Genius*, argues that a person's creative force is not a function of divine inspiration in a literal sense. Dispelling the myth of supernatural forces acting on an individual's mind is important, but Weisberg takes the issue one step further: he proposes that a 'big C' creator's brain is every bit as ordinary as everyone else's. However, Weisberg is wrong when he states that all brains are created equal. Even though they may *look* the same, different brains do *function* somewhat differently. On the surface, the genius' brain looks exactly like an average brain. Early in this century, this observation became the big disappointment of those anatomists who had made the discovery of differences one of their goals in life. Their concept, also known as phrenology, soon was replaced by another, similarly simplistic model derived from the discovery of neurotransmitters: chemical balances determine a brain's abilities or deficiencies. This chemical reincarnation of phrenology again ignores the fact that brain function depends on the concerted action of vast numbers of neuronal circuits comprising many different types of synapses—each with its own chemistry.

Galler describes how deprivation in childhood may result in a permanent change in brain function. Stevens, Damasio and Pfenninger explain the complex pathways through which sensory information is processed and recreated in the brain, and they point out how function modulates the brain's circuitry—a concept echoed in Adolphe's comment that the music shapes the musician. Palade makes the point that creativity is a human condition only—and thus genetic. This point is reflected in the well-known phenomenon of inherited special talents, for example, in musical families (the Bachs, the Mozarts). All of these observations suggest that subtle differences among normal human brains render some of them more creative than others.

Howard Gardner certainly is right when he states, 'You could know every bit of neurocircuitry in somebody's head, and you still would not know whether or not that person was creative.' This can be taken to mean that there is no relationship between creativity and circuitry. Yet, Gardner's statement is correct *not* because neuronal circuits are irrelevant or identical in people of variable intelligence or creativity. The real reasons actually are twofold. First, our analytical tools and our understanding of brain function are inadequate to perform the study. We are incapable of analyzing the entire circuitry of an individual human brain and of understanding how all these circuits function in detail and together. Even if the analysis were possible today, we would not know which small deviations from 'the norm' of the circuitry would be meaningful functionally. Second, the function of highly complex systems such as the brain is dependent on a very large number of determinants that are partially unknown or not measurable without introducing perturbations, and very small differences in the determinants may have very large consequences for the function of the ensemble. This is the realm of chaos theory, which describes such non-linear systems—systems that behave in an essentially unpredictable fashion. So, on both theoretical and experimental grounds, Gardner's statement is correct.

However, Gardner is right for the wrong reasons. Therefore, his argument fails to dissociate the source of creative behavior from brain circuitry. It does not argue at all against Stevens' and Damasio's evidence of discrete circuits involved in specific aspects of higher brain function. We know that some of these circuits malfunction in pathologic conditions, for example, in certain mental disorders. *Subtle* modifications in the function of such circuits are likely to account for the different cognitive capabilities and talents observed in the normal human population. This view is entirely consistent with the neurobiological explanation of the mind presented by Damasio: the human brain is characterized by an abundance of recursive and bidirectional pathways that interconnect cortical areas holding mapped representations (resembling actual images) with higher association areas that store 'acquired dispositional, non-mapped (i.e. abstract) representations'. Thus, mapped representations ('mental images') can be driven by sensory input as well as by higher association areas. It is this functional feature of the cerebral cortex that enables us to generate mental representations internally, i.e. that gives us the mind. So, differences in the abundance and nature of the recursive and bidirectional pathways in the cerebral cortex may well result in different mental powers.

Concluding that an important, innovative work of art or science is the product of a particularly capable brain, we must seek the answers to the question of the origin of creativity in the biology of the brain. As a philosopher of psychology, Paul Churchland, has stated (1981), 'Our common sense conception of psychological phenomena ... will eventually be displaced ... by completed neuroscience ... Our mutual understanding and even our introspection may then be reconstituted within the conceptual framework of completed neuroscience.' It follows that any theory on creativity must be consistent and integrated with the contemporary understanding of brain function. This conclusion is a critical basic premise for the discussions to follow.

Influence of the environment

Gardner introduced the 'creative triangle' to describe the relationships between the individual, the creative work and its domain and the creator's peers (the field). Damasio also acknowledges the important role of the creator's environment, and he lists, among his requirements for creativity, courage to face criticism by the field and insight into the workings of other minds. Yet another important facet of the multipersonal quality of creativity is the issue of how much is nurture and how much is nature. Or, more explicitly formulated: does the environment—the society, the times, as well as the immediate sphere—influence the creative mind's activities; and to what degree is that brain's exceptional ability predetermined genetically? We must answer these questions if we are to develop an understanding of the origins of creativity. We will begin by examining the creator's macroenvironment, then explore his or her microenvironment and, finally, discuss the brain itself.

The macroenvironment: where are the golden flowers?

The societal factors, the settings and circumstances that foster creative behavior, play an important role—more or less explicitly—in almost all of the chapters. Palade uses the Italian Renaissance masters and masterworks to epitomize an outburst of creativity in a particular society at a particular time. He points out the importance of affluence in Northern Italy as a critical factor for the blooming of the 'golden flower'. Simonton and Csikszentmihalyi would agree (see Gardner's chapter), but they would also argue that the intrigue and rivalry between the city states of the region added an important stimulus for creative output. Furthermore, the beginning of the Renaissance witnessed a shift away from the contemplative state of the Middle Ages, characterized by anonymous works and slow evolution of the society. The revolutionary spirit of the Renaissance began to value the acquisition of new knowledge and the creation of original works. Ever since, innovative creations would no longer be expected to satisfy traditional norms and could be identified with a particular creator, the scientist or the artist.

Where do we stand today? Progress in the natural sciences—as illustrated, for example, in the chapters by Cech, Damasio, Pfenninger and Stevens—has been unprecedented, even though the twentieth century hardly was a time of unperturbed happiness and prosperity. Nevertheless, Palade's thesis that an affluent environment nurtures creativity is illustrated in Gardner's biographical analysis of major creators of this century: they all came from bourgeois, comfortable environments that provided ample education and stimulus.

Galler provides an interesting counterpoint. She documents how desperate poverty and malnutrition, especially in the Third World and often in our inner cities, deprive large population segments of participation in the creative acts that move society forward. It has become very clear that simply handing out food to the poor does not fundamentally change this situation, and that the damage may be irreversible. So, the effect of deprivation may not primarily be a 'hardware' problem (i.e. organic change or damage in the brain due to the lack of nutrients). In fact, the brain seems to be well protected against all but the most severe malnutrition. Instead, deprivation seems to generate a severe 'software' problem resulting from the lack of stimulus and education in a critical phase of development. This is consistent with what we know about brain development. As Stevens and Pfenninger explained, many of the brain's functions are modified or tuned by the use of the relevant neuronal circuits. Actually, proper usage of such circuits is a prerequisite for normal brain development.

Using the Italian Renaissance as the shining example, a true golden flower draws its sap from both the sciences and the arts. What about the arts in the last century? George Palade is skeptical. Have the arts suffered from the sciences' move to center stage? One can argue that the last hundred years already have produced an impressive array of painters, sculptors, architects, writers, composers and musicians. The arts, like the sciences, never have been more available physically, but they may have become less accessible to the human mind. Or are we reaching the end of a cycle of creative output? Musicologist Jan Swafford (1997) recently wrote in his Brahms biography: 'Every creative era contains the seeds of its own destruction; each plays out its decadence in its own way. Modernism expired over the last decades of the twentieth century, lost in the wilderness it had thrashed into but turned out to be incapable of settling.' How long can the golden flower last? Are signs of decay apparent? And will the lack of understanding of contemporary creative works by a large segment of our society eventually cause the golden flower to wither?

What is the relationship between a creative era and a creative individual? Howard Gardner and Mihaly Csikszentmihalyi feel that one should ask, 'Where is creativity' and not, 'Who is creative?' Their reasoning is that a work must be validated first on the basis of its impact on the field—on the culture—in order to be deemed creative. However, it is evident there are many known—and probably many more unknown—examples of truly novel, creative works that are not understood by the field or the society when they are generated. Gunther Stent discusses 'premature' discoveries in science, discoveries whose importance is seen only much later, when other information has become available. Picasso's *Les Demoiselles d' Avignon* was revolutionary at the time it was painted, but it was acknowledged as important only much later. Validation by the *field* (the multipersonal) is important for the impact of the work, its incorporation into the cultural repertoire. So, the fate of many twentieth-century creations remains to be assessed. Yet, any work of art or science is the product of an individual mind (or a few minds), and its intrinsic value and originality are not changed by the field's judgment.

The creator's microenvironment: always a lonely place?

'Let me think for a moment' is a common phrase used to shut out distractions so that we can evaluate an idea or go systematically through a sequence of thoughts or deductions. Bruce Adolphe would say, 'We listen to our minds'; Antonio Damasio might call it, 'Recreating, and operating on, circumstances in representational memory.' Our diverse creators exist each in his or her own microcosm, like islands in a sea of societal interactions. What is the nature of these microcosms?

A recurring theme, emerging in many different contexts, is that creativity requires deep submersion in a thought process. Scientists often describe how a great idea may suddenly strike them. However, the scientist does not just walk into the laboratory and conduct the key experiment: Cech shares with us the trials and tribulations surrounding the discovery of catalytic RNA. Scientists—like artists—struggle for extended periods of time with the solution of a particular problem or the expression of a particular idea (linguistic or other). Especially telling is Françoise Gilot's account of her battles with a particular concept, of the many false tries that litter the path to a masterwork, and of the necessity to be able to be alone and self-absorbed for extended periods of time. Picasso had an entourage of hangers-on during daytime, but stayed up alone all night to struggle with his ideas. Adolphe, Gardner, Mandelbrot and Rogers make the same point from different perspectives.

Damasio explains how recreating complex contexts in one's mind, evaluating them and reading them out in the appropriate language are major steps in the creative process. Not surprisingly, the process is time-consuming and delicate: shutting out parts of the external world is critical for the thoughts to proceed unperturbed. As Howard Gardner points out, this leads to increasing isolation of the 'big C' creative mind. While feeling integrated and fulfilled in his or her domain, in the personal construct of virtual reality, the creator may be prone to unhappiness or frustration in the external world, a world that may present a different set of realities. Eccentricity may ensue.

Is creative behavior, by necessity, linked to eccentricity, or is this a cliché—often used as an excuse to escape from the realities of the external world? Creative acts come in many different guises, from contributions to everyday activities to major achievements in a wide range of areas, as Gardner and Galler have pointed out. There *are* creative individuals who strive for a balance between their primary domain, creative activity in another domain and connectedness to the real world. Rogers, for example, is an acknowledged scientist, leader in the medical world and sculptor. When he says, 'My artwork gives me some personal security', he reveals that he gains strength from the submersion into the creative act of sculpting for his role as a leader of a large and complex organization. One can conclude that long times of submersion are prerequisite for the creative process, but that to be creative does not necessitate eccentricity or disconnectedness from the world.

The evolving mind

Once you accept that intelligence and creativity are brain products, you must conclude, in our post-Darwinian world, that cognitive functions have a genetic basis and have evolved alongside the nervous system. This fundamental belief of the biologist is now receiving strong support from an unusual ally, the evolutionary psychologist. Pinker (1994) points out that 'language . . . is a distinct piece of the biological makeup of our brains' and makes the argument that natural selection favored those primates that were endowed with the capacity to use this new and efficient form of communication. An equally convincing argument can be made for the full range of cognitive functions of the brain. The increasing ability to recognize cause and consequence and to act accordingly—as opposed to following blind instincts (see Pfenninger's chapter)—provided a huge advantage for the evolution of *Homo sapiens*.

So, is there a mind gene or a creativity gene? Without question, the brain's cognitive functions are inherited. Yet, the proper establishment and operation of the brain's circuits are controlled by a vast array of different genes, suggesting that the cooperation of a large number of genes is required to make one brain more intelligent or creative than another. In other words, creative powers are inherited, but inheritance does not follow the simple laws of Mendel. Does this contradict everything that has been said about the effects of the environment on the developing brain? Not by any means.

One of the most important lessons neuroscientists have learned in the recent past is that the brain is a highly adaptive machine, especially during development (see the chapters by Stevens and Pfenninger): normal development of the brain depends on the use of its circuits. This is not really different from the adaptation (i.e. growth) of muscle to exercise. However, increased use of the brain does not change its size or shape, as stated already. The adaptation is more refined, specifically tailored to its function. The neurobiologist, Greenough, and his collaborators (1991) have shown this in a striking set of studies on the rat. Simple, monotonous exercise, on a treadmill for example, improves blood circulation in the cerebellum (a brain structure involved in motor control and coordination). More interestingly, an enrichment in the rat's environment that requires the application of diverse motor skills (e.g. to get to a food source) results in an increase in the number of synapses in the cerebellum. In other words, the use of the cerebellum modifies its circuits. Inevitably, one is drawn to conclude that the cerebellum of the violinist, Isaac Stern, must be wired somewhat differently from that of the Brazilian soccer star, Pelé. As Adolphe says, the music shapes the musician.

Extrapolating from here to creativity does not take a great leap of faith. A brain whose imaginative powers have been stimulated from an early age is likely to exhibit differently wired regions in the cerebral cortex, to be richer in synaptic connections and to be more creative than the brain that has grown up in a deprived, unstimulating environment—assuming both were built with the same, favorable genes. The genes control the basic blueprint of the brain's circuitry; use of these circuits refines and enhances their function. This is where Galler's, Gardner's and Pfenninger's messages converge. As Pfenninger points out, neuroscience explains Galler's observations regarding the effects of childhood deprivation on intelligence and behavior, and it provides the reasons for Gardner's finding that a nurturing, stimulating environment is very important in the development of major creators. So, nature and nurture are not mutually exclusive. In fact, environmental stimulus is necessary to make the most of one's genetic endowment.

Perception, imagination, reason, emotion and modern brain science

Gunther Stent states, 'In the preconscious process of converting the primary sensory data step by step into structures, information is necessarily lost because the creation of structures, or the recognition of patterns, is nothing other than the selective destruction of information. The mind creates a pattern from the mass of sensory data by throwing away this, throwing away that. Finally, what's left of the data is a structure in which the mind perceives something meaningful.' Using knowledge of how the brain processes visual information, rather than philosophical arguments, Charles Stevens reaches a very similar conclusion. Because of the way the visual system is wired, our brains select specific features from what our eyes see—lines, color or icons, such as the elements of a face. Antonio Damasio climbs higher on the ladder of brain function, from the recognition of icons and symbols to imagination and the emotional response. Integrating Stent's, Stevens' and Damasio's insights makes possible the transition from epistemology to the natural science of pattern perception, the aesthetic experience and imagination. The enabling steps are recent advances in neuroscience, and the resulting views are complementary to the artist's perspective.

Concepts of order: recognition of symbols

Works of art or science are forms of communication between human beings. The function of any form of communication is to transmit meaning, and as Hofstadter pointed out (1979), meaning acts upon intelligence in a predictable way. All forms of communication among animals or humans consist of symbols. They may be words, gestures, shapes, colors or musical motifs. For the stickleback fish mentioned earlier (see Pfenninger's chapter), it is the red belly of the male that signifies to the female his readiness for mating. For the bees, it is a 'dance' in a figure of eight that communicates to the other bees the location of a source of nectar. The figure of eight is the framework of the 'language'; the orientation of the figure, the speed of the dance and other variables indicate the direction, distance and size of the source. The bases for these forms of communication between animals are genetically transmitted instincts, not learned behaviors (see Pfenninger's chapter). Is there evidence for genetically encoded recognition of symbols in humans?

The majority of symbols used in human communication are learned. Yet, our spoken languages are not the great example of acquired knowledge they initially seem to be: even though human languages are highly diverse, modern linguists have elucidated ground rules (phrase structure, grammar) that are common to all of them. And even though we have to learn the sounds and vocabularies of these languages, humans seem to recognize the ground rules from an early age, suggesting an inborn ability. The evolutionary psychologist Pinker speaks of the 'language instinct', a code word for his evolutionary theory of the development of language: humans have the innate ability to decipher the contextual meaning of words in the message of a sentence based on its structure. This ability has evolved along with our brains and, thus, is genetic and depends on the way certain circuits in our cerebral cortex are constructed. This is consistent with Damasio's discovery that words for entities (nouns) and those for actions (verbs) are handled by distinct circuits.

Other forms of communication, such as the visual arts and music, are likely to be based on ground rules analogous to those of language, and they also may contain symbols whose recognition is a genetic trait of humans. Stevens and Damasio pointed out the importance of the elements of the face in human communication and art. The ability to recognize facial features and expressions, so necessary in our social structure and starting immediately after birth, may have been selected for genetically because it confers a clear advantage on those endowed with it. Other symbols have sprung up independently, in totally unrelated cultures, and prompted the Swiss psychiatrist, C.G. Jung, to develop the theory of the 'collective unconscious' and its 'archetypes'. Jung's concept was that similar religious or mythical symbols appeared in the imagery of diverse cultures because the symbols were innate in the human psyche.

Stevens presented the example of specific neurons in the cerebral cortex that respond selectively to the recognition of certain facial features, such as a smiling mouth. There may be other neurons in the human brain that respond selectively to the presentation of particular symbols or icons. This would mean that data processing in the brain and the relevant circuitry of neurons are constructed in such a way that specific symbols evoke a unique response (see Damasio's chapter and page 231). Indeed, it is tempting to conclude that the recognition by specific neuronal circuits of such symbols—for example, the circle, the pyramid, the mandala, the cross, the spiral or the eye—is an ability encoded genetically, like an animal's instinct. In this case, they would be part of Damasio's innate dispositional representations. Is this the genetic foundation of the collective unconscious? Stevens' perspective strongly suggests that works combining such symbols are especially decipherable and recognizable by the cerebral cortex because of its design (i.e. the structure and function of its circuitry). Why do particular symbols or combinations of symbols evoke much stronger responses than others—a phenomenon observed in art as well as in science? To try to understand this, we must first ask the question, what are the shared features of particularly evocative sets of symbols in art or science.

Order and abstraction in scientific thought

> Most people find the haphazard profusion of nature so intensely pleasing, even spiritually profound, that it seems plain common sense to say that there is an invigorating, even mystical, order to the variable shapes of waves as they break, swallows on a summer evening, and weather. Yet for centuries scientists have dismissed such common-sense order. For a long time, their attitude made good sense. The traditional task of science has

been to simplify nature, expose its underlying logic, and then use that logic as a means of control.

John Briggs, 1992

An early morning bucolic scene has roosters crowing, daylight appears in the East and the sun is rising. These observations are linked by temporal correlation. Does the sun rise because the roosters are crowing? Certainly not! Copernicus and Galileo demonstrated that the day/night cycle depends on the earth's rotation. So, works of science reveal causal relationships between different natural phenomena and thus create a system of order.

The universe encompasses many different levels of organization: solar systems with planets; ecosystems that are home to humans, animals and plants; the living creatures composed of organs; and, eventually, cells and atoms and subatomic particles. Natural science describes the laws that connect the different levels of organization and that govern the organization at each level. The interactions among a particular set of subunits explain many of the properties of the next-higher unit. A creative work of science presents a novel hypothesis regarding such relationships and contains a set of data supporting it. We call a work of science particularly beautiful or elegant when the conclusions are unambiguous and unexpected, and when a simple theory illuminates a broad range of phenomena.

Stent explained that the natural scientist usually works in a much more abstract world than is generally assumed: a protein may be 'seen' as a band of stain in a gel slab used to isolate it, a curve plotting counts of radioactivity may represent an enzyme activity, and a complex set of peaks on a chart may contain information on the three-dimensional structure of a molecule. Even when all the information on a particular organizational unit of the external world is assembled and synthesized, we cannot see it, we only visualize it as a concept. But we do not see this unit as it really exists, as a composite of subunits and their sub-subunits, and ultimately as a myriad of atoms that follow the laws of chemistry and physics. Instead, we selectively eliminate information and see each unit as a system, an abstraction. In other words, we visualize the universe as an incredibly complex *set of nested abstractions*. This is, in essence, an extension of structuralist realism, the philosophical view rooted in Kant's work. As Stent explained, structuralists see reality as a 'set of structural transforms abstracted from the phenomenal world'.

Is there fractal order in these nested systems? As shown by Mandelbrot, fractal rules apply to many natural phenomena, such as the structure of a mountain range, a cauliflower or a snowflake. The case is more difficult to make for the logical structure of the universe discussed here. Yet, the nested arrangement of systems and subsystems iterated over and over is fractal as such. Now let us try to think of a world—or just a cell in an organism—in terms of individual atoms: it would first appear to us as totally random and disorganized. Surprisingly though, there is order in this chaos at each level, and the human mind is capable of recognizing it.

Chaos

> *VALENTINE . . . Real data is messy. There's a thousand acres of moorland that had grouse on it, always did till about 1930. But nobody counted the grouse. They shot them. So you count the grouse they shot. But burning the heather interferes, it improves the food supply. A good year for foxes interferes the other way, they eat the chicks. And then there's the weather. It's all very, very noisy out there. Very hard to spot the tune.*
> *. . . But yes. The unpredictable and predetermined unfold together to make everything the way it is. It's how nature creates itself, on every scale, the snowflake and the snowstorm. It makes me so happy. To be at the beginning again, knowing almost nothing.*
>
> Tom Stoppard, Arcadia (1993)

Watch a stream and you will discover spots of smooth water surrounded by eddies and whorls that may stay put or may appear and disappear in cyclic fashion. Then a few pebbles suddenly move and total disorder ensues. But after a little while, a new, stable pattern of eddies emerges. Or you may observe on a windy day the coming and going of little whorls of dust in your backyard or the image of a hurricane beamed to earth from a weather satellite. All are self-similar structures generated by air currents and distinct only by their scale.

Mandelbrot discussed these phenomena but did not mention chaos theory. Indeed, fractals yield the mathematics to describe the patterns in these apparently disordered systems. So fractal organization in nature goes well beyond obvious forms, such as cauliflower florets and snowflakes, and penetrates the universe at every scale. As Valentine explains to Hannah in *Arcadia*, real nature is very messy. Moving bodies experience friction, and energy is lost to heat; fluids and gases usually move with turbulence (i.e. non-linearly); and when the foxes have feasted on the grouse and depleted their supply, the foxes will face hard times, and their population will shrink until the grouse have recovered. There is a further, equally important issue: it is true, the grouse gets killed and eaten if it walks into the fox's path, but even a very small distraction to the fox, for example, a rustle of leaves in the background, may let the grouse escape.

> *One way to make the task manageable is to look at the world from the point of view of information. When we do that, we see that the basic*

pattern is one of complexity emerging from very simple rules, initial order, and the operation, over and over again, of chance. In the case of the whole universe, the fundamental laws of physics constitute those simple rules.

M. Gell-Mann, 1995

Chaos theory (or 'non-linear dynamics') deals with the dynamics of very large, apparently random populations of entities, for example, molecules, people or celestial bodies (so-called dynamical systems)—the stuff nature is made of in reality, not the simple, idealized systems Newtonian physics describe. When Galileo and Newton isolated mechanical phenomena from surrounding interferences (see Mandelbrot's chapter), they simplified them to a degree that the underlying fundamental principles became accessible to analysis. This enabled them to reveal the (linear) relationships describing such principles. This research strategy evolved into reductionism, the thinking that complex phenomena can be explained readily by the sum of underlying mechanisms, ultimately by the laws of chemistry and physics. This approach has been extraordinarily successful in the natural sciences in general, and absolutely essential for the twentieth century's progress in biology. In fact, essentially all the advances in biology up to the very recent past are based on reductionist thinking. However, this cannot explain the oft-quoted image that a butterfly flapping its wings in the Amazon basin might influence the weather in North America two months later.

In the real world, natural phenomena form intricately and elaborately interconnected systems determined by vast numbers of parameters, and they are affected by very small changes in some of these parameters. Such 'dynamical systems' behave non-linearly, in a manner that seems totally unpredictable and is not amenable to traditional mathematical analysis. In other words, chaos theory is needed to explain nature. Together with fractal mathematics, chaos theory has initiated a revolution in science by beginning to describe natural phenomena that have been refractory to treatment with the reductionist approach. Returning to our concept of the universe as a 'set of nested abstractions', fractals not only provide the overall organizational pattern of nested systems, they also describe complex, non-linear interactions at each organizational level. It is the manipulation of these abstractions, the investigation of the interactions among these nested systems, the examination of their innate order and the analysis of the causes that govern this order, hidden in chaos, that characterize the creative work of science. And the scientist appears to be under the spell of this elusive fractal order hidden everywhere in the universe.

David Rogers and Howard Gardner discussed non-traditional forms of creativity, such as the successful management of large and complex organizations. Such organizations, consisting of large numbers of people, are dynamical systems. To lead such organizations necessitates at least intuitive knowledge of non-linear dynamics: a small misunderstanding between two employees that results in a quarrel may destroy a whole branch of the organization! Also necessary is a vision of the organizational structure, a structure that consists of nested systems and subsystems. The creative leader, like the scientist, worships at the altar of fractal order.

Symbols and order in art

'Picasso sent a bowl of cherries to our table, that was his introduction . . . Cherries became a symbol in his paintings and next to the cherries, three glasses', Gilot told us. She discusses symbols extensively. A circle indicates movement, it rolls; a horizontal line is at rest; if a line is diagonal or zigzag, it is very active. Gilot describes the artist's struggles with the placement of such symbols on the canvas: placing the symbol into a context. Is there a system of order in that context?

The composer Adolphe works with musical symbols, consonant and dissonant tone intervals, harmonic progression and rhythm. To create a work of art, he places a musical thought composed of such symbols into a context or structure. Adolphe observes that a fugue is a 'fractal thing because its structure is completely self-similar all over the place', and he draws attention to the similarity between Mandelbrot's fractal images and Dale Chihuly's multi-colored glass. This similarity is all the more remarkable because of the spontaneity needed in the process of shaping the hot medium—which renders most glass sculpture highly intuitive. It captures a 'fluid thought', as Chihuly says. Surprisingly a connection appears to exist between this highly intuitive art form and fractal order determined by a mathematical formula. 'That's why Professor Mandelbrot's fractal concept actually has me deeply worried. Because I think that maybe everything is like that' to quote Adolphe again.

So, is art fractal or at least self-similar? Self-similarity is an attribute of, for example, the 'golden section', which divides a line of length a into two segments, b and c, so that $a/c = c/b$. Each segment can be subdivided further and *ad infinitum* according to the same rule to generate a highly self-similar structure. The proportions thus created, as well as those of the 'golden rectangle', where the side c' equals c, have been used extensively in art and architecture for hundreds of years. Humans find these proportions pleasing. Another self-similar structure is the logarithmic spiral, used as a symbol in many different cultures. Beyond Euclidean geometry, fractals abound in the arts from a great variety of cultures and ages. For example, there are fractal images in African art long before 1877, when George Cantor (1845–1918) produced a first fractal.

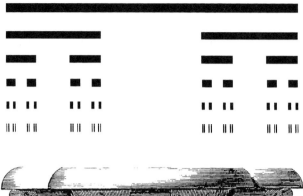

Fig. 5.1 Several stages of construction of a very simple fractal, called 'Cantor dust' (top). Drawing of a Pharaonic column capital (bottom) that first appeared in a report by Joseph Fourier (1768–1830) on Napoleon's expedition to Egypt (1821) and was brought to wider attention by R. Eglash. The capital bears a lotus design that becomes ominously Cantorian if continued *ad infinitum*, to quote Mandelbrot. (From Eglash, 1999)

Fourier's record of Napoleon's expedition to Egypt contains a drawing of an ancient fractal on the capital of an Egyptian temple column (Fig. 5.1; Eglash, 1999). In music, Adolphe and others have made the case for the fractal structure of many compositions. Works of art seem to share with nature, in an abstract way, a principle of order that follows rules of self-similarity and/or fractal geometry. However, the attentive listener or viewer does not need to understand the fractal concept to enjoy the music or the painting or the glass sculpture. Somehow, even without ever having heard of fractals, we recognize them as distinct from randomness or Euclide an geometric figures.

In abstract art the linguistic element is gone, and order may be difficult to recognize. When Mandelbrot discusses the connection between abstract art and fractals, he invokes the little-known Swiss painter Augusto Giacometti. We can be sure that Giacometti never heard of fractals. But his idea of breaking natural form into increasingly formalized, repetitive elements—in the extreme, just differently sized color patches—and of the quasi endless continuation of his canvas bears all the trademarks of fractal organization. Giacometti viewed each of his abstract paintings as only a piece of a much larger, ongoing whole: try to block off different portions of the image and you will find self-similarity at different scales. The paintings may look random, but they are not.

Augusto Giacometti, like his much better known cousin, the sculptor Alberto Giacometti, was born in Stampa (in 1877), a small mountain village in south-eastern Switzerland (Stutzer and Windhöfel, 1991). He spent the years from 1897 to 1901 as Eugène Grasset's student in Paris. Grasset, an art theoretician and leader of the *art nouveau* movement, preached that artists should study and discover the principles in natural forms, and that they should reduce the natural forms to their ornament-like essence. Giacometti adopted Grasset's views, and much of his work contains, as an important stylistic element, iterated ornamental forms taken from nature.

Giacometti did not stop with the use of ornamental forms, however. Around 1900, he started to paint totally abstract color compositions which he called *Versuche über abstrakte Farbenwirkungen and Farbentranspositionen* [Experiments on abstract color effects and color transpositions]. He pushed stylization by simplifying natural forms to the extreme and focusing on color. It is in a series called *Chromatic Phantasies*, created between 1910 and 1917, where the connection with fractal shapes is most obvious. As in *Memory of Italian Primitives II* (Plate 12) natural forms blur into apparently random, self-similar patterns. These paintings share with the percolation cluster (Plate 13) an underlying fractal order. (Giacometti showed his abstract works for a long time only in private, to friends; the field did not recognize the importance of his pioneering work for another ten to fifteen years. This identifies Giacometti as one of the earliest abstract painters.)

Thus, Augusto Giacometti represents an important bridge between art and painting on the one hand and computer-generated fractal images, mathematics and science on the other. Is the connection between those two worlds the art of fractals—or the fractal nature of art? This also raises the question of the role of the artist in this new, fractal-conscious world.

If a computer-generated fractal image can mimic a work of art, conceived by a mind and executed by hand, then they must share some properties. Using Stent's definition of art as conveying new knowledge about the *inner subjective world* of the emotions, it is difficult to argue that fractal images, generated by a computer from a mathematical formula, are art. So, do fractals threaten the artist? Fractal images and art may evoke similar feelings based on the one shared property: the intrinsic beauty of fractal order so evident in the composition of many paintings and in Mandelbrot's images. In a way, the fractal image tricks our brains into thinking that it is a work of art. So, this fractal order evokes a reaction in the viewer; it is perceived and recognized by the viewer's brain, whether the viewer knows anything about fractals or not, and regardless of whether it was conceived by a computer or a brain. In other words, the fractal order (perhaps like the ground rules of human language) is recognized by a subconscious, innate mechanism—an extraordinary phenomenon.

The perspective of fractal order in the universe, from natural phenomena to works of art, provides the basis for the thesis that true works of art and science exhibit an inherent order. One may call it 'beauty' in art and 'logic' in science. It would explain why the scientist may find a particular hypothesis or a set of research data beautiful and exciting. For the artist, the organization of shapes in a painting or motifs in a sonata may follow fractal order. This may be diffi-cult to discern (consciously) by the untrained eye or ear but, nevertheless, has its uniquely evocative effect.

The thesis that factual order is a critical element of creative and evocative works, indicates to the neuroscientist that the human brain or some of its circuits are designed so they can detect fractal order. If such circuits do indeed exist, why did they ever develop? Being able to recognize and abstract from fractal forms in nature, such as specific types of trees or clouds, may have been an important and very useful evolutionary step. In modern humans, the pro-posed innate ability to respond to fractal order may play a critical role in the aesthetic experience.

Do you have to be Mozart to enjoy Mozart?

A step towards understanding the audience's experience with a work of art is understanding the role of the performer. In the performing arts, the work's message is conveyed to the spectator through an intermediary who typically is not the creator of the work. Is Yehudi Menuhin a creative artist or a mere mechanic? This clearly is a matter of great concern to the composer Adolphe. The performer must be able to recreate at least some of the meaning the creator intended. He or she may or may not recreate the composer's inner music accurately, but in either case, his or her playing should carry a powerful message. Adolphe feels strongly that the performer is an artist contributing creatively to the work as it is heard and/or seen at that particular moment. The same applies to the members of a creative team, such as Chihuly's collabora-tors—many of them well-known glass artists with independent careers—who transform his vision into a glass sculpture. The differences between creator and collaborator or interpreter blur.

How about the audience? The listener, viewer or reader must somehow, and at least in part, recreate in his or her mind what occurred in the original creator's brain. The aesthetic or logic of the creative work may then evoke an emotional response. Goethe wrote on 14 October 1771, on the occasion of Shakespeare's name day, 'Wir ehren heute das Andenken des grössten Wanderers und tun uns dadurch selbst eine Ehre an. Von Verdiensten, die wir zu schätzen wissen, haben wir den Keim in uns.' [We honor today the memory of the greatest wanderer and thus honor ourselves. Of achievements that we can appreciate, we carry the seed in us.]

Do you have to be an artist to relive the artist's experience? Probably, to some degree: the ability to reconstitute the work in one's mind is required; we carry the seed in us. It is clear, however, that you do not have to be Mozart to enjoy the products of his creative genius. Interestingly, many of us can somehow make the distinction between 'good' music and 'bad' or 'trivial' music. In fact, validation of a work of art is performed by the field and the society (see Gardner's chapter)—that means by people whose creative powers usually do not equal those of the work's creator. The spectator also contributes to the work of art, in a very broad sense. The onlooker and the society, Gilot argues, shape the work of art in the context of their personal experiences, culture and history. Remember Gardner's question, 'Where is creativity?' It appears that Goethe was right: the audience reached by a work of art may not be capable of creating the work *de novo*; but it certainly must be able to recreate at least parts of it in its mind.

Does the same hold for science? Any educated audience may understand the contents of a work of science. To appreciate its creative nature, however, the reader must recreate in his or her mind the elegant arguments and deductions presented by the author. This elicits a response. Don't think such reactions are foreign to the supposedly cool and rational scientist! The scientist often reacts emotionally to an idea of his or her own if he or she thinks it is particularly unusual and original, and many scientists respond with equally raised emotions when they listen to a fellow scientist presenting a particularly elegant set of experiments with exciting results—or, for that matter, a set of data or conclusions they consider seriously flawed. In science—as in the arts—the audience reached by the creative work carries the seed.

The aesthetic experience and the body loop

Stent comments that 'at the musical end of the continuum, where symbolism is incommensurable with language' verbal descriptions fail. Indeed, Adolphe, in his latest book, felt compelled to use poetry to express his thoughts on music. But how does the artist's language reach the audience? Gilot and Adolphe focus their discussion on the artist's personal experiences. Yet, when Adolphe describes the tools used in composition he also addresses the issue of how he shapes abstract sounds to evoke a particular response. This may offer some clues. He says that 'you can have ... a wonderful melody ... but when you create a context, or structure, then you have an art form'. He demonstrates how a melody or motif may sound—or be perceived—very differently in different tonal environments, and how harmonic progression and rhythm can further change the mood or color or flavor of the music. For example, the listener's response is quite different if a motif appears in a dissonant or a consonant context.

The *New Harvard Dictionary of Music* states: 'In Western tonal music, consonant intervals (pairs of pitches) are those that are treated as stable and not requiring resolution. Dissonant intervals are those regarded as having an instability that requires resolution to a consonance.' These considerations of tone intervals apply to simultaneous sounds or to sounds heard in succession. This explanation is not scientific, but nevertheless indicates that the human brain perceives tension in dissonance. How dissonance can be used as a communication tool or symbol can be illustrated particularly well in Richard Wagner's extraordinarily evocative opera, *Tristan and Isolde*. In the ancient legend upon which the opera is based, the hero Tristan and his king's intended bride, Isolde, unwittingly drink a love potion and fall under an all-consuming spell. Upon discovery of their illicit relationship, Tristan is mortally wounded by the king's courtier and brought to a distant land. The opera closes with the famous 'Liebestod,' when Isolde reaches the dying Tristan. She follows him by transfiguration, to be united with him in love and death forever. Musically, the opera offers countless references to specific circumstances or relationships, in the form of musical fragments or 'leitmotives', most notably the motifs of 'longing,' 'love-glance' and 'Liebestod.' However, these motifs change constantly to reflect the situation and evolution of the drama and often appear in a dissonant tonal context. The Liebestod motif in particular does not emerge in its pure form until the end of the four-hour work. Tension increases in anticipation of the resolution of the music to consonant tonality and of the drama in the Liebestod.

Wagner had liberated himself from conventional tonal (diatonic) constraints. Musicologists (see von Westernhagen, 1956), such as Arnold Schönberg and Alfred Lorenz, explain that *Tristan* starts in A-minor, but that the hallmark chord, the tonic triad, is never heard. The opera ends with a B-major chord. Between beginning and end, the key shifts continually, leaving the tonality ambiguous along the way—but defining E-major as a 'virtual tonality' at the center. Wagner's device for achieving this result is called chromaticism—the use of tones (or semitones) from outside the diatonic scale (any major or pure minor scale). The resulting harmonies evoke a new kind of dissonance, and the extensive inclusion of half-tones enhances color, tension and the evocative power of the music. Chromatic harmonies had never been used as extensively before; *Tristan* makes the leap from conventional tonality to the 'total chromaticism' and atonality of twentieth-century music.

The revolutionary use of chromaticism and, thus, dissonance in Wagner's opera conveys to the listener the intensity and progression of the unfolding drama and of the emotional worlds of its protagonists. Even the non-musicologist, who may not understand the harmonic devices employed by Wagner, feels the tension developing in the opera and longs for the anticipated tonal resolution. It is only in the final measures that the pure 'Liebestod' motif resolves the tension and produces a climax on stage—and a climactic experience off stage.

> Tristan *illustrates two additional issues discussed in this book: Adolphe's and Gilot's comments that they understand their works to the full extent only after they have been created; and the recurring problems of 'premature discovery' and delayed acceptance of revolutionary works, discussed by Stent, Gardner and Mandelbrot. Wagner had planned to create in* Tristan *a serviceable, practical work—a love story that would give him a pause from the strains of the composition of the monumental* Ring des Nibelungen. *He also hoped that the new opera would generate badly needed revenue. Not until after* Tristan *was nearly complete did Wagner realize that he had written a revolutionary, unique operatic work way ahead of its time.* Tristan *was completed in 1859. The Vienna Royal Opera dropped it as unperformable after 54 rehearsals, so that* Tristan *was not seen until 1865, at the Munich Opera. The composer Richard Strauss observed in 1935 that* Tristan, *rather than resurrecting the romantic era, ended all romanticism, and that the longings of the entire nineteenth century were summarized in this opera and brought to rest in Isolde's Liebestod (see von Westernhagen, 1956; Ewen, 1965).*

Is there a *biological* explanation for our perception of dissonance and consonance and the evocative experience? It is clear that the artist can create in his or her mind, and then transmit in a language, new truths about the inner world that may be perceived by many non-artists. Even though the audience cannot create a similar work, it can perceive the musical images and tension. To understand this, it helps to recall Stevens' explanations of visual processing. Not unlike visual processing in the retina, the ear is known to resolve sounds into their component frequencies. The numerical relationships between these component frequencies determine consonance or dissonance. Thus, the brain is wired so it can discern the order inherent in tonal frequency relationships (in addition to tempo, rhythm, etc.). Via such an analytic process in the ear and the brain, music ultimately elicits images in mapped and non-mapped representational memory and activates an aesthetic experience. To understand this better, one must turn to Damasio's unorthodox integration of mind and body. This concept definitively rejects the dualism of mind and body, of the Apollinian and the Dionysian, of the rational and the emotional.

At the core of Damasio's concept are the following four observations:

(1) The brain—like other organs of the body—is subject to the influence of body control mechanisms, such as hormonal effects. Hormones, like Tristan and Isolde's love potion, may overcome all reason!

(2) The brain holds both innate and acquired dispositional representations (mental images), and the association of such representations with aural or visual experiences (such as the viewing of a work of art) may trigger an emotional response.

(3) Emotions and feelings depend on physical reactions i.e. a change in body state, and on the signalling of this change to the brain.

(4) This sequence of events i.e. the association of experiences and/or newly generated representations with representations already held in the brain, the emotional body response and the resultant feeling, plays a crucial role in decision making, rational or otherwise.

Damasio is putting back together emotion and reason and mind and body, while Descartes and Kant had them strictly separate. They would turn in their graves if they knew.

Let us now apply Damasio's points to the creator and his or her audience. The creative individual has lots of imagination: he or she generates, in the association cortex and its working memory, large numbers of diverse mental images (dispositional representations) that place experiences or facts into novel contexts. These are abstract representations, but they can reconstitute 'mapped' (iconic) representations in lower-level cortical areas. The creator then sorts through these images, and the criteria are novelty and association with important (innate or acquired) images stored in memory. Associations with such representations elicit an emotional response, a change in body state mediated via the autonomic nervous system and hormones. The resultant changes are signalled back to the somatic sensory cortex and perceived as feelings ('body loop'). However, familiar associations may be signalled directly from the association cortex to the somatic sensory cortex, thus evoking feelings without changes in body state ('as-if loop'). Selected (non-mapped) representations probably are then reconstituted into mapped representations, e.g. iconic images or tone sequences, and, from there, translated into the external world as works of art or science. (The execution of the work requires another form of the mind–body continuum e.g. eye–hand coordination for painting.)

The audience viewing the work of art first forms a mapped dispositional representation, then a non-mapped representation in the association cortex. If the image triggers acquired or innate representations in the limbic system or diencephalon, an emotional response ensues ('body loop'), or a feeling can be elicited directly via the 'as-if loop'. So, modern cognitive neuroscience can logically connect imagination and intuition with artistic decision making, and it can link scientifically the audience's experience of a work of art with emotions and feelings. One of the most remarkable outcomes of the synthesis of the many different views expressed here is that we can move beyond the psychologists' phenomenology of creative behavior to an internally consistent theory founded on natural science.

Toward a new definition of creativity

Current neuroscience says that the aesthetic experience depends on the associations that the brain's cortical circuits can make with innate and learned representations, and on the re-creation of a body response in the somatosensory cortex (the feeling). (Note that the learned representations were acquired based on their association with, ultimately, innate symbols.)

One has to infer that the innate or acquired representations eliciting feelings and emotions must include not only specific symbols, color combinations and tonal sequences, but also specific forms of order, such as sentence structures, logical connections and fractal geometry. How else could images based on a fractal formula and synthesized by a computer mimic works of art and elicit feelings?

So what is creativity? Creativity must be the ability to generate in one's brain (the association cortex), novel contexts and representations that elicit associations with symbols and principles of order. Such symbols or principles of order are innate to the human brain or part of the repertoire of acquired dispositional representations in the brains that form one's culture or society. Creativity further must include the ability to translate the selected representations into a work of art or science. Much of these abilities depend upon the highly developed human association cortex.

Evolution clearly favored the human ability to integrate observations, identify problems and seek solutions. The highest level of primate brain function must have evolved through an ever-widening spectrum of associations, from intelligence or learned adaptation (understanding of contexts between different facts in the environment) to creativity, the generation of novel contexts and representations in the mind. Eventually, this led to the invention of tools or the design of cave paintings. Unquestionably, this was based on the continued evolution of the association cortex, which enables its owner to generate more associations and representations, to hold them in memory, and to modify and select them. Along this evolutionary path of simple genetic encoding of circuits and Darwinian selection, additional factors must have contributed to the emergence of creativity. Teaching the known contexts (through language, the drawing of symbols, etc.) and exercising one's mind must have played an increasingly important role in the shaping of human creativity—while innate emotional responses continued their crucial role at the root of decision making. Finally, the collective societal or cultural repertoire of innate (Jung's collective unconscious?) and acquired representations must have become an increasingly important reference point for all creative works.

Are our brains evolving further and becoming more creative, individually or collectively, in our societies? Teilhard de Chardin would want to think so, but the fact that the golden flower of the twentieth century seems hidden from large segments of humanity may make this questionable.

Remarkably, the views and definition of creativity presented here are compatible with a great variety of perspectives—of artist, scientist, philosopher, psychologist and neurobiologist. Advances in modern neuroscience have demystified creativity, but they also are reshaping our understanding of creativity. As the principles of how the human brain works are being revealed, the realization and appreciation of this marvel of biology turns into a new aesthetic experience of its own.

References and further reading

The entangled bank: An introduction

References

Darwin, C. (1859/1964). *On the origin of species.* A facsimile of the first edition with an introduction by Ernst Mayr, Harvard University Press, Cambridge, MA and London.

Freud, S. (1891/1954). *On aphasia.* International Universities Press, New York.

Russell, B. (1954/1985). *My philosophical development.* Unwin Hyman Ltd., London.

Part 1 Eureka! Discovery versus creation

References

Chargaff, Erwin (1968). A quick climb up Mount Olympus. *Science* **159**: 1448–9.

Chihuly, D. (1986). *Chihuly: color, glass, and form.* Kodanska International Ltd., Tokyo, Japan.

Chihuly, D. (1989). *Venetians.* Twin Palms Publishers, Altadena.

Chihuly, D. (1993). *Chihuly: Form from fire.* The Museum of Arts and Sciences, Inc., Daytona Beach, in association with University of Washington Press, Seattle.

Crick, Francis H.C. (1974). The double helix; a personal view. *Nature* **248**: 766–71 (Reprinted in Watson (1980) pp. 137–45.)

Gadamer, Georg (1976). *Philosophical hermeneutics* (Trans D.E. Linge). University of California Press, Berkeley.

Langer, S.K. (1948). *Philosophy in a new key.* Mentor Books, New York.

Medawar, P. (1991). *The threat and the glory. Reflections on science and scientists.* Oxford University Press, Oxford, UK.

Meyer, Leonard B. (1967). *Music, the arts and ideas.* University of Chicago Press.

Meyer, Leonard B. (1974). Concerning the sciences, the arts – AND the humanities. *Critical Inquiry* **1**: 163–217.

Perreault, J. (1996). Conversation with Suzanne Ramljak. *Glass: The Urban Glass Art Quarterly* **No. 64**, pp. 12–13.

Read, H. (1964). *Modern sculpture. A concise history.* Thames and Hudson, New York.

Snow, C.P. (1959). *The two cultures and the scientific revolution.* Cambridge University Press, New York.

Stent, G.S. (1968). What they are saying about honest Jim. *Quarterly Review of Biology* 43: 179–184. (Reprinted and expanded in Watson, 1980, pp. 161–175).

Stent, Gunther S. (1972). Prematurity and uniqueness in scientific discovery. *Scientific American* 227: 84–93. (Reprinted in Gunther S. Stent (1978), *Paradoxes of progress*, pp. 95–113. Freeman, San Francisco.)

Thomas, L. (1980). *Science and 'science.' Late night thoughts on listening to Mahler's Ninth Symphony.* The Viking Press, New York.

Watson, James D. and Crick, Francis H.C. (1953). A structure for deoxyribonucleic acid. *Nature* 171: 737–8. (Reprinted in Watson (1980) pp. 237–41.)

Watson, James D. (1968). *The double helix.* Atheneum, New York.

Watson, James D. (1980). *The double helix. A critical edition* (ed. Gunther S. Stent). Norton, New York.

Further reading

Alberts, B., Bray, D., Lewis, J., Raff, M., Roberts, K. and Watson, J.D. (1994). *Molecular biology of the cell* (3rd edition) Garland Publishing Inc., New York.

Bryan, T.M. and Cech, T.R. (1999). Telomerase and the maintenance of chromosome ends. *Current Opinion in Cell Biology* 11: 318–24.

Brockman, J. (1995). *The third culture.* (First Touchstone edition, 1996.) Touchstone, New York.

Cairns, J., Stent, G.S., Watson, J.D. (1966). *Phage and the origins of molecular biology.* Cold Spring Harbor Laboratory Press, Plainview, New York.

Cech, T.R. and Uhlenbeck, O.C. (1994). Ribozymes. Hammerhead nailed down. *Nature* 372: 39–40.

Cech, T.R. (1993). The efficiency and versatility of catalytic RNA: implications for an RNA world. *Gene* 135: 33–6.

Delbrück, M. (1986). *Mind from matter?: an essay on evolutionary epistemology.* Edited by G.S. Stent. Blackwell Scientific Publications, Palo Alto.

Frantz, S.K. (1989). *Contemporary glass.* Harry N. Abrams Inc., New York.

Kuspit, D.B. (1997). *Chihuly.* Portland Press, Seattle (distributed by Harry N. Abrams Inc., New York).

Stent, G.S. (1971). *Molecular genetics: and introductory narrative.* W.H. Freeman, San Francisco.

Part 2 Body, brain, and mind: emotion and reason

References

Adolphe, B. (1991). *The mind's ear: exercises for improving the musical imagination.* MMB Music, St Louis.

Adolphe, B. (1996). *What to listen for in the world.* 1st Limelight Edition with illustrations by Vijay Kumar. Limelight Editions, New York.

Brockman, J. (1995). Introduction: the emerging third culture. In Brockman, J., *The third culture.* (First Touchstone edition, 1996.) Touchstone, New York.

Churchland, P. (1981). Eliminative materialism and the propositional attitudes. *Journal of Philosophy* 78: 67–90. (Reprinted in Boyd, R., Gasper, P. and Trout, J.D. (ed) 1991. *The philosophy of science.* The MIT Press, Cambridge).

Damasio, A.R. (1994). *Descartes' error: emotion, reason, and the human brain.* Grosset/Putnam, New York.

Damasio, A.R. (1999). *The feeling of what happens: body and emotion in the making of consciousness.* Harcourt Brace & Company, New York.

Darwin, C. (1859/1964). *On the origin of species.* A facsimile of the first edition with an introduction by Ernst Mayr, Harvard University Press, Cambridge, MA.

Goleman, D., **Kaufman,** P. and **Ray,** M. (1992). *The creative spirit.* Penguin Books USA Inc., New York.

Kandel, E.R. and **Schwartz,** J.H. (1981). *Principles of neural science* (1st edition). Elsevier/North-Holland, New York, Amsterdam, Oxford.

Marr, D. (1982). *Vision.* W.H. Freeman and Company, New York.

Medawar, P. (1991). *The threat and the glory. Reflections on science and scientists.* Oxford University Press, Oxford, UK.

Pfenninger, K.H. (1986). Of nerve growth cones, leukocytes and memory: on the growth cone's second messenger systems and growth-regulated proteins. *Trends in Neuroscience* 9: 562–5.

Pinker, S. (1994). *The language instinct.* William Morrow & Co./Harper Collins Publishers Inc., New York.

Read, H. (1964). *Modern sculpture. A concise history.* Thames and Hudson, New York.

Reeke, G.N. Jr. and **Sporns,** O. (1993). Behaviorally based modeling and computational approaches to neuroscience. *Annual Review of Neuroscience* 16: 597–623.

Selverston, A.I. (1993). Modeling of neural circuits. What have we learned? *Annual Review of Neuroscience* 16: 531–46.

Further reading

Adolphe, B. (1999). *Of Mozart, parrots and cherry blossoms in the wind: a composer explores mysteries of the musical mind.* Limelight Editions, New York.

Damasio, A.R., **Damasio,** H. and **Christen,** Y. (eds.) (1996). *Neurobiology of decision-making.* Springer Verlag, Berlin, New York.

Damasio, A.R. (1989). The brain binds entities and events by multiregional activation from convergence zones. *Neural Computation* 1: 123–32.

Damasio, H., **Grabowski,** T.J., **Tranel,** D., **Hichwa,** R. and **Damasio,** A.R. (1996). A neural basis for lexical retrieval. *Nature* 380: 499–505.

Greenough, W.T. and **Anderson,** B.J. (1991). Cerebellar synaptic plasticity. Relation to learning versus neural activity. *Annals of the New York Academy of Science* 627: 231–47.

Kandel, E.R., **Schwartz,** J.H. and **Jessell,** T.M. (2000). *Principles of neural science* (4th edition). McGraw-Hill, New York.

Klintsova, A.Y. and **Greenough,** W.T. (1999). Synaptic plasticity in cortical systems. *Current Opinion in Neurobiology* 9: 203–8.

McCutchan, A. (1999). *The muse that sings: Composers speak about the creative process.* Oxford University Press, Oxford, UK.

Purves, D. and **Lichtman,** J.W. (1985). *Principles of neural development.* Sinauer Associates Inc., Sunderland.

Ralston, H.J. III (1998). Untying the Gordian Knot: contemporary studies of neuronal organization. *Anatomical Record (New Anat.)* 253: 139–42.

Rogers, D.E. (1988). Clinical education and the doctor of tomorrow. In *Adapting clinical medical education to the needs of today and tomorrow* (eds. B. Gastel and D.E. Rogers). New York Academy of Medicine, New York.

Rogers, D.E. and **Ginzberg,** E. (eds.) (1993). *Medical care and the health of the poor.* Cornell University Medical College Eigth Conference on Health Policy. Westview Press, Boulder.

Rogers, D.E. and **Ginzberg,** E. (eds.) (1995). *The metropolitan academic medical center: its role in an era of tight money and changing expectations.* Cornell University Medical College Ninth Conference on Health Policy. Westview Press, Boulder.

Widnell, C.C. and **Pfenninger,** K.H. (1990). *Essential cell biology.* Williams & Wilkins, Baltimore.

Part 3 The adaptive mind: deprivation versus rich stimulation

References

Aronson, L.R., **Tobach,** E., **Rosenblatt,** J.S., **Lehrman,** D.S. (editors) (1972). *Selected writings of T.C. Schneiria.* W.H. Freman, San Francisco.

Crnic, L.S. (1990). The use of animal models to study effects of nutrition on behavior.

In *Diet and behavior: multidisciplinary approaches* (ed-in-chief G.H. Anderson), chapter 5. Springer Verlag, London, Berlin.

Csikszentmihalyi, M. (1996). *Creativity, flow and the psychology of discovery and invention.* Harper Collins Publishers Inc., New York.

Dobbing, J. (1968). Vulnerable periods in developing brain. In *Applied neurochemistry* (eds. A.N. Davidson and J. Dobbing), pp. 287–316. Blackwell Scientific Publications, Oxford, UK.

Gardner, H. (1983). *Frames of the mind. The theory of multiple intelligences.* Basic Books (Harper Collins Publishers Inc.), New York.

Gardner, H. (1993*a*). *Creating minds: an anatomy of creativity seen through the lives of Freud, Einstein, Picasso, Stravinsky, Eliot, Graham and Gandhi.* Basic Books, (Harper Collins Publishers Inc.) New York.

Gardner, H. (1993*b*). *Multiple intelligences. The theory in practice.* Basic Books (Harper Collins Publishers Inc.), New York.

Goleman, D., **Kaufman,** P. and **Ray,** M. (1992). *The creative spirit.* Penguin Books USA Inc., New York.

Grantham–McGregor, S. (1987). Field studies in early nutrition and later achievement. In *Early nutrition and later achievement* (ed. J. Dobbing). Academic Press Inc., London, UK.

Lashley, K. (1963). *Brain mechanisms and intelligence; a quantitative study of injuries to the brain.* With new introduction by D.O. Hebb. Dover Publications, New York.

Levitsky, D.A. and **Strupp,** B.J. (1987). Discussion quoted in *Early nutrition and later achievement* (ed. J. Dobbing), p. 198. Academic Press Inc., London, UK.

Sinisterra, L. (1987). Studies on poverty, human growth and development: the Cali experience. In *Early nutrition and later achievement* (ed. J. Dobbing). Academic Press Inc., London, UK.

Stravinsky, I. (1962). Igor Stravinsky: an autobiography. W.W. Norton, New York.

Tanner, J.M., **Preece,** M.A. (editors) (1989). *The physiology of human growth.* Cambridge University Press, Cambridge, New York.

Further reading

Alberts, B., **Bray,** D., **Lewis,** J., **Raff,** M., **Roberts,** K. and **Watson,** J.D. (1994). *Molecular biology of the cell* (3rd edition). Garland Publishing Inc., New York.

Anderson, G.H. (ed-in-chief) (1990). *Diet and behavior: multidisciplinary approaches.* Springer Verlag, London, Berlin.

Boorstin, D.J. (1992). *The creators. A history of heroes of the imagination.* Random House, New York.

Durant, W. (1953). *The story of civilization: Part V, the Renaissance.* Simon and Schuster, New York.

Feldman, D., **Csikszentmihalyi,** M. and **Gardner,** H. (1994). Changing the world: a framework for the study of creativity. Greenwood Publishing Co., Westport.

Galler, J.R. (1987). The interaction of nutrition and environment in behavioral development. In *Early nutrition and later achievement* (ed. J. Dobbing). Academic Press, New York.

Gardner, H. (in press). *Intelligence reframed.* Basic Books, New York.

Palade, G.E. (1975). Intracellular aspects of the process of protein secretion (Nobel lecture). *Science* 189: 347–58.

Palade, G.E. (1991). Major basic research discoveries. Supplement to *Discovering new worlds in medicine.* Farmitalia Carlo Erba, Milan, Italy.

Palade, G.E. (1995). Summary in *Cold Spring Harbor Symposia on Quantitative Biology,* vol. LX, pp. 821–31.

Widnell, C.C. and **Pfenninger,** K.H. (1990). *Essential cell biology.* Williams & Wilkins, Baltimore.

Part 4 Patterns of perception

References

Cowart, J. and **Hamilton,** J. (1987). *Georgia O'Keeffe, Art and letters.* Letter to John I.H. Baur, dated 22 April 1957. New York Graphic Society Books/Little, Brown and Company Inc.

Dyson, F.J. (1978). Characterizing irregularity. *Science* 200: 677–8.

Edgerton, S.Y. Jr (1991). *The heritage of Giotto's geometry: art and science on the eve of the scientific revolution.* Cornell University Press, Ithaca.

Galilei, G. (1990). Discoveries and opinions of Galileo: including The starry messenger (1610), Letter to the Grand Duchess Christina (1615), and excerpts from Letters on sunspots (1613), The assayer (1623). Translated with an introduction by Stillman Drake. Anchor Books, New York.

Gardiner, M. (1988). *A scatter of memories.* Free Association Books, London.

Huffington, A.S. (1993). *The gods of Greece.* Paintings by F. Gilot. 1st Atlantic Monthly Press ed., New York.

Kandel, E.R. (1981). In *Principles of neural science* (eds. E.R. Kandel and J.H. Schwartz) (1st edition), p. 247. Elsevier/North-Holland, New York, Amsterdam, Oxford.

Mandelbrot, B. (1983). *The fractal geometry of nature.* W.H. Freeman, New York.

Picasso, P. (1945). Similar quotation in *Les Lettres Francaises* V, no. 48, Paris, 24 March.

Picasso, P. (1947). Originally published in 'Picasso speaks'. In *The Arts,* New York, May 1923, pp 315–26.

Read, H. (1960). *The forms of things unknown: essays towards an aesthetic philosophy.* Faber & Faber Ltd., London, UK.

Stent, Gunther S. (1972). Prematurity and uniqueness in scientific discovery. *Scientific American* **227**: 84–93. (Reprinted in Gunther S. Stent, *Paradoxes of progress*, pp. 95–113. Freeman, San Francisco.)

Further reading

Gilot, F. (1964). *Life with Picasso* (with Carlton Lake). McGraw-Hill, New York.

Gilot, F. (1983). *Interface: the painter and the mask/Le regard et son masque.* English translation by Françoise Gilot. The Press at California State University, Fresno.

Gilot, F. (1987). *An artist's journey/Un voyage pictural.* Atlantic Monthly Press, New York.

Gilot, F. (1990). *Matisse & Picasso: a friendship in art.* Doubleday, New York.

Gilot, F. (2000). *Sixty years of her art (1940–2000).* ACATOS, Lausanne, Switzerland.

Harmon, L.D. (1973). The recognition of faces. *Scientific American* **229**: 70–82.

Kandel, E.R., **Schwartz,** J.H. and **Jessell,** T.M. (2000). *Principles of neural science* (4th edition). McGraw-Hill, New York.

Mandelbrot, B. (1981). Scalebound or Scaling Shapes: A Useful Distinction in the Visual Arts and in the Natural Sciences. *Leonardo* **14**: 45–7.

Mandelbrot, B. (1986). Fractals and the rebirth of iteration theory. In *The beauty of fractals* (eds. H-O Peitgen and P.H. Richter). Springer, New York.

Mandelbrot, B. (1988). People and events behind the science of fractal images. In *The science of fractal images* (eds. H-O Peitgen and D. Saupe). Springer, New York.

Mandelbrot, B. (1989). Fractals and an art for the sake of science. *Leonardo* Supplemental Issue: 21–4.

Mandelbrot, B. (1991). Fractals and the rebirth of experimental mathematics. In *Fractals for the classroom* (eds. H-O Peitgen, H. Jürgens, D. Saupe, E.M. Matelski, T. Perciante, and L.E. Yunker). Springer, New York.

Stevens, C.F. (1996). Spatial learning and memory: the beginning of a dream. *Cell* **87**: 1147–8.

Synthesis

References

Briggs, J. (1992). *Fractals, The patterns of chaos.* Touchstone Books (Simon and Schuster), New York.

Churchland, P. (1981). Eliminative materialism and the propositional attitudes. *Journal of Philosophy* 78: 67–90. (Reprinted in Boyd, R., Gasper, P. and Trout, J.D. (ed) (1991). *The philosophy of science.* The MIT Press, Cambridge).

Eglash, R. (1999). *African fractals: modern computing and indigenous design.* Rutgers University Press, New Brunswick.

Ewen, D. (1965). *The complete book of classical music.* Prentice-Hall Inc., Englewood Cliffs.

Gell–Mann, M. (1995). Plectics. In *The third culture* (ed. J. Brockman), chapter 19. Touchstone Books, (Simon and Schuster), New York.

Greenough, W.T. and **Anderson,** B.J. (1991). Cerebellar synaptic plasticity. Relation to learning versus neural activity. *Annals of the New York Academy of Science* **627**: 231–47.

Hofstadter, D.R. (1979). *Gödel, Escher, Bach: an eternal golden braid.* Basic Books (Harper Collins Publishers Inc.) New York.

Heisenberg, W. (1958). *Physics and philosophy; the revolution in modern science.* Harper, New York.

Martin, S. (1996). *Picasso at the lapin agile and other plays.* Grove Press, New York.

Pinker, S. (1994). *The language instinct.* William Morrow & Co./Harper Collins Publishers Inc., New York.

Stoppard, T. (1993). *Arcadia.* Faber and Faber, London, Boston.

Stutzer, B. and **Windhöfel,** L. (1991). *Augusto Giacometti, Leben und Werk.* Verlag Bündner Monatsblatt, Chur, Switzerland.

Swafford, J. (1997). *Johannes Brahms. A biography.* Alfred A. Knopf, New York.

Weisberg, R.W. (1993). *Creativity: beyond the myth of genius.* W.H. Freeman and Company, New York.

Westernhagen, C. von (1956). *Richard Wagner, Sein Werk, sein Wesen, seine Welt.* Atlantis Verlag, Zürich, Switzerland.

Further reading

Coffey, D.S. (1998). Self-organization, complexity and chaos. The new biology for medicine. *Nature Medicine* 4: 882–5.

Deacon, T.W. (1997). *The symbolic species. The co-evolution of language and the brain.* W.W. Norton & Company, New York, London.

Fisk, J. (1997). *Composers on music. Eight centuries of writings.* Northeastern University Press/Panteon Books Inc., Boston.

Gleick, J. (1987). *Chaos: making a new science.* Penguin Books USA Inc., New York.

Kandel, E.R., **Schwartz,** J.H. and **Jessell,** T.M. (2000). *Principles of neural science* (4th edition). McGraw–Hill, New York.

Popper, K.R. and **Eccles,** J.C. (1977). *The self and its brain. An argument for inter-actionism.* (Reprinted 1995 by Routledge, London, New York.)

Biographies

Bruce Adolphe

A composer's mental images play a central part in the creation of new music, but real musical thinking takes place in the mind's ear alone. Composer, author, educator and performer, Bruce Adolphe has explored the mysteries of the musical mind and devised a series of exercises that are designed to link memory, the mind and musical imagination. He found that inspiration is a mode of perception which can be cultivated when he tested his exercises on young musicians in classes at Juilliard and the Chamber Music Society of Lincoln Center (where he is Music and Education Advisor). He is also permanent composer-in-residence at SummerFest La Jolla and Artistic Director of PollyRhythm Productions.

Bruce Adolphe has composed music for Itzhak Perlman, Sylvia McNair, David Shifrin, the Beaux Arts Trio, the Orpheus Chamber Orchestra, the National Symphony, the Caramoor Festival, the Metropolitan Opera Guild, the Brentano String Quartet, the Miami Quartet, David Finckel and Wu Han and many others.

His over fifty compositions include four operas. His Bridgehampton Concerto was performed at the Aspen Music Festival. Formerly on the faculties of the Juilliard School and New York University and a visiting lecturer at Yale, Adolphe has been the lecturer of the Chamber Music Society of Lincoln Center since 1992, and has been featured in nationally broadcast 'Live from Lincoln Center' television programs. In 1999, he created a cross-disciplinary lecture series on music, science, art and literature for SummerFest La Jolla in collaboration with the University of California, San Diego.

He has been composer-in-residence at festivals throughout the United States, including the Santa Fe Chamber Music Festival, Chamber Music Northwest, Music from Angel Fire, Bravo! Colorado, the Grand Canyon Festival, the Perlman Music Program, the Bridgehampton Chamber Music Festival, Chamber Music Virginia, the OK Mozart Festival and Summerfest La Jolla.

With Julian Fifer, Bruce Adolphe co-founded PollyRhythm Productions, a company devoted to the creation of educational repertoire and materials in a wide range of media specifically aimed at children and families. (The company is named after Adolphe's opera-and-jazz singing parrot, Polly Rhythm.)

A regular writer for Sony Classical Records and a prolific author, Adolphe's books include *The Mind's Ear: Exercises for Improving the Musical Imagination,* *What to Listen for in the World* and *Of Mozart, Parrots and Cherry Blossoms in the Wind: A Composer Explores Mysteries of the Musical Mind.* Adolphe's music has been recorded on the Telarc, CRI, Delos, Koch and Summit labels. His film scores include the permanent documentary at the Holocaust Museum in Washington, DC.

Thomas R. Cech PhD

Thomas R. Cech was awarded the Nobel Prize in Chemistry in 1989 for pioneering studies which showed that RNA can play a catalytic role in cellular metabolism rather than being only a passive carrier of genetic information.

In 1982, Cech and his research group announced that an RNA molecule from *Tetrahymena*, a single-celled pond organism, cut and rejoined chemical bonds in the complete absence of proteins. This discovery of self-splicing RNA provided the first exception to the long-held belief that biological reactions are catalyzed exclusively by proteins and offered a plausible foundation for a new theory of the origin of life on earth. Because RNA can be both an information-carrying molecule and a catalyst, perhaps the first self-reproducing system consisted of RNA alone. Only years later was it recognized that RNA catalysts, or 'ribozymes,' might provide a new class of highly specific pharmaceutical agents, able to cleave and thereby inactivate viral or other RNAs involved in disease.

Currently, he is the Distinguished Professor of Chemistry and Biochemistry and also of Molecular, Cellular and Developmental Biology at the University of Colorado, Boulder. In addition, he is an investigator and the recently appointed head of the Howard Hughes Medical Institute.

Born in Chicago, Illinois on 8 December 1947, Cech was educated in Iowa and received his BA in Chemistry from Grinnell College. Graduating from the University of California, Berkeley, he was awarded his PhD in 1975, and then did post-doctoral research in the Department of Biology at MIT in Cambridge, Massachusetts. In 1978, he joined the faculty of the University of Colorado, Boulder, in the Department of Chemistry and Biochemistry.

Cech's pioneering studies on catalytic RNA have earned him many prestigious national and international awards, including an American Cancer Society Lifetime Professorship (1987). In 1987, he was elected to the National Academy of Sciences. His work has been recognized by the Heineken Prize of the Royal Netherlands Academy of Sciences (1988), the Albert Lasker Basic Medical Research Award (1988), the Louisa Gross Horwitz Prize (1988), the Nobel Prize in Chemistry (1989), the National Medal of Science (1995), the Mike Hogg Award of the M.D. Anderson Cancer Center, University of Texas

(1997), the Wright Prize awarded by Harvey Mudd College (1998) and many others.

Cech teaches, writes and lectures extensively. In his own words, he spends his time as 'teacher, father and discoverer'.

Dale Chihuly MFA

Chihuly's homage to Jerusalem on the eve of the millennium weighs over 42 tonnes and is made up of some 15 large installations in the courtyard of the Tower of David, one of which is a 13.5-meter tower of some 2000 pieces of glass. At the Tower of David Museum, *The Moon*–a 3.5-meter-diameter blue globe made from 500 pieces of glass that hang above the fortress—is visible from the new city. The exhibition 'Chihuly in the Light of Jerusalem 2000' opened on 1 July 1999 and drew more than 70 000 people in its first month.

Born in 1941 in Tacoma, Washington, Dale Chihuly first thought about glass as an art medium while studying interior design at the University of Washington. After graduating with honors in 1965, he enrolled in Harvey Littleton's seminal glass program at the University of Wisconsin. He continued his studies at the Rhode Island School of Design (RISD) where he was awarded an MFA in 1968. He established the Glass Department at RISD, and later became head of the Sculpture Department. In 1980, he resigned to become an artist-in-residence so that he could devote more time to his own work.

In 1968, Chihuly was awarded a Fulbright Fellowship to work at the Venini factory in Venice, Italy. While in Venice, he observed the Italians' team approach to blowing glass, which is critical to his studio today. In 1971, Chihuly co-founded Pilchuck Glass School in Stanwood, Washington. This school is now an international glass communications center which leads the way in the development of glass blowing as an art form. He has been the recipient of many awards, including honorary doctorates from the University of Puget Sound, the Rhode Island School of Design and the California College of Arts and Crafts. Chihuly has also been honored with two fellowships from the National Endowment for the Arts, the American Council for the Arts Visual Artist's Award and the Louis Comfort Tiffany Foundation Award. In 1992, he was named the first National Living Treasure by the United States' fifty governors.

His glass sculptures are included in over 170 museum collections, from New York to Kyoto. Dale Chihuly has created many well-known series of works, among them the *Baskets*, *Persians* and *Seaforms*, but he is most celebrated for large architectural installations. In 1986, Kodansha International Ltd. published *Dale Chihuly: Color, Glass, and Form*. He was honored by a one-man exhibition at the Musée des Arts Decoratifs in Paris—only the fourth American to have their work shown in the Louvre. In 1988, Henry Geldzahler curated an exhibition of *Persians* for the Dia Art Foundation. The University of Washington Press documented his work with full-color illustrations of the drawings and maquettes in *Pelleas + Melisande + Chihuly*. In 1995, he embarked on the multifaceted international project, 'Chihuly over Venice', which involved collaborative glass blowing at factories in Finland, Ireland and Mexico, and included a trip to Waterford, Ireland, where glass was blown, etched and installed in and around Lismore Castle. The resultant sculptures were mounted over the canals and *piazze* of Venice as part of that city's first glass biennial. The project was the subject of a documentary television program, the first HD-TV broadcast by PBS. The next year, Chihuly traveled to the Virgin Islands and created over 100 drawings of the island scenery. In 1998, he was the guest of honor at the Sydney Arts Festival and he blew glass on the island of Niijima in Japan.

Antonio R. Damasio MD PhD

Antonio R. Damasio is the Van Allen Distinguished Professor and Head of the Department of Neurology at the University of Iowa, and an Adjunct Professor at The Salk Institute in La Jolla, California.

Damasio's work has focused on elucidating fundamental problems in the neuroscience of mind and behavior, at the level of large-scale systems in humans. His contributions have had a major influence on our understanding of the neural basis of decision making, emotion, language and memory.

In collaboration with Hanna Damasio, a distinguished neurologist who is independently recognized for her achievements in neuroimaging and neuro-anatomy, Damasio moved lesion studies away from clinical descriptions and placed them at the service of hypothesis-driven research. The laboratories that he and Hanna Damasio created at the University of Iowa are a leading center for the investigation of cognition using both the lesion method and functional imaging.

Damasio is a member of the National Academy of Sciences' Institute of Medicine, a fellow of the American Academy of Arts and Sciences, a member of the Neurosciences Research Program, a member of the National Advisory Council on Neurological Diseases and Stroke, a fellow of the American Academy of Neurology, a member of the European Academy of Sciences and Arts and of the Royal Academy of Medicine in Belgium, a member of the American Neurological Association and of the Association of American Physicians and a board member of leading neuroscience journals. He is a past President of the Academy of Aphasia and of the Behavioral Neurology Society.

Damasio's distinguished lectureships include the Tanner Lecture (Michigan), the Wilson Lecture (Wellesley), the Steubenbord Lectures (Cornell University), the Aird Lectures (University of California, San Francisco), the Nobel Conference, the Karolinska Research Lecture at the Nobel Forum and the Presidential Lecture at The University of Iowa. Since 1981, he has delivered an annual series of lectures on the neurology of behavior at Harvard Medical School.

Among other awards, he has received the William Beaumont Prize from the American Medical Association (1990), the Golden Brain Award (1995), the Ipsen Prize (1997) and the Kappers Medal of Neuroscience (1999). In 1992, he and his wife shared the Pessoa Prize.

Antonio Damasio's book *Descartes' Error: Emotion, Reason and the Human Brain* (Putnam, 1994) has been published in over 20 countries. His new book *The Feeling of What Happens: Body, Emotion, and the Making of Consciousness* is published by Harcourt Brace.

Damasio was born in Portugal. He received both his MD and his doctorate from the University of Lisbon, and began his research in cognitive neuroscience with the late Norman Geschwind.

Janina Galler MD

Since 1973, Janina Galler has studied the effects of childhood malnutrition on brain function and behavior in animal models and in long-term studies of children in Barbados and Mexico. Her research explores the impact of a child's early experiences on the later plasticity and adaptive functioning of that individual's brain. Her studies have provided some of the clearest data on the relationship of the infant's early environment to adult performance.

After graduating summa cum laude from Sophie Newcomb College, Tulane University, New Orleans, she received her MD degree in 1972 from the Albert Einstein College of Medicine in New York. She was trained in child psychiatry at the Massachusetts General Hospital, and was a Research Associate in the Department of Nutrition and Food Science at the Massachusetts Institute of Technology. Currently, Janina Galler is Professor of Psychiatry and Public Health and the Director of the Center for Behavioral Development and Mental Retardation at the Boston University School of Medicine.

Galler is the recipient of numerous awards, including the Irving B. Harris Lectureship Award, the Society for Behavioral Pediatrics, St Louis, Missouri, which was awarded in 1992, and the Centennial Award from the Sophie H. Newcomb College at Tulane University in that same year. She also received the Blanche F. Ittleson Award for Research in Child Psychiatry from the American

Psychiatric Association and the Joseph P. Kennedy Jr Foundation Public Policy Leadership Award in Mental Retardation.

A past Director of Residency Training, Division of Psychiatry at the Boston University School of Medicine, Galler is a fellow of the American Psychiatric Association and a past Chairperson of the Planning and Policy Committee of the National Advisory Child Health and Human Development Council at the National Institutes of Health (NIH). She is a member of numerous advisory committees including the Pediatric and SIDS Brain Bank, NICHD, the International Maternal PKU Study Committee, NICHD, the Functional Aspects of Undernutrition Steering Committee, US Agency for International Development (USAID), the Advisory Committee on Future Directions for Research on Nutrition and Delinquency, The Ford Foundation; a past Chairperson of the Workshop on Behavioral Correlates of Malnutrition; and a member of the Workshop on Children of Holocaust Survivors (1981–95).

Galler is an active participant in US Congressional committees and on the boards of various philanthropic organizations including the Scientific Advisory Board of the Joseph P. Kennedy Foundation, the Board of Directors of The Trasher Research Fund, Salt Lake City, the Board of Directors of the New England Council of Child Psychiatry and the Douglas A. Thom Clinic in Boston.

Howard E. Gardner PhD

Widely recognized for his work in the areas of developmental psychology, neuropsychology, education, aesthetics and the social sciences, Howard Gardner is an educator who has written more than 353 articles in scholarly journals, 20 books and 166 topical articles, introductions and book reviews. His book *Frames of Mind: The Theory of Multiple Intelligences* (1983) was translated into 10 foreign languages, selected by three book clubs and received the National Psychology Award for Excellence. His most recent book is *Intelligence Reframed* (1999).

For more than 25 years, Howard Gardner has researched and written about creativity. In addition to *Frames of Mind*, he has written other books that examine the creative experience: *Art, Mind, and Brain: A Cognitive Approach to Creativity* (1982); *Art Education and Human Development* (1990); *Multiple Intelligences: The Theory in Practice* (1993); *Creating Minds: An Anatomy of Creativity Seen Through the Lives of Freud, Einstein, Picasso, Stravinsky, Eliot, Graham, and Gandhi* (1993); with the collaboration of Emma Laskin, *Leading Minds: An Anatomy of Leadership* (1997); *Extraordinary Minds: Portraits of Exceptional Individuals and An Examination of Our Extraordinariness* (1997) and *The Disciplined Mind: What All Students Should Understand* (1999).

Currently, he is the John H. and Elisabeth A. Hobbs Professor of Cognition and Education (1998–present) and Co-Director (1972–present) and Chairman of the Steering Committee (1995–present) of Harvard Project Zero at the Harvard Graduate School of Education. He is also Adjunct Research Professor of Neurology at Boston University School of Medicine (1987–present) and on the editorial boards of *Creativity Research Journal, Journal of Creative Behavior* and *The Handbook of Neuropsychology.*

Born on 11 July 1943, Howard Gardner graduated summa cum laude from Harvard College in 1965, read philosophy and sociology at the London School of Economics on a Frank Knox Fellowship (1965–6) and received a PhD in Developmental Psychology in 1971. From 1971 to 1972, he was a post-doctoral fellow at Harvard Medical School and Boston University Aphasia Research Center. In 1972, he joined the Harvard faculty, and in 1987, he also had a faculty appointment at the Boston University School of Medicine.

Gardner's interdisciplinary approach to creativity has earned him numerous awards, fellowships and honorary degrees, including a MacArthur Prize Fellowship (1981–6); the University of Louisville's Grawemeyer Award in Education (1990); Doctor of Music, *honoris causa*, New England Conservatory of Music (1993); Teachers College Medal for Distinguished Service to Education, Teachers College, Columbia University (1994); Center for Advanced Study in the Behavioral Sciences, Fellow, Stanford University (1994–5); Distinguished Achievement Award for Excellence in Educational Journalism, Educational Press Association of America (1996); subject of exhibit, *Contemporary Educational Leaders*, at the Museum of Education, Columbia, South Carolina (1998); Doctor of Humane Letters, *honoris causa* from Princeton University and Tel Aviv University, Israel (1998); Presidential Citation, American Psychological Association (1998); the John P. McGovern Award in Behavioral Sciences, Smithsonian Associates (1998) and the Walker Prize, Museum of Science, Boston (1999).

He is also a fellow of the American Association for the Advancement of Science and a past Vice-President of the National Academy of Education, American Academy of Arts and Sciences.

Françoise Gilot BA (Philosophy)

Françoise Gilot, since the first exhibition of her paintings in the Madeleine Decre Gallery in Paris at the age of 22, has been dedicated to painting. From 1951, when she exhibited her paintings at the Galerie La Hune in Paris, her work has been a bridge between the school of Paris and today's American art scene. Her early work was exhibited in galleries in Paris, England, New York,

Germany and Italy. Her paintings, influenced in the early years by her association with Picasso and Matisse, seek to establish a visual order through the timeless language of symbols.

Born in 1921 in Neuilly-sur-Seine, France, she is the daughter of a French industrialist. Graduating from the University of Paris in 1938, she received a Bachelor of Arts Degree in Philosophy and a Diploma in English Literature from the British Institute (Cambridge University) in Paris in 1939. From 1939 until 1942, she studied law and literature at the University of Paris.

In the 40 years since her first exhibition, Gilot's paintings have been exhibited all over the world and are in the permanent collections of many museums including the Musée d'Art Moderne in Paris; the Musée Picasso, in Antibes, France; the Musée de Tel Aviv in Tel Aviv, Israel; the Women's Museum in Washington, DC; the Museum of Modern Art in New York; the El Paso Museum of Art, El Paso, Texas; the Museum of the University of New Mexico, Albuquerque, New Mexico; the University Art Museum, California State University, Long Beach, California; and in the permanent collection of Scripps College, Claremont, California.

She has designed the sets and costumes for five different theatrical performances including 'La Frange des Mots' [At the Edge of Words] (1952), 'Herakles' [Hercules] at the Theatre des Champs Elysées in Paris (1953), 'Satyavan: Dream Twilight' in the Solomon R. Guggenheim Museum Auditorium (1985), 'Shi-me' at the Walker Art Center (1987) and 'Septet' at the Museum of Contemporary Art in San Diego.

Françoise Gilot is also well known for her original prints and monotypes. She contributes text and or prefaces for the exhibition catalogs of some of her most important exhibitions, which include those at the Musée Picasso, Antibes, France (1987); the Georges Pompidou National Centre in Paris (1990); the Philip and Muriel Berman Museum of Art at Ursinus College, Pennsylvania (1995) (1997); the Fall Galerie, Paris (1998) and the Elkon Gallery, New York (1998). She has created original lithographs for Paul Eluard's *Pouvoir Tout Dire* (1951), André Verdet's *Pages d'Amour* (1951) and André Miguel's *Infus Amour* (1952), as well as illustrating Colette's *Break of Day* (1983) and Lisa Alther's *Birdman and the Dance* (1993).

Although painting is her principal interest, she is a writer as well as a visual artist. Gilot is the author of six books including the best-selling *Life With Picasso* (with Carlton Lake) (1964), *Matisse & Picasso, A Friendship in Art* (1990) and, in 1996, *1946, Picasso et la Méditerranée Retrouvée*.

From 1976 to 1983, she was the Chairperson, Department of Fine Arts, University of Southern California of the Isomata Program, and for five years in the 1970s, the Art Director of the *Virginia Woolf Quarterly*.

Benoit B. Mandelbrot PhD

Benoit B. Mandelbrot is Abraham Robinson Professor of Mathematical Sciences at Yale University and IBM Fellow Emeritus (Physical Sciences) at the IBM T.J. Watson Research Center. For nearly 50 years, he has been seeking a measure of order in physical, mathematical or social phenomena that are characterized by abundant data but extreme sample variability. The surprising aesthetic value of many of his discoveries and their unexpected usefulness in teaching have made him an eloquent spokesman for 'the unity of knowing and feeling'.

Mandelbrot is best known as the founder of fractal geometry and author of the books *Les Objets Fractals* (1975, 1984, 1989 and 1995; translated into Chinese, Italian, Spanish, Portugese, Rumanian, Bulgarian and Basque) and *The Fractal Geometry of Nature* (1982; translated into Chinese, Korean, Japanese, Spanish and German). His multi-volume *Selecta* began with *Fractals and Scaling in Finance: Discontinuity, Concentration, Risk* (1997), *Fractales, Hasard et Finance* (1997) and *Multifractals and 1/f Noise: Wild Self-Affinity in Physics* (1999).

He is a fellow of the American Academy of Sciences, Foreign Associate of the US National Academy of Sciences, Foreign Member of the Norwegian Academy of Science and Letters, and Membre Titulaire de l'Académie Européenne des Sciences, des Arts et des Lettres.

He received the 1993 *Wolf Prize for Physics*. His other awards include the 1985 *F. Barnard Medal for Meritorious Service to Science* ('Magna est Veritas'), granted by the US National Academy of Sciences and Columbia University, the 1986 *Franklin Medal for Signal and Eminent Service in Science* from the Franklin Institute of Philadelphia, the 1988 *Charles Proteus Steinmetz Medal from* IEEE and Union College, the 1988 (first) *Science for Art Prize* from Moet-Hennessy-Louis Vuitton, the 1989 *Harvey Prize for Science and Technology* from the Technion in Haifa, the 1991 *Nevada Prize* and the 1994 *Honda Prize*. He also received a *Distinguished Service Award for Outstanding Achievement* from the California Institute of Technology and a *Humboldt Preis* from the Alexander von Humboldt Stiftung.

Graduate of the Paris Ecole Polytechnique, MS and AeE in Aeronautics, California Institute of Technology and Docteur ès Sciences Mathématiques, University of Paris, Mandelbrot received honorary doctorates from a number of universities including Boston University, State University of New York, University of Guelph, University of Buenos Aires, University of St Andrews, Universität Bremen and the University of Tel Aviv.

Mandelbrot had no formal teacher, but his early work was strongly influenced by Paul Levy, Norbert Wiener and John von Neumann. His positions before joining IBM included the CNRS in Paris, MIT, the Princeton Institute for Advanced Study and Ecole Polytechnique. On leave from IBM, he served as Institute Lecturer at MIT and Visiting Professor of Economics, later of Applied Mathematics and then of Mathematics at Harvard, of Engineering at Yale, of Physiology at the Albert Einstein College of Medicine and of Mathematics at the University of Paris-Sud and as Professor of the Practice of Mathematics at Harvard. In 1995, he served as Professeur de l'Académie des Sciences a l'Ecole Polytechnique, Paris. In 1999, he visited Cambridge, UK as G.C. Steward Visiting Fellow, Gonville and Caius College, Scott Lecturer, Cavendish Laboratory and member, I. Newton Institute of Mathematical Sciences.

George E. Palade MD

George E. Palade is one of the fathers of modern cell biology. Using the electron microscope and biochemical methods, he described many subcellular components for the first time. His pioneering work in cell biology—in the early years with A. Claude, K.R. Porter and C. de Duve—created a new discipline by assigning selected functions of the cell to specific subcellular structures. In 1974, he was awarded the Nobel Prize for Physiology and Medicine, which he shared with A. Claude and C. de Duve.

Dean for Scientific Affairs at the University of California, San Diego, George E. Palade is also Professor of Medicine in Residence at the University of California, San Diego, School of Medicine in La Jolla, California.

Born in Jassy, Moldavia, Romania, he received his MD in his native Romania, and was on the faculty of the Institute of Anatomy at the University of Bucharest until he went to the Rockefeller Institute in New York. He was a Visiting Investigator in the Department of Biology in 1946, and the following two years a Visiting Investigator in the Department of Pathology and Bacteriology. In 1948, he became a member of the faculty. From 1956 until 1973, he was the Professor of the Laboratory of Cell Biology, and from 1961–73, he was the Head of the Cell Biology Laboratories at the Rockefeller University. Between 1973 and 1990, he was on the Yale faculty, the Head of the Section of Cell Biology. In 1990, he joined the faculty of the University of California, San Diego.

Palade has produced over 186 selected publications on the organization of living matter. He elucidated the structure in collaboration with several notable biochemists, the functions of the principal components of the cell (namely the mitochondria, the endoplasmic reticulum and the ribosomes). In addition, he described the structure of the synapses in the nervous system, aspects of muscle structure and morphological and functional properties of the vascular endothelium. Palade can be said to have made the major contribution to our understanding of the structure and function of living organisms in this century.

His pioneering work was honored by numerous prestigious awards and 12 honorary doctorates including honorary degrees from Yale University, the University of Chicago, Columbia University, Rockefeller University, the University of Siena in Italy, the University of Paris, Sud, the University of Jassy in Romania, the Scripps Research Institute in La Jolla, the University of Rome 'La Sapienza' in Rome and the University of Milan. For his distinguished contributions to science, he received the Warren Triennial Prize (1962), the Passano Award (1964) (shared with K.R. Porter), the Lasker Award (1966), the Gairdner Special Award (1967), the Louisa Gross Horwitz Prize (1970) (shared with A. Claude and K.R. Porter), the Dickson Prize (1971) and the Nobel Prize for Physiology and Medicine (1974) (shared with A. Claude and C. de Duve). Palade also received the Brown—Hazen Award (1983), the Schleiden Medallie from the Leopoldina Academy (1985), the Henry Gray Award (1986) and the National Medal of Science (1986).

Karl H. Pfenninger MD

Karl H. Pfenninger is Professor and Chairman of Cellular and Structural Biology at the University of Colorado School of Medicine.

Born in 1944, he grew up in Switzerland and received his MD from the University of Zurich in 1971. As a medical student, he made a commitment to the neurosciences, doing experimental research on synapses with Dr K. Akert at the Brain Research Institute of the University of Zurich. He received postgraduate training first at Washington University in St Louis, Missouri, and then with George Palade at Yale University in the Section of Cell Biology.

In 1976, he joined the faculty of Columbia University's College of Physicians and Surgeons in New York as an Associate Professor (through to 1981) and then as Professor of Anatomy and Cell Biology (1982–6). In 1986, the University of Colorado recruited him to become Professor and Chairman of the Department of Cellular and Structural Biology in the School of Medicine. In 1990, he published, together with Dr C. Widnell, the textbook *Essential Cell Biology*.

His research interests include mechanisms and control of directed neurite growth, regulation of cell adhesion and pseudopod activity and cancer cell motility and invasiveness. He has made important contributions to an understanding of molecular aspects of nerve growth and growth cone function in the developing brain. His work crosses over the boundary lines that separate molecular cell biology, neurobiology and developmental biology.

In addition to research and teaching, Pfenninger has assumed numerous administrative and advisory positions. He holds several leadership positions at the University of Colorado and is a past Chairman of the Scientific Advisory Board, Colorado Cancer League (1998–9), served as NIH Study Section Chair from 1992 to 1994 and is a past President of the Association of Anatomy, Cell Biology and Neurobiology Chairpersons.

Pfenninger's honors include several Swiss and US fellowship awards. In 1977, he received the C.J. Herrick Award in Comparative Neurology and an I.T. Hirschl Career Scientist Award. He is also one of very few US investigators to receive two consecutive Sen. Jacob Javits Neuroscience Investigator Awards (1984–91 and 1991–8) from the National Institutes of Health.

David E. Rogers MD

Physician, educator, author and artist, David Elliott Rogers completed his MD at Cornell University in 1948 and devoted much of his scientific career to the study of infectious diseases including, more recently, AIDS. His major contributions in the field of infectious disease, health care and its delivery, and the AIDS problem have been recognized by numerous awards including seven honorary degrees. He is also an accomplished wood sculptor who has had a number of one-man exhibitions.

Born in New York City on 17 March 1926, he attended Ohio State University from 1942–4, and received his MD from Cornell University Medical College in 1948. After an internship at Johns Hopkins, he was a USPHS post-doctoral fellow in the Division of Infectious Diseases at the New York Hospital where he became an attending physician. He was appointed as the first Walsh McDermott University Professor of Medicine at the New York Hospital–Cornell University Medical Center (1986–94). He died in 1994.

In the 1950s, Rogers was the Lowell M. Palmer Sr Fellow in Medicine (1955–7) and the Chief of the Division of Infectious Diseases at the Cornell University Medical College in New York City (1955–9). Simultaneously, he held academic appointments at the neighboring Rockefeller Institute of Medical Research in New York City.

Professor and Chairman of Medicine at Vanderbilt University from 1959 until 1968, he was also physician-in-chief of the Vanderbilt University Hospital. In 1968, he became Professor and Dean of the School of Medicine at Johns Hopkins, and later its Vice-President for Medical Affairs. From 1972 until 1986, he was President of the Robert Wood Johnson Foundation in Princeton,

New Jersey. He wrote *American Medicine: Challenge for the 1980s* and was the editor of the *Year Book of Medicine* from 1966 until 1993.

Recognized for his research and treatment of infectious diseases, and especially AIDS, Rogers was a visiting professor at numerous universities. He also acted in an advisory capacity to the Office of the Surgeon General, Public Health Service, HEW, and was a member of the Science Advisory Board of the Scripps Clinic and Research Foundation. He was the Vice-Chairman of the National Committee on AIDS from 1989 until 1993 and the Senior Advisor to the New York Academy of Medicine (1990–4).

His many honors include the John Metcalf Polk prize, the Alfred Moritz prize from Cornell University Medical School (1948), the Flexner Award (1986), the John W. Gardner Leadership Award (1991), the Special Recognition Award from the American College of Preventive Medicine (1993), the John Sterns Award for Lifetime Achievement in Medicine (1994) and the Gustav O. Lienhard Award (1993).

Carving in wood was an important part of his life. From his earliest years, he collected unusual pieces of wood. His work was often focused on the human or animal figure. In later years, he was invited to exhibit his sculpture in university and private galleries.

Valerie Reid Shubik PhD

Valerie Reid Shubik has been educated both in art and in English and American literature. She has taught at the University of Nebraska and the George Washington University in Washington, DC. Her career as a biographer, an associate editor of two scientific journals and a writer of popular science articles, as well as her training in the fine arts has given her an unusually broad base from which to co-edit this complex volume of interdisciplinary essays.

She received her BA from Cornell University in Ithaca, New York, where she majored in creative writing and art history. She was in a tutorial program with David Daiches, and studied Milton with William Keast. After a creative workshop with Helen Frankenthaler, she was trained in drawing and painting at the Art Institute of Chicago, Illinois. She then moved to Omaha, Nebraska, and received a BFA from the University of Nebraska in 1972 after completing three years of study at the Chicago Art Institute. She taught art at the University of Nebraska as a graduate assistant to Wayne Higby, was an Officer of the American Crafts Council, Nebraska Chapter and first heard Dale Chihuly lecture when she was a Nebraska representative at the national meeting. She was a member of the Committee for Sculpture in Public Places, the Chairperson of the Riverfront Urban Renewal Arts Committee, lectured on art in the public schools and founded the Unicorn Studio together with a painter and a studio art potter. At the Anderson Ranch Art Center in Aspen, Colorado, she worked with several notable craftsmen and artists.

In 1976, she received an MA from the University of Nebraska at Omaha and subsequently a PhD in English Literature from the University of Nebraska in Lincoln, Nebraska. She is a member of the Nebraska Chapter of the Educational Honorary Society. Her thesis, an analysis of the philosophical ethos of the major works of the American writer, Willa Cather, was among the first dissertations on the works of a woman writer. She has written articles about the relationship of Sir Yehudi Menuhin and Willa Cather, based on a collection of letters given to her by the musician, and has lectured at Brigham Young University on 'A new dimension: the best years and the Menuhin letters'. Her article entitled 'Living in a sea of carcinogens' was published in *Harper's* whilst she was in the English Department at the University of Nebraska.

In 1980, she studied German at the University of Heidelberg for one year, and worked at Deutsches Krebsforschungszentrum as a scientific editor. She edited a textbook on oncology, to be translated into Chinese, for Dieter Schmahl, Professor and Chairman of the Department of Chemotherapy at Deutsches Krebsforschungszentrum, as well as scientific manuscripts for Professor George Kolar and others.

From 1986 to 1989, she was a senior associate member of St Antony's College, Oxford. At that time, she was awarded the Hokin Scholarship for Advanced Studies in English Literature. While an associate professor at the George Washington University in Washington, DC (1989), she designed a new course of lectures on technical writing. During the past five years, she has been associate editor of two international scientific journals, *Cancer Letters* and *Teratogenesis, Carcinogenesis and Mutagenesis*, and continues to edit the latter journal. She has in preparation a biography of Willa Cather. Currently she is a Member of Common Room at Green College, Oxford University.

Gunther S. Stent PhD

In 1948, Gunther Stent went to the California Institute of Technology as a post-doctoral fellow of the National Research Council, to join Max Delbrück's 'Phage Group'—the fountain-head of the discipline that, a few years later, came to be called 'molecular biology'. He has been on the faculty of the University of California, Berkeley since 1952, as Professor of Molecular Biology since 1959, as Chairman of the Department from 1980 until 1992 and as Professor Emeritus of Neurobiology since 1994. His current research interest is the development of the nervous system.

Besides writing scientific textbooks and contributing to the scientific litera-ture in his fields, Stent has looked at the history and the metaphysics of science. His work ranges from bacterial molecular biology in earlier years to neuro-science and the history and philosophy of science in more recent times. He wrote *Phage and the Origins of Molecular Biology*, with J. Cairns and J. D. Watson (1966, 1992). *The Coming of the Golden Age* (1969) was his next book, which was followed by *Paradoxes of Progress* (1978) and *Morality as a Biological Phenomenon* (1978, 1981). In 1980, he wrote a critical review of J.D. Watson's *The Double Helix* and followed that with *Truth and Spiritual Awakening; Metaphysics of Science and Oriental Philosophy* (1981). The fall of 1998 marked the appearance of his autobiographical memoir, *Nazis, Women and Molecular Biology: The Memoirs of a Lucky Self-Hater*.

Born in Berlin in 1924, he fled from Nazi Germany in 1938 and settled in Chicago where he attended the same high school as James Watson. He went on to study physical chemistry at the University of Illinois (BS 1945; PhD 1948). His fellowship at the California Institute of Technology was the first of many. A National Science Foundation fellowship at the Universities of Kyoto and of Cambridge in the 1960s was followed by a Guggenheim fellowship at Harvard Medical School in Boston. From 1985–90 he was a fellow of the Institute for Advanced Study in Berlin; from 1990–2 he was a Fogarty Scholar in Residence at the National Institutes of Health in Bethesda, Maryland. Currently, he is an external member of the Max Planck Institute for Molecular Genetics in Berlin.

Stent has held many national and international leadership positions and his many seminal contributions have been honored by numerous awards including the Runstrom Medal (Stockholm), 1986 and the Urania Medal (Berlin), 1990.

Professor Stent is a scientist–philosopher who is recognized for his elucida-tion of scientific paradoxes as well as his contributions to basic science. He is a member of the National Academy of Sciences, the American Philosophical Society, the American Academy of Arts and Sciences, the Akademie der Wissenschaften und der Literatur, Mainz, the Max–Planck–Gesellschaft and the European Academy of Sciences and Arts.

Charles F. Stevens MD PhD

Charles Stevens' research centers on mechanisms responsible for synaptic transmission. These problems—central to an understanding of brain func-tion—are approached in an inter-disciplinary manner using a combination of molecular biology, electrophysiology, anatomy and theoretical methods. Stevens studies neurons both in cell culture and in brain slices, and also investigates the function of individual membrane proteins of importance for synaptic transmission. It is his belief, based on research into the structure and function of the brain, that the principles of brain organization provide insight into the aesthetic experience. For example, how we appreciate line drawings and see color has its basis in the fundamental organization of the brain. Art appreciation is determined through brain function. The language of art is shaped by the constraints imposed by the brain's processing capabilities.

Prior to his appointment at the Salk Institute, he held faculty positions at the University of Washington School of Medicine and at the Yale University School of Medicine. In 1990, he became the Professor of Molecular Neurobiology at the Salk Institute and Adjunct Professor of Pharmacology and Neuroscience at the University of California in San Diego. He is also an investigator of the Howard Hughes Medical Institute. Teacher and researcher, he has made many contributions in molecular neuroscience and has used a combination of methods to elucidate the molecular basis to neurotransmitter release at synapses.

In 1956, he graduated with a BA in psychology from Harvard University, Cambridge, Massachusetts. He received his MD from the Yale University School of Medicine in New Haven, Connecticut in 1960, and he was awarded a PhD in biophysics from Rockefeller University, New York in 1964.

His outstanding contributions in molecular neuroscience have earned him many honors and awards. From 1969 until 1970, he was the Guest Investigator at the Lorentz Institute for Theoretical Physics at Leiden University in the Netherlands. He received the Alden Spencer Award from Columbia University in 1979 and was the Grass National Lecturer at the Society for Neuroscience in 1981. He has been a member of the National Academy of Sciences since 1982 and is a member of the American Academy of Arts and Sciences.

In the last ten years, Stevens has focused on the various mechanisms used by the central nervous system for the short- and long-term regulation of synaptic strength, which is central to an understanding of the functioning of the brain, especially learning and memory.

Index

childhood, influence of 71, 96, 101–16, 132
Churchland, Paul 89, 217
Close, Chuck 178
  No.6 in Keith Series, 1979 **Fig. 4.4**
cognitive functions 89
cognitive neurosciences 60, 66–8
cognitive psychology and study of creativity
  127, 143
composing, the process of; *see* Adolphe, Bruce
computer graphics 201, 205–7, 210
computer modelling, link with biology 90
consciousness, role in creativity 68
contents of works of art or science 37, 38
  presentational 37
  propositional 37, 38
  semantic 33, 34, 35, 41
  continuum 214, 231–2
  between art and science 39–41, **Table 1.1**
  from a painter's perspective 164, 166
cortex, visual; *see* visual system
Count de Gobineau (1816–1882) 147, 156
courtyard exhibitions; Honolulu Academy of
  Arts (Chihuly)
  Central Courtyard 24, **Plate 8**
  lighting of 24
  Mediterranean Courtyard 24
  Oriental Courtyard 24
creative individuals, or innovators 117,
  118–25, 129, 131, 140, 141
creative process
  in art; *see* Chihuly, Adolphe, Gilot
  in science; *see* Cech
creative triangle 117–8, **Table 3.1**, 130, 142,
  217
creativity
  biological or neural basis of 59–60, 65, 67–8,
  96, 189, 213, 215–17, 220–1
  flowering of 146–50, 152–6, 217–18
  of mathematics 205, 212
  requirements for 63–6, 177
  role of emotions 67–8
  tests for 125–6
creativity, defined 68, 117, 128, 129, 145,
  234–6
creativity gene 146–7, 220–1
Crick, Francis 31–7, 154, 200; *see also* Watson
  (James), deoxyribonucleic acid (DNA)
Csikszentmihhalyi, Milhaly 117, 128, 129,
  130, 132, 217

da Vinci, Leonardo (1452–1519) 147–8, 167,
  196
  Mona Lisa 174
Damasio, Antonio R. 59–68, 223–4
  cognitive neuroscience 60–3
  interactions of brain with environment
  59–60
  requirements for creativity 63–6

  role of emotions 67–8
Damasio, Hannah 57, 61
Darwin, Charles 89–90, 127
  Darwinian selection 236
Debussy, 25, 26, 27, 29, 81; *see Pelléas* and
  Mélisande
determinisim, historical 32
De Humuni Corporis Fabrica (Vesalius) 148,
  Fig. 3.13
deoxyribonucleic acid (DNA) 6–9, 32, 37, 92,
  155
  configuration 7, **Fig. 1.1**
  copying 8–9, **Fig. 1.4**
  information storage 92
  significance of discovery 155
deprivation, effect of 218, 221; *see also*
  malnutrition
Descartes, René (1596–1650) 194, 234
diffusion limited aggregation (DLA) 208
discovery 35, 37, 41, 88, 166
  premature 200, 219, 229, 233,
  versus creation; *see* antinomy
domains of creativity 118, 129, 130, 143
Duchamp, Marcel 174

economic prosperity, creativity and 148,
  217–18
Einstein, Albert (1879–1955) 121, **Fig. 3.6**
  123, 130, 131, 135,136,137, 138, 214
Eliot, T.S. (1888–1965) 121, **Fig. 3.9**, 123,
  131, 134, 135
emotions; *see also* body loop, feelings, intuition
  ability to signal response 67–8, 234–5
  role in aesthetic experience 67–8
  role in painting 171–2
Emerson, Ralph Waldo (1803–82) 197
environment, influence of 59–60, 96 101–2,
  110, 115–16, 141, 146, 213, 217–19, 221
  on artist's perceptions 171
  on brain circuitry 59, 94–6
  relationship of individual, *domain* and *field*
  142
epistemology 36, 41, 222
Euclid (founder of geometry, about 330–270 BC)
  193, 194, 198, 212
Euclidean geometry 198
'Eureka!' experience concept 14–15, 35,
  172–3, 204, 205
evolutionary perspective, brain 59, 91–5,
  220–1
exhibitions, *see also* courtyard exhibitions,
  Honolulu Academy of Art
  Dale Chihuly Installations (1964–1992) 22–3,
  Fig. 1.10

faces, recognition of 66–7, 178, 181, 188–9,
  223